THE ENGLISH LANGUAGE

THE ENGLISH LANGUAGE

ESSAYS BY ENGLISH AND
AMERICAN MEN OF LETTERS
1490–1839

SELECTED AND EDITED BY
W. F. BOLTON

Professor of English in the University of Reading

CAMBRIDGE
AT THE UNIVERSITY PRESS
1966

PUBLISHED BY
THE SYNDICS OF THE CAMBRIDGE UNIVERSITY PRESS

Bentley House, 200 Euston Road, London, N.W. 1
American Branch: 32 East 57th Street, New York, N.Y. 10022
West African Office: P.M.B. 5181, Ibadan, Nigeria

Printed in Great Britain at the University Printing House, Cambridge
(Brooke Crutchley, University Printer)

LIBRARY OF CONGRESS CATALOGUE
CARD NUMBER: 66–11030

CONTENTS

CONTENTS

ACKNOWLEDGEMENTS

I wish to thank all who assisted me in compiling this book, especially my colleagues, the Librarian and staff of Reading University Library, and my wife, as well as the Syndics and those responsible for its production at the Cambridge University Press. Miss J. M. Field gave great help with the proofs and index.

W. F. B.

Reading
June 1965

INTRODUCTION

The twenty essays in this book illustrate both the internal and the external history of literary English prose since the end of the fifteenth century; that is, they are examples of the structure of the language and of attitudes toward it over some 350 years. The point of view is that of men of letters, not because their usages and opinions are the only 'correct' ones, but because they are the most articulate members of the linguistic community and the most readable and influential writers, and because they provide the most revealing manifestations of the importance of linguistic resources and linguistic theory for literary style.

The order of the selections is chronological, but readers may find other arrangements which correspond to their own interests, such as the idea of an English academy, spelling reform, neologisms, the American language, the phenomenon of human speech, or the history of English orthography, clause structure, the essay and letter genres themselves. But for the history of linguistic science, men of letters supply very imperfect illustrations, showing sometimes its motivating concerns, sometimes its published conclusions, more often only the gulf between professional writers and professional students of language.

For Caxton and the sixteenth and seventeenth centuries, there was little linguistic science that had English as its subject. The renewed study of the classical languages left the vernacular with an uncertain reputation, and the debate over the sufficiency of English ended only in the eighteenth century when its elevation to 'classical' status was made to depend on the provision of inflexible authorities for its employment. Defoe, Addison, and Swift called for an English academy on the French and Italian models; Chesterfield proposed, and Johnson supplied, a lexical standard; and Lowth wrote a prescriptive grammar, of which Cobbett's is a proletarian offshoot, outdoing the classicists in its rigour. America sought an independent standard.

The growth of historical philology in the nineteenth century, dispensing with the idea of a fixed standard and increasingly technical in its description of language, ended the age in which a writer who knew schoolboy Greek and Latin could regard himself as a linguistic authority. Some, like Hazlitt, investigated the new methodology, but the man of letters was no longer *ipso facto* a well-informed philologist, and many declined to regard their profession as a commitment to the study of language. The century produced philologists from amongst its amateurs—the schoolmaster Murray, the archbishop Chenevix Trench—but few from amongst even the most liberal critics and writers: De Quincey, who gives up the ideal of linguistic permanence, elsewhere challenges the 'justification' of some neologisms. Those who wrote about the theoretical aspects of language subordinated observation to the demands of their philosophical systems, as Hobbes had to nominalism, Locke to empiricism, Emerson to transcendentalism.

The literary eminence of these writers has added its force to the traditions they voiced, so that Swift's proposed moratorium on linguistic change recommends itself to students and teachers of English as that of the author of *Gulliver's Travels* (and as a view consistent with most school textbooks of the 250 years since he wrote). But the interplay of literary practice and linguistic history has not been limited to the strictures of men of letters on the common language. Johnson's *Dictionary* (on the model of classical dictionaries) employed examples to illustrate the words; these Johnson called his 'authorities', and regarded in some way as attesting or supporting, as well as illustrating, his lexicon. The literary dialect of Modern English, as it developed from Caxton to the present, provided a criterion by which all English utterances might be judged, a surrogate for the academy which Defoe and the others desired. Swift, to be sure, complained of 'Corruptions very few of the best Authors in our Age have wholly

escaped', and so did Cobbett, but the authority of literary eminence endowed one form of the written language with a propriety which has been extended to the spoken language as well.
In consequence, other forms have suffered neglect when they were
fortunate enough to escape persecution, and an artificial notion of
the structure of English has been fostered.

The exaltation of the literary dialect as the authority for the
entire language in turn limits the range of linguistic materials
available to serious writers. In the nineteenth century, the Englishman William Barnes and the Americans Joel Chandler Harris and
James Russell Lowell wrote in non-standard dialects, but not
without a measure of self-consciousness, or even condescension.
The state of the language in any age provides the basis from which
a writer can work: he cannot direct the language, he can only
employ it, and the range of possible employment, though wide
enough, is not infinite. Johnson, who feared a gallicized English,
latinized it; and Franklin, who complained that verbs were being
created from nouns, used a number formed in that way. The
'errors' here lie neither in latinizing nor in changing the class or
adapting the meaning of words, but in assuming that the writer
is an influence on, but is not influenced by, the habits of his
linguistic community. Caxton drew heavily on French and Latin
when he attempted to emulate the syntactical systems of those
languages, but he was limited by the actual clausal conventions
of fifteenth-century English. He could no more mould the language by extension than Johnson or Franklin could mould it by
restriction.

The influence of literary men on linguistic opinion; the adoption
of literary English as the premier dialect of the language; the
dependence of the literary dialect itself on the resources of
English in each age; these associate the history of English literature
with the internal and external history of the language continuously
and intimately.

The preceding pages outline the ideas that controlled the selection of texts for this book. Some were excluded because they

duplicated those already chosen; some were not the work of important literary figures; for some there was simply no room. A number of these rejected essays are referred to in the study questions. Except where otherwise noted, the texts are those of the first edition, save that obvious errors have been silently corrected, abbreviations have been expanded, marginal summaries have been omitted, typography has been modernized (notably the black letter of Caxton and Harrison, and the long *s* of the first sixteen items), and a few small matters of style like footnote conventions and the use of inverted commas in quotations have been standardized. Nearly all the essays, letters or chapters are complete; only nos. 5 and 10 are excerpts. The selections consequently illustrate the development of English literary and linguistic forms as well as the opinions of men of letters about their language. Neither the introductory paragraphs nor the study questions are exhaustive. The reader may find them a useful way of relating the texts to one another, but he may prefer to follow his own interests, using the topical index. Footnotes provide translations and some other clarifications where necessary.

WILLIAM CAXTON

(1422?–1491)

Confronted with the need to render the polished French original in a close English translation, Caxton questions the adequacy of his native tongue for the task. Its diversity makes its speakers unintelligible to one another, and its alterations close the books of one age to the readers of the next. Yet attempts to supply its shortcomings by newly coined words and constructions fail when the unfamiliar is rejected. Caxton's is an early voice doubting the capacity of English in an ungoverned state to measure up to the elegant languages of literary and scholarly fashion.

Prologue to his translation of *Eneydos* (1490)

After dyuerse werkes made / translated and achieued / hauyng noo werke in hande. I sittyng in my studye where as laye many dyuerse paunflettis and bookys. happened that to my hande cam a lytyl booke in frenshe. whiche late was translated oute of latyn by some noble clerke of fraunce whiche booke is named Eneydos / made in latyn by that noble poete & grete clerke vyrgyle / whiche booke I sawe ouer and redde therin. How after the generall destruccyon of the grete Troye. Eneas departed berynge his olde fader anchises vpon his sholdres / his lityl son yolus on his honde. his wyfe wyth moche other people folowynge / and how he shypped and departed wyth alle thystorye of his aduentures that he had er he cam to the achieuement of his conquest of ytalye as all a longe shall be shewed in this present boke. In whiche booke I had grete playsyr. by cause of the fayr and honest termes & wordes in frenshe / Whyche I neuer sawe to fore lyke. ne none so playsaunt ne so wel ordred. whiche booke as me semed sholde be moche requysyte to noble men to see as wel for the eloquence as the historyes / How wel that many honderd yerys passed was the sayd booke of eneydos wyth other werkes made and lerned dayly in scolis specyally in ytalye & other places / whiche historye the sayd vyrgyle made in metre / And whan I had aduysed me in this sayd boke. I delybered and concluded to translate it in to englysshe And forthwyth toke a penne & ynke and wrote a leef or tweyne / whyche I ouersawe agayn to correcte it / And whan I sawe the fayr & straunge termes therin / I doubted that it sholde not please some gentylmen whiche late blamed me sayeng y^t[1] in my translacyons I had ouer curyous termes whiche coude not be vnderstande of comyn peple / and desired me to vse olde and homely termes in my translacyons. and fayn wolde I satysfye euery man / and so to doo toke an olde boke and redde therin / and certaynly the englysshe was so rude and brood that I coude not wele vnderstande it. And also my lorde abbot of westmynster ded do shewe to me late certayn euydences[2] wryton in olde englysshe for to reduce it in to our englysshe now vsid / And certaynly it was wreton in suche wyse that it was more lyke to dutche[3] than englysshe I coude not reduce ne brynge it to be vnderstonden / And certaynly our langage now vsed varyeth ferre from that. whiche was vsed and spoken whan I was borne / For we englysshe men / ben borne vnder the domynacyon of the mone. whiche is neuer stedfaste / but euer wauerynge / wexynge one season / and waneth & dyscreaseth another season / And that comyn englysshe that is spoken in one shyre varyeth from a nother. In so moche that in my dayes happened that certayn marchauntes were in a shippe in tamyse for to haue sayled ouer the see into zelande / and for lacke of wynde thei taryed atte forlond. and wente to lande for to refreshe them And one of theym named sheffelde a mercer cam in to an hows and axed for mete. and specyally he axyd after eggys And the good wyf answerde. that she coude speke no frenshe. And the marchaunt was angry. for he also coude speke no frenshe. but wold haue hadde egges / and she vnderstode hym

---

[1] [y^t that (cf. y^e, the).]   [2] [euydences documents.]
[3] [dutche German.]

2

not / And thenne at laste a nother sayd that he wolde haue eyren / then the good wyf sayd that she vnderstod hym wel / Loo what sholde a man in thyse dayes now wryte. egges or eyren / certaynly it is harde to playse euery man / by cause of dyuersite & chaunge of langage. For in these dayes euery man that is in ony reputacyon in his countre. wyll vtter his commynycacyon and maters in suche maners & termes / that fewe men shall vnderstonde theym / And som honest and grete clerkes haue ben wyth me and desired me to wryte the moste curyous termes that I coude fynde / And thus bytwene playn rude / & curyous I stande abasshed. but in my Iudgemente / the comyn termes that be dayli vsed ben lyghter to be vnderstonde than the olde and auncyent englysshe / And for as moche as this present booke is not for a rude vplondyssh man to laboure therin / ne rede it / but onely for a clerke & a noble gentylman that feleth and vnderstondeth in faytes of armes in loue & in noble chyualrye / Therfor in a meane bytwene bothe I haue reduced & translated this sayd booke in to our englysshe not ouer rude ne curyous but in suche termes as shall be vnderstanden by goddys grace accordynge to my copye. And yf ony man wyll entermete in redyng of hit and fyndeth suche termes that he can not vnderstande late hym goo rede and lerne vyrgyll / or the pystles of ouyde / and ther he shall see and vnderstonde lyghtly all / Yf he haue a good redar & enformer / For this booke is not for euery rude and vnconnynge man to see / but to clerkys and very gentylmen that vnderstande gentylnes and scyence ¶ Thenne I praye alle theym that shall rede in this lytyl treatys to holde me for excused for the translatynge of hit. For I knowleche my selfe ignorant of connynge to enpryse on me so hie and noble a werke / But I praye mayster Iohn Skelton late created poete laureate in the vnyuersite of oxenforde to ouersee and correcte this sayd booke. And taddresse and expowne where as shalle be founde faulte to theym that shall requyre it. For hym I knowe for suffycyent to expowne and englysshe euery dyffyculte that is therin / For he hath late translated the epystlys of Tulle / and the boke of dyodorus syculus. and diuerse other werkes oute of latyn in to englysshe not in rude and olde langage. but in polysshed and ornate termes craftely. as he that hath redde vyrgyle / ouyde. tullye. and all the other noble poetes and oratours / to me vnknowen: And also he hath redde the ix. muses and vnderstande theyr musicalle scyences. and to whom of theym eche scyence is appropred. I suppose he hath dronken of Elycons well. Then I praye hym & suche other to correcte adde or mynysshe where as he or they shall fynde faulte / For I haue but folowed my copye in frenshe as nygh as me is possyble / And yf ony worde be sayd therin well / I am glad. and yf otherwyse I submytte my sayd boke to theyr correctyon / Whiche boke I presente vnto the hye born. my tocomynge naturell & souerayn lord Arthur by the grace of god Prynce of Walys Duc of Cornewayll. & Erle of Chester fyrst bygoten sone and heyer vnto our most dradde naturall & souerayn lorde & most crysten kynge / Henry the vij. by the grace of god kynge of Englonde and of Fraunce & lord of Jrelonde / byseching his noble grace to receyue it in thanke of me his moste humble subget & seruaunt / And I shall praye vnto almyghty god for his prosperous encreasyng in vertue / wysedom / and humanyte that he may be egal wyth the most renommed of alle his noble progenytours. ¶ And so to lyue in this present lyf / that after this transitorye lyfe he and we alle may come to euerlastynge lyf in heuen / Amen:

2

RICHARD MULCASTER

(1530?–1611)

Mulcaster, headmaster of the Merchant Taylors' School (where Edmund Spenser was his pupil, and where he may have provided the inspiration for Holofernes in Shakespeare's *Love's Labour's Lost*), presented in this book a reformed spelling. Others who had done so, he says, had failed through an underestimation of the strengths of English, or through a neglect of the demands of custom. Implicitly answering doubts like Caxton's, he marshals his four arguments for the adequacy of the language, confident in the very antiquity that had worried Caxton and reassured by the century of literary accomplishment that lay between them.

'That the English tung hath in it self sufficient matter to work her own artificiall direction, for the right writing thereof'

(Chapter XIII from *The First Part of the Elementarie*, 1582)

It must nedes be that our English tung hath matter enough in hir own writing, which maie direct her own right, if it be reduced to certain precept, and rule of Art, tho it haue not as yet bene thoroughlie perceaued.

The causes why it hath not as yet bene thoroughlie perceaued, ar, the hope & despare of such, as haue either thought vpon it, and not dealt in it, or that haue delt in it, but not rightlie thought vpon it.

For som[1] considering the great difficultie, which theie found to be in the writing thereof, euerie letter almost being deputed to manie, and seuerall, naie to manie and wellnigh contrarie sounds and vses, euerie word almost either wanting[2] letters, for his neces-

---

[1] [*For som...requireth* For some people who considered the great difficulty which they found in English spelling, where almost every letter stands for many and different sounds, nay for many and opposite sounds, and where almost every word has either too few or too many letters for its sound, etc.]   [2] [*wanting* lacking.]

sarie sound, or hauing some more then necessitie requireth, began to despare in the midst of such a confusion, euer to find out anie sure direction, whereon to ground Art, and to set it certain. And what if either theie did not seke, or did not know how to seke, in right form of Art, and the compòsing method? But whether difficultie in the thing, or infirmitie in the searchers, gaue cause thereunto, the parties them selues gaue ouer the thing, as in a desperat case, and by not medling thorough despare, theie helped not the right.

Again som others bearing a good affection to their naturall tung, and resolued to burst thorough the midst of all these difficulties, which offered such resistence, as theie misliked the confusion, wherewith the other were afraid, so theie deuised a new mean,[1] wherein theie laid their hope, to bring the thing about. Wherevpon som of them being of great place and good learning, set furth in print particular treatises of that argument, with these their new conceaued means, how we ought to write, and so to write right. But their good hope by reason of their strange mean, had the same euent, that the others despare had, by their either misconceauing the thing at first, or their diffidence at the last.[2] Wherein the parties them selues no dout deserue some praise, and thanks to, of vs and our cuntrie in both these extremities of hope and despare, tho theie helped not the thing, which theie went about, but in common apparence, did somwhat hinder it rather. For both he, that despared in the end, took great pains, before diffidence caused him giue ouer to despare: and he that did hope by his own deuise to supply the generall want, was not verie idle both in brain, to deuise, and in hand to deliuer the thing, which he deuised. Which their trauell[3] in the thing, and desire to do good, deserue great thanks, tho that waie which theie took, did not take effect.

[1] [*mean* means.]
[2] [*But their...last* But because of their approach, their optimism had the same outcome as the pessimism of the others had either through their misunderstanding the thing in the beginning, or through their diffidence at the end.]
[3] [*trauell* labour.]

The causes why theie took not effect, and thereby in part did hinder the thing, by making of manie think the case more desperat then it was in dede, bycause such fellowes did so faill, were these. Their despare, which thought, that the tung was vncapable of anie direction, came of a wrong cause, the falt rising in dede not of the thing, which theie did condemn, as altogether rude and vnrulie, but of the parties them selues, who mistook their waie. For the thing it self will soon be ordered (our custom is grown so orderable) tho it require som diligence, and good consideration, in him that must find it out. But when a writer taketh a wrong principle, quite contrarie to common practis, where triall must be tuch,[1] and practis must confirm the mean, which he conceaueth, is it anie maruell if the vse of a tung ouerthwart such a mean, which is not conformable vnto it? Herevpon proceded the desparc to hit right, bycause theie missed of their minde, whereas in dede theie should haue changed their minde, to haue hit vpon that right, which as it is in the thing, so will it soon be found out, if it be rightlie sought for.

Again the others hope deceiued them to as much. For theie considered not, that whereas common reason, and common custom haue bene long dealers in seking out of their own currant, themselues wilbe councellers, and will neuer yeild to anie priuat conceit, which shall seme euidentlie either to force them or to crosse them, as theie themselues do, neuer giuing anie precept, how to write right, till theie haue rated at custom, as a most pernicious enemie to truth and right, euen in that thing, where custom hath most right, if it haue right in anie. Wherefor when theie proceded on in a customarie argument, with the enemitie of him, which is Lord of the soill, was it anie wonder if theie failed of their purpos, & hindered the finding out of our right writing, which must nedes be compased by customs consent, and reasons frindship? So in the mean time, while despare deceiues the one, and hope begiles the other, the one missing his waie, the the other making a fo, and both going astraie, theie both lease their

---

[1] [*tuch* touchstone, test.]

7

labor, and let the finding out of our right in writing, by their ill led, and worse laid labor, bycause the artificiall course, in finding out such a thing, hath another currant, as I haue shewed before in the last title.

Yet notwithstanding all this, it is verie manifest, that the tung it self hath matter enough in it self, to furnish out an art, & that the same mean, which hath bene vsed in the reducing of other tungs to their right, will serue this of ours, both for generalitie of precept, and certaintie of ground, as maie be easilie proued by these four arguments, the antiquitie of our tung, the peples wit, their learning, and their experience. For how can it be, but that a tung, which hath continewed manie hundred years, not onelie a tung, but one of good account, both in speche, and pen, hath growen in all that time to som finesse, and assurance of it self, by so long and so generall an vse, tho it be not as yet founded, the peple that haue vsed it, being none of the dullest, and trauelling continuallie in all exercises that concern learning, in all practises that procure experience, either in peace or war, either in publike, or priuat, either at home or abrode?

As for the antiquitie of our speche, whether it be measured by the ancient *Almane*, whence it cummeth originallie, or euen but by the latest terms which it boroweth daielie from foren tungs, either of pure necessitie in new matters, or of mere brauerie, to garnish it self withall, it cannot be young. Onelesse the *Germane* himself be young, which claimeth a prerogatiue for the age of his speche, of an infinit prescription: Onelesse the *Latin* and *Greke* be young, whose words we enfranchise to our own vse, tho not all-waie immediatlie from them selues, but mostwhat thorough the *Italian*, *French*, and *Spanish*: Onelesse other tungs, which be neither *Greke* nor *Latin*, nor anie of the forenamed, from whom we haue somwhat, as theie haue from ours, will for companie sake be content to be young, that ours maie not be old. But I am well assured, that euerie one of these, will striue for antiquitie, and rather grant it to vs, then forgo it themselues. So that if the verie newest words, which we vse do sauor of great antiquitie, and the

8

ground of our speche be most ancient, it must nedes then folow, that our hole tung was weined[1] long ago, as hauing all her tethe.

For the account of our tung, both in pen and speche, no man will dout thereof, who is able to iudge what those thinges be, which make anie tung to be of account, which things I take to be thré, the autoritie of the peple which speak it, the matter & argument, wherein the speche dealeth, the manifold vse, for which the speche serueth. For all which thré, our tung nedeth not to giue place, to anie of her peres.

First to saie somwhat for the peple, that vse the tung, the *English* nation hath allwaie bene of good credit, and great estimation, euer since credit and estimation by historie came on this side the *Alps*, which appeareth to be trew, euen by foren cronicles (not to vse our own in a case of our own) which would neuer haue said so much of the peple, if it had bene obscure, and not for an historie, or not but well worthie of a perpetuall historie.

Next, for the argument, wherein it dealeth, whether priuat or publik, it maie compare with som other, that think verie well of their own selues. For not to tuch ordinarie affairs in comon life, will matters of learning in anie kind of argument, make a tung of account? Our nation then, I think, will hardlie be proued to haue bene vnlearned at anie time, in anie kinde of learning, not to vse anie bigger speche. Wherefor hauing learning by confession of all men, & vttering that learning in their own tung, for their own vse, of verie pure necessitie (bycause we learn to vse, and the vse is in our own) theie could not but enrich the tung, and purchace it account.

Will matters of war, whether ciuill or foren, make a tung of account? Our neighbor nations will not deny our peple to be verie warrious, and our own cuntrie will confesse it, tho loth to fele it, both by remembring the smart, & comparing with som other, neither to vaunt our selues, nor to gall our frinds, with anie mo words.

Now in offring matter to speche, war is such a bréder, as tho it

[1] [*weined* weaned.]

9

be opposit to learning, bycause it is enemie to the Muses, yet it dare compare with anie point in learning, for multitude of discourses, tho not commonlie so certain, ne yet of so good vse, as learned arguments be. For war (besides all graue and sad considerations about it, which be manie and wise) as somtime it sendeth vs trew reports, either priuatelie in proiects and deuises, that be entended, or publikelie in euents, which be blased abrode, bycause theie be don, so mostwhat it giueth out infinit and extreme, I dare not saie lies, but verie incredible newes, bycause it maie hatch them at will, being in no danger of controllment, and comonlie in such practises and places, as haue not manie witnesses, while euerie man seketh as well to saue him self, as to harm his enemie, besides som curteous entertainment, which a deuising referendarie hath euen by telling that, which is not trew, to such as loue to hear, and either like or will like. All which occasions, and infinit mo, about stratagemes & engins, giue matter to speche, and cause of new words, and by making it so redie, do make it of renoun.

Will all kindes of trade, and all sorts of traffik, make a tung of account? If the spreading sea, and the spacious land could vse anie speche, theie would both shew you, where, and in how manie strange places, theie haue sene our peple, and also giue you to wit, that theie deall in as much, and as great varietie of matters, as anie other peple do, whether at home or abrode. Which is the reason why our tung doth serue to so manie vses, bycause it is conuersant with so manie peple, and so well acquainted with so manie matters, in so sundrie kindes of dealing. Now all this varietie of matter, and diuersitie of trade, make both matter for our speche, & mean to enlarge it. For he that is so practised, will vtter that, which he practiseth in his naturall tung, and if the strangenesse of the matter do so require, he that is to vtter, rather then he will stik in his vtterance, will vse the foren term, by waie of premunition, that the cuntrie peple do call it so, and by that mean make a foren word, an English denison.[1]

---

[1] [*denison* denizen, naturalized inhabitant.]

All which reasons concerning but the tung, and the account thereof, being put together, as of themselues, theie proue the nations exercise in learning, and their practis in other dealings: so theie seme to infer no base witted pcple, not to amplify it with more, bycause it is not for foulls to be so well learned, to be so warrious, to be so well practised. I shall not nede to proue anie of these my positions, either by foren or home historie: seing my reader stranger, will not striue with me for them, and mine own nation, will not gainsaie me in them, I think, which knoweth them to be trew, and maie vse them for their honor.

Wherefor I maie well conclude my first position: that if *vse* and *custom* hauing the help of so long time, and continuance, wherein to fine[1] our tung: of so great learning and experience, which furnish matter for the fining: of so good wits and iudgements, which can tell how to fine, haue griped at nothing in all that time with all that cunning, by all those wits, which theie will not let go, but hold for most certaine, in the right of our writing: that then our tung hath no certaintie to trust to, but writeth all at randon. But the antecedent in my opinion, is alltogether vn-possible, wherefor the consequent, is a great deall more then probable, which is, that our tung hath in hir own possession, and writing verie good euidence to proue hir own right writing: Which tho no man as yet, by anie publik writing of his, semeth to haue sene, yet the tung it self is redie to shew them, to anie whosoeuer, which is able to read them, and withall to iudge, what euidence is right in the right of writing. Wherefor seing I haue proued sufficientlie in mine own opinion, that there is great cause, why our tung should haue som good right, in her own writing, and take my self to haue had the sight of that euidence, whereby that same right appeareth most iustifiable, and am not alltogither ignorant, how to giue sentence thereof, I will do my best, accord-ing to that course, which I said was kept in the first, and generall fining of anie speche, which also hath bene translated to euerie secondarie, and particular tung, to set furth som certaintie for the

English writing, by those notes, which I haue obserued in the tung it self, the pure best and finest therein, offering mean by comparison with them selues, both to correct, and to direct the worse and more grosse, without either innouating anie thing, as theie do, which set furth new deuises, or by mistaking my waie, as theie do, which despare, that our tung can be brought to anie certaintie, without som maruellous foren help. Thus much for the artificiall stuf in our tung, now to the obiections which charge it with infirmities.

3

WILLIAM HARRISON

(1534–1593)

The second edition of Raphael Holinshed's *Chronicles* included Harrison's *Descriptions* of Britain and of England as prefatory matter. They were indebted to earlier studies, but through their publication with the *Chronicles* the material in them achieved wide readership, including Shakespeare, who used this edition as a source, and Spenser, who said the book 'hath much furthered and advantaged me'. Harrison shares Mulcaster's patriotic confidence in the English language as it had developed among Elizabethan writers, and his linguistic geography of Britain singles out the southern dialect as the most excellent. In addition he employs linguistic data, including etymology, for historical purposes.

'Of the languages spoken in this Iland'

(Chapter vi from *The Description of Britaine*, 1587)

What language came first with SAMOTHES and afterward with ALBION, and the giants of his companie, it is hard for me to determine, sith nothing of sound credit remaineth in writing, which may resolue vs in the truth hereof. Yet of so much are we certeine, that the speach of the ancient Britons, and of the Celts, had great affinitie one with another, so that they were either all one, or at leastwise such as either nation with small helpe of interpretors might vnderstand other, and readilie discerne what the speaker meant. Some are of the opinion that the Celts spake Greeke, and how the British toong resembled the same, which was spoken in Grecia before HOMER did reforme it: but I see that these men doo speake without authoritie and therefore I reiect them, for if the Celts which were properlie called Galles did speake Gréeke, why did Cesar in his letters sent to Rome vse that language, because that if they should be intercepted they might

13

not vnderstand them, or why did he not vnderstand the Galles, he being so skilfull in the language without an interpretor? Yet I denie not but that the Celtish and British speaches might haue great affinitie one with another, and the British aboue all other with the Greeke, for both doo appéere by certeine words, as first in TRI for three, MARCH for an horsse, & TRIMARCHIA, whereof PAUSANIAS speaketh, for both. ATHENEUS also writeth of BATHANASIUS a capitaine of the Galles, whose name is méere British, compounded of BATH & YNAD, & signifieth a noble or comelie iudge. And wheras he saith that the reliques of the Galles tooke vp their first dwelling about Isther, and afterward diuided themselues in such wise, that they which went and dwelled in Hungarie were called SORDSAI, and the other (that inhabited within the dominion of Tyroll) Brenni, whose seate was on the mount Brenhere parcell of the Alpes, what else signifieth the word ISCAREDICH in British, from whence the word SCORDISCI commeth, but to be diuided? Hereby then, and sundrie other the like testimonies, I gather that the British and the Celtish speaches had great affinitie one with another, as I said, which Cesar (speaking of the similitude or likenesse of religion in both nations) doth also auerre, & TACITUS *in vita* AGRICOLÆ, in like sort plainlie affirmeth, or else it must needs be that the Galles which inuaded Italie and Greece were meere Britons, of whose likenes of speech with the Grécke toong I need not make anie triall, sith no man (I hope) will readilie denie it. APPIANUS talking of the Brenni calleth them Cymbres, and by this I gather also that the Celts and the Britons were indifferentlie called CYMBRI in their owne language, or else that the Britons were the right CYMBRI, who vnto this daie doo not refuse to be called by that name. BODINUS writing of the means by which the originall of euerie kingdome and nation is to be had and discerned, setteth downe thrée waies whereby the knowledge thereof is to be found, one is (saith he) the infallible testimonie of the sound writers, the other the description and site of the region, the third the relikes of the ancient speech remaining in the same. Which later if it be of any force, then I must conclude, that the spéech of the Britons and Celts was sometime either all one or verie like one to another, or else it must follow that the Britons ouerflowed the continent vnder the name of Cymbres, being peraduenture associat in this voiage, or mixed by inuasion with the Danes, and Norwegiens, who are called CYMBRI and CYMMERIJ, as most writers doo remember. This also is euident (as PLUTARCH likewise confesseth *In vita Marij*) that no man knew from whence the Cymbres came in his daies, and therfore I beleeue that they came out of Britaine, for all the maine was well knowne vnto them, I meane euen to the vttermost part of the north, as may appeare furthermore by the slaues which were dailie brought from thence vnto them, whom of their countries they called DAUI for DACI, GETÆ for GOTHES, &c: for of their conquests I need not make rehearsall, sith they are commonlie knowne and remembred by the writers, both of the Greekes and Latines.

The British toong called CAMBERAEC dooth yet remaine in that part of the Iland, which is now called Wales, whither the Britons were driuen after the Saxons had made a full conquest of the other, which we now call England, although the pristinate integritie thereof be not a little diminished by mixture of the Latine and Saxon speaches withall. Howbeit, manie poesies and writings (in making whereof that nation hath euermore delited) are yet extant in my time, wherby some difference betwéene the ancient and present language may easilie be discerned, notwithstanding that among all these there is nothing to be found, which can set downe anie sound and full testimonie of their owne originall, in remembrance whereof, their BARDS and cunning men haue béene most slacke and negligent. GIRALDUS in praising the Britons affirmeth that there is not one word in all their language, that is not either Gréeke or Latine. Which being rightly vnderstanded and conferred with the likenesse that was in old time betwéene the Celts & the British toongs, will not a little helpe those that thinke the old Celtish to haue some sauour of the Gréeke. But how soeuer that matter standeth, after the British speach came once ouer into this Iland, sure it is, that it could neuer be extinguished for all the attempts that the Romans, Saxons, Normans, and Englishmen could make against that nation, in anie maner of wise.

Petigrées and genealogies also the Welsh Britons haue plentie in their owne toong, insomuch that manie of them can readilie deriue the same, either from Brute or some of his band, euen vnto ÆNEAS and other of the Troians, and so foorth vnto Noah without anie maner of stop. But as I know not what credit is to be giuen vnto them in this behalfe, although I must néeds confesse that their ancient BARDS were verie diligent in there collection, and had also publike allowance or salarie for the same; so I dare not absolutelie impugne their assertions, sith that in times past all nations (learning it no doubt of the Hebrues) did verie solemnelie preserue the catalogs of their descents, thereby either to shew themselues of ancient and noble race, or else to be descended from some one of the gods. But

Stemmata quid faciunt? quid prodest Pontice longo
Sanguine censeri? aut quid auorum ducere turmas? &c.[1]

Next vnto the British speach, the Latine toong was brought in by the Romans, and in maner generallie planted through the whole region, as the French was after by the Normans. Of this toong I will not say much, bicause there are few which be not skilfull in the same. Howbeit, as the speach it selfe is easie and delectable, so hath it peruerted the names of the ancient riuers, regions, & cities of Britaine in such wise, that in these our daies their old British denominations are quite growne out of memorie, and yet those of the new Latine left as most vncertaine. This remaineth also vnto my time, borowed from the Romans, that all our déeds, euidences, charters, & writings of record, are set downe in the Latine toong, though now verie barbarous, and therevnto the

---

[1] [*Stemmata...turmas?* What use are pedigrees? What use, Ponticus, to be thought of ancient lineage? Or to display the throngs of your forefathers? etc. (Juvenal, *Sat.* 8. 1–2, reading *pictos ostendere uultus* for *aut...turmas*).]

copies and court-rolles, and processes of courts and leets registred in the same.

The third language apparantlie knowne is the Scithian or high Dutch, induced at the first by the Saxons (which the Britons call SAYSONAEC, as they doo the speakers SAYSON) an hard and rough kind of speach, God wot, when our nation was brought first into acquaintance withall, but now changed with vs into a farre more fine and easie kind of vtterance, and so polished and helped with new and milder words, that it is to be aduouched how there is no one speach vnder the sunne spoken in our time, that hath or can haue more varietie of words, copie[1] of phrases, or figures and floures of eloquence, than hath our English toong, although some haue affirmed vs rather to barke as dogs, than talke like men, bicause the most of our words (as they doo indéed) incline vnto one syllable. This also is to be noted as a testimonie remaining still of our language, deriued from the Saxons, that the generall name for the most part of euerie skilfull artificer in his trade endeth in HERE with vs, albeit the H be left out, and ER onlie inserted, as Scriuenhere, writehere, shiphere, &c: for scriuener, writer, and shipper, &c: beside manie other relikes of that spéech, neuer to be abolished.

After the Saxon toong, came the Norman or French language ouer into our countrie, and therein were our lawes written for a long time. Our children also were by an especiall decrée taught first to speake the same, and therevnto inforced to learne their constructions in the French, whensoeuer they were set to the Grammar schoole. In like sort few bishops, abbats, or other clergie men, were admitted vnto anie ecclesiasticall function here among vs, but such as came out of religious houses from beyond the seas, to the end they should not vse the English toong in their sermons to the people. In the court also it grew into such contempt, that most men thought it no small dishonor to speake any English there. Which brauerie tooke his hold at the last likewise in the countrie with euerie plowman, that euen the verie carters

---

[1] [*copie* abundance, copiousness.]

began to wax wearie of there mother toong, & laboured to speake French, which as then was counted no small token of gentilitie. And no maruell, for euerie French rascall, when he came once hither, was taken for a gentleman, onelie bicause he was proud, and could vse his owne language, and all this (I say) to exile the English and British speaches quite out of the countrie. But in vaine, for in the time of king Edward the first, to wit, toward the latter end of his reigne, the French it selfe ceased to be spoken generallie, but most of all and by law in the midst of Edward the third, and then began the English to recouer and grow in more estimation than before; notwithstanding that among our artificers, the most part of their implements, tooles and words of art reteine still their French denominations euen to these our daies, as the language it selfe is vsed likewise in sundrie courts, bookes of record, and matters of law; whereof here is no place to make any particular rehearsall. Afterward also, by diligent trauell of GEFFRAY CHAUCER, and IOHN GOWRE, in the time of Richard the second, and after them of IOHN SCOGAN, and IOHN LYDGATE monke of Berrie, our said toong was brought to an excellent passe, notwithstanding that it neuer came vnto the type of perfection, vntill the time of Quéene Elizabeth, wherein IOHN IEWELL Bishop of Sarum, IOHN FOX, and sundrie learned & excellent writers haue fullie accomplished the ornature of the same, to their great praise and immortall commendation; although not a few other doo greatlie séeke to staine the same, by fond affectation of forren and strange words, presuming that to be the best English, which is most corrupted with externall termes of eloquence, and sound of manie syllables. But as this excellencie of the English toong is found in one, and the south part of this Iland; so in Wales the greatest number (as I said) retaine still their owne ancient language, that of the north part of the said countrie being lesse corrupted than the other, and therefore reputed for the better in their owne estimation and iudgement. This also is proper to vs Englishmen, that sith ours is a meane[1] language, and neither too rough nor too

[1] [*meane* in-between.]

smooth in vtterance, we may with much facilitie learne any other language, beside Hebrue, Gréeke & Latine, and speake it naturallie, as if we were home-borne in those countries; & yet on the other side it falleth out, I wot not by what other meanes, that few forren nations can rightlie pronounce ours, without some and that great note of imperfection, especiallie the French men, who also seldome write any thing that sauoreth of English trulie. It is a pastime to read how NATALIS COMES in like maner, speaking of our affaires, dooth clip the names of our English lords. But this of all the rest dooth bréed most admiration with me, that if any stranger doo hit vpon some likelie pronuntiation of our toong, yet in age he swarueth so much from the same, that he is woorse therein than euer he was, and thereto peraduenture halteth not a litle also in his owne, as I haue séene by experience in REGINALD WOLFE, and other, whereof I haue iustlie maruelled.

The Cornish and Deuonshire men, whose countrie the Britons call CERNIW, haue a speach in like sort of their owne, and such as hath in déed more affinitie with the Armoricane toong than I can well discusse of. Yet in mine opinion, they are both but a corrupted kind of British, albeit so far degenerating in these daies from the old, that if either of them doo méete with a Welshman, they are not able at the first to vnderstand one an other, except here and there in some od words, without the helpe of interpretors. And no maruell (in mine opinion) that the British of Cornewall is thus corrupted, sith the Welsh toong that is spoken in the north & south part of Wales, doth differ so much in it selfe, as the English vsed in Scotland dooth from that which is spoken among vs here in this side of the Iland, as I haue said alreadie.

The Scottish english hath beene much broader and lesse pleasant in vtterance than ours, because that nation hath not till of late indeuored to bring the same to any perfect order, and yet it was such in maner, as Englishmen themselues did speake for the most part beyond the Trent, whither any great amendement of our language had not as then extended it selfe. Howbeit in our time the Scottish language endeuoreth to come neere, if not altogither to match our toong in finenesse of phrase, and copie of words, and this may in part appeare by an historie of the Apocrypha translated into Scottish verse by HUDSON, dedicated to the king of that countrie, and conteining sixe books, except my memorie doo faile me.

Thus we sée how that vnder the dominion of the king of England, and in the south parts of the realme, we haue thrée seuerall toongs, that is to saie, English, British, and Cornish, and euen so manie are in Scotland, if you accompt the English speach for one: notwithstanding that for bredth and quantitie of the region, I meane onelie of the soile of the maine Iland, it be somewhat lesse to see to than the other. For in the north part of the region, where the wild Scots, otherwise called the Redshanks, or rough footed Scots (because they go bare footed and clad in mantels ouer their saffron shirts after the Irish maner) doo inhabit, they speake good Irish which they call Gachtlet, as they saie of one Gathelus, whereby they shew their originall to haue in times past béene fetched out of Ireland: as I noted also in the chapiter precedent, and wherevnto VINCENTIUS *cap. de insulis Oceani* dooth yéeld his assent, saieng that Ireland was in time past called SCOTIA; *Scotia eadem* (saith he) *& Hibernia, proxima Britanniæ insula, spatio terrarum angustior, sed situ fœcundior; Scotia autem à Scotorum gentibus traditur appellata, &c.*[1] Out of the 14. booke of ISIDORUS intituled *Originum*, where he also addeth that it is called HYBERNIA, because it bendeth toward IBERIA. But I find elsewhere that it is so called by certeine Spaniards which came to seeke and plant their inhabitation in the same, wherof in my Chronologie I haue spoken more at large.

In the Iles of the ORCHADES, or Orkeney, as we now call them, & such coasts of Britaine as doo abbut vpon the same, the Gottish or Danish speach is altogither in vse, and also in Shetland, by reason (as I take it) that the princes of Norwaie held those Ilands

---

[1] [*Scotia...appellata* Scotland, or Ireland, the island next to Britain, is narrower in space of land, but of a more fertile situation; Scotland takes its name from the peoples of the Scots, etc. (Vincent of Beauvais, *Speculum Naturale*, XXXII. 16, 'Of the islands of the ocean', reading *creditur* for *traditur*).]

so long vnder their subiection, albeit they were otherwise reputed as rather to belong to Ireland, bicause that the verie soile of them is enimie to poison, as some write, although for my part I had neuer any sound experience of the truth hereof. And thus much haue I thought good to speake of our old speaches, and those fiue languages now vsuallie spoken within the limits of our Iland.

4

WILLIAM CAMDEN

(1551–1623)

Camden was a friend of Sir Philip Sidney, and patron and tutor of Ben Jonson, who dedicated two plays to him and wrote in *Epigram xiv* of

> Camden, most reverend head, to whom I owe
> All that I am in arts, all that I know
> ...to whom my countrey owes
> The great renowne, and name wherewith shee goes.

He rejected linguistic mythologizing and advanced the objective study of factual material, pondering the interrelationship of languages, comparing the changes in a text over a thousand years, accepting the idea of linguistic change without either decrying or overpraising the earlier language. His attitude toward the adequacy of English, and particularly toward its spelling, recalls Mulcaster.

'The Languages'

(From *Remaines Concerning Britain*, 1605)

From the people we will now proceede to the languages. Heere would Schollers shew you the first confusion of languages out of *Moses*, that the gods had their peculiar tongue out of *Homer*, that brute beasts, birdes, and fishes, had their owne proper languages out of *Clemens Alexandrinus*. They would teach you out of *Euphorus*, that there were but 52. tongues in the world, because so many soules out of *Iacob* descended into *Ægypt*, and out of *Arnobius*, that there were seaventie and two: Albeit *Timosthenes* reporteth that in *Dioscurias* a mart towne of *Colchis*, their trafficked 300. Nations of divers languages: And howsoever our *Indian* or *American* discouerers say, that in every fourescore mile in *America*, and in every valley almost of *Peru* you shall finde a new language. Neither would they omit the Iland where the people have cloven tongues out of the fabulous *Narrations* of *Diodorus Siculus*: yea, they would lash out of the *Vtopian* language with

Volvola Barchin hemam, la lalvola drame pagloni.[1]

whenas it is a greater glory now to be a *Linguist*, then a *Realist*. They would moreover discourse at large, which I will tell you in a word. First the British tongue or Welsh (as we now call it) was in vse onely in this Island, having great affinitie with the olde *Galliqua* of *Gaule*, now *Fraunce*, from whence the first inhabitants in all probability came hither. Afterward the *Latin* was taken vp when it was brought into the forme of a Province, about the time of *Domitian*, according to that notable place of *Tacitus*, where he reporteth that *Iulius Agricola* Governour heere for the *Romans*, preferred the *Britans*, as able to doe more by witte, then the *Gaules* by studie: *Vt qui* (saieth he) *modò linguam Romanam abnuebant, eloquentiam concupiscerent. Inde etiam habitus nostri honor & frequens toga.*[2] But the *British* overgrewe the *Latine*, and continueth yet in *Wales*, and some villages of *Cornwall* intermingled with some *Provinciall Latine*. Afteı ɟlιc Irish tongue was brought into the Northwest partes of the Isle, out of *Ireland* by the auntient Scottishmen, and there yet remaineth. Lastly, the *English-Saxon* tongue came in by the *English-Saxons* out of *Germany*, who valiantly and wisely performed heere all the three things, which implie a full conquest, viz. the alteration of lawes, language, and attire.

This English tongue extracted out of the olde *German*, as most other from *Island*[3] to the *Alpes*, is mixed as it is now, of the olde *English-Saxon* & *Norman-French*, as the *French* of *Latine*, *German*, and the olde *Gallique*, the *Italian* of *Latine* and *German-Gotish*, and the *Spanish* of *Latine*, *Gotish-German* and *Arabique*, *Saracen*, or

---

[1] [*Volvola...pagloni* the last line, somewhat misquoted, of a quatrain 'in the Utopian tongue' prefixed to Sir Thomas More's *Utopia* (1516). Although a hexameter line and accompanied with a Latin 'translation', it is meaningless.]

[2] [*Vt...toga* So that those who used to reject the Latin language, came to desire eloquence. And our costume became a distinction, our toga a fashion (Tacitus, *Agricola*, 21).]

[3] [*Island* Iceland.]

Morisquo. And to the honour of our progenitors the *English-Saxons* be it spoken, their conquest was more absolute heere over the *Britaines*, than either of the *Francs* in *Fraunce* over the *Gaules*, or the *Gothes* and *Lombardes* in *Italie* over the *Romans*, or of the *Gothes*, *Vandales*, and *Moores* over the auntient *Spaniards* in *Spaine*. For in these nations much of the provinciall Latine (I meane the Latine vsed whilest they were Provinces of the *Romans*) remaineth, which they politikely had spread over their Empire, by planting of Colonies and enfranchising all Nations subiect vnto them. But the *English-Saxon* conquerors, altred the tongue which they found here wholy: so that no *British* words, or provinciall *Latine* appeared therein at the first: & in short time they spread it over this whole *Iland*, from the *Orcades* to the Isle of *Wight*, except a few barren corners in the *Westerne* parts, wherevnto the reliques of the *Britans* and *Scots* retyred, reserving in them both their life and their language. For certainely it is that the greatest and best parts, the East and South of *Scotland*, which call themselves the *Lawland-men*, speake the English tongue varied onely in *Dialect*, as descended from the *English-Saxons*: and the old *Scottish*, which is the verie *Irish*, is vsed onely by them of the West, called the *Hechtland-men*,[1] who call the other as the Welsh call vs *Sassons*, *Saxons*, both in respect of language and originall, as I shewed before.

I dare not yet heere affirme for the antiquitie of our language, that our great-great-great-grandsires tongue came out of *Persia*, albeit the wonderfull Linguist *Ioseph Scaliger* hath observed, *Fader*, *Moder*, *Bruder*, *Band*, &c. in the *Persian* tongue in the very sence as we now vse them.

It will not be vnproper I hope to this purpose, if I note out of the epistles of that learned Ambassadour *Busbequius*, how the inhabitants of *Taurica Chersonessus*, in the vttermost part of *Europe* eastward, have these words, *Wind*, *Silver*, *Korne*, *Salt*, *Fish*, *Son*, *Apple*, *Waggen*, *Singen*, *Ilanda*, *Beard*, with many other in the very same sence and signification, as they now are in vse with vs, whereat I mervailed not a little when I first read it. But nothing

[1] [*Hechtland* Highland.]

can bee gathered thereby, but that the *Saxons* our progenitours, which planted themselves heere in the West, did also to their glorie place *Colonies* likewise there in the East.

As in the Latine tongue, the learned make in respect of time, foure *Idioms*, the *Antient*, the *Latine*, the *Roman*, the *Mixt*: so we in ours may make the *Antient English-Saxon*, and the *Mixt*. But that you may see how powerable time is in altering tongues as all things else, I will set downe the Lords prayer as it was translated in sundrie ages, that you may see by what degrees our tongue is risen, and thereby coniecture how in time it may alter and fall againe.

If we could set it downe in the antient *Saxon*, I meane in the tongue which the English vsed at their first arrivall heere, about 420. yeares after Christs birth, it would seeme most strange and harsh Dutch or Gebrish,[1] as women call it; or when they first embraced Christianitie, about the yeare of Christ 600. But the antientst that I can finde, was about 900. yeare since, about the yeare of Christ 700. found in an antient *Saxon*, glossed *Evangelists* in the hands of my good friend Maister *Robert Bowyer*, written by *Eadfride* the eight Bishop of *Lindisfarne*, (which after was translated to *Durham*,) and divided according to the antient *Canon* of *Eusebius*, not into chapters, for *Stephen Langton*, Archbishop of *Canturburie*, first divided the holy Scriptures into chapters, as *Robert Stephan*[2] did lately into verse; and thus it is.

Our Father which art   in heaven   be   hallowed   thin   name.
Vren Fader thic   arth in heofnas, Sie gehalgud thin noma,

  come   thy   kingdom. Be   thy   will   so   as in heaven   and
to cymeth thin ric.   Sie thin willa sue is in heofnas, and

in earth.   Oure lofe Super-substantiall give vs to day,   and
in eortho. Vren hlaf ofer   wirtlic   sel   vs to daeg, and

forgive vs debts   oures so   we forgive   debts   oures, and
forgef vs scylda urna, sue we forgefan scyldgum vrum, and

---

[1] [*Gebrish* gibberish.]
[2] [*Robert Stephan* Robert Estienne, scholar, printer and lexicographer.]

do not led vs   into temptation. But deliver everyone from   evill.
no inlead vsith in   custnung, Ah gefrig vrich   from ifle.
Amen.

Some two hundred yeeres after, I finde this somewhat varied
in two translations.

Thu vre fader the eart on heofenum Si thin nama gehalgod.
Cum thin ric. Si thin willa[1] on eorthan, swa swa on heofenum.

dayly   *trespasses*
Syle vs to dæg vrn dægthanlican hlaf. And forgif vs vre gyltas

against vs have trespassed
swa, swa we forgifath tham the with vs agyltath.[2]   And

Be it so.
ne led the vs on costnung, Ac alys vs from yfle. Si it swa.[3]

About an hundred and three score yeeres after, in the time of
king *Henry* the second, I find this in rime sent from *Rome* by
Pope *Adrian* an Englishman, to be taught to the people.

> *Vre fadyr in heaven rich,*
> *Thy name be halyed everlich:*
> *Thou bring vs thy michell blisse,*
> *Als hit in heaven y-doe,*
> *Evar in yearth beene it also:*
> *That holy bread that lasteth ay,*
> *Thou send it ous this ilke day.*
> *Forgive ous all that we havith don,*
> *As wee forgivet vch other mon:*
> *Ne let ous fall into no founding,*
> *Ac sheild ous fro the fowle thing. Amen.*

Neither was there any great variation in the time of king *Henry*
the third, as appeereth in this of that age, as I coniecture by the
Character;   *Fader that art in heavin blisse,*
             Thin helge nam it wurth the blisse.

---

[1] Gewurth thin willa.   [2] Vrum gyltendum.   [3] Sothlice.

Cumen & mot thi kingdom,
Thin holy will it be all don,
In heaven and in erdh also,
So it shall bin full well Ic tro.
Gif vs all bread on this day,
And forgif vs vre sinnes,
As we do vre wider winnes:
Let vs not in fonding fall,
O ac fro evill thu syld vs all. Amen.

In the time of king *Richard* the second about a hundred and odde yeeres after, it was so mollified, that it came to be thus, as it is in the Translation of *Wickliffe*, with some Latine wordes now inserted, whereas there was not one before.

Our fadyr, that art in heaven, halloed be thy name, thy kingdom com to,
be thy will done, so in heaven, and in erth: gif to vs this day our bread
over other substance: and forgif to vs our dettis, as we forgeven to our
detters, and leed vs nott into temptation, but deliver vs fro evill. Amen.

Hitherto will our sparkefull Youth laugh at their great grand-fathers *English*, who had more care to do well, than to speake minion-like, and left more glory to vs by their exploiting of great actes, than we shall do by our sonnetting.

Great verily was the glory of our tongue before the *Norman* Conquest in this, that the olde *English* could expresse most aptly, all the conceiptes of the minde in their owne tongue without borrowing from any. As for example:

The holy service of God, which the *Latines* called *Religion*, because it knitted the mindes of men together, and most people of *Europe* have borrowed the same from them, they called most significantly *Ean-fastnes*, as the one and onely assurance and fast anker-holde of our soules health.

The gladsome tidings of our salvation, which the *Greekes* called *Evangelion*, and other Nations in the same word, they called *Godspel*, that is, *Gods speech.*

For our *Saviour*, which wee borrowed from the *French*, and they from the *Latin Salvator*, they called in their owne word, *Haelend* from *Hael*, that is, *Salus*, safetie, which we retaine still in *Al-hael*, and *Was-hael*, that is, *Ave*, *Salve*, *Sis salvus*.

They could call the disciples of Christ, *Leorning Cnihtas*, that is, *Learning Servitours*. For *Cniht* which is now a name of worship, signified with them an *Attendant*, or servitour.

They could name the *Pharises* according to the *Hebrew*, *Sunder-halgens*, as holy religious men which had sundred and severed themselves from other.

The Scribes they could call in their proper signification, as *Booke-men*, *Bocer*. So they called parchment which wee have catcht from the Latine *Pergamenum*, *Boc-fell* in respect of the vse.

So they could call the sacrament *Haligdome*, as holy iudgement. For so it is according as we receive it.

They could call *Fertilitie* and fruitfulnesse of land significatively *Eordes-wela*, as wealth of the earth.

They could call a *Comet*, a *Faxed starre*; which is all one with *Stella Crinita*, or *Cometa*. So they did call the iudgement seate *Domesettle*.

That which we call the *Parlament* of the *French Parler* to speake, they called a *Witten mot*, as the meeting and assembly of wise men.

The certaine and inward knowledge of that which is in our minde, be it good or bad, which in the Latine word we call *Conscience*, they called *Inwit*, as that which they did inwardly wit and wote, that is, know certainely.

That in a river which the Latines call *Alveus*, and *Canalis*, and from thence most nations of *Europe* name the *Chanel*, *Kanel*, *Canale*, *&c.* they properly called the *Streame-race*.

Neither in the degrees of kinred they were destitute of significative woordes; for he whom we of a *French* & *English* compound word call *Grandfather*, they called *Eald-fader*, whom we call *Great Grandfather* they called *Thirda-fader*. So *Proavus*, which we call *Great Great Grandfather*, they called *Fortha-fader*, as *Abavus*, *Fiftha-fader*.

An *Eunuch*, for whome we have no name, but from the *Greekes*, they could aptly name *Vnstana*, that is, without stones, as we vse *Vnspotted* for without spotte, *Vnlearned*, for, without learning.

A Covetous man whome we so call of the *French Convoitise*, they truely called *Git-sor*, as a sore & eagre *Getter*, and *Gatherer*.

That which the Latines call *Abortus*, and wee in many wordes, *Vntimely Birth*, or, *Borne before the full time*, they called *Miss-borne*.

A *Porter*, which wee have received from the *French*, they could in their own word as significatively call *A Doreward*.

I could particulate in many more, but this woulde appeare most plentifully, if the labours of the learned Gentlemen Maister *Laurence Nowell* of *Lincolnes Inne*, who first in our time recalled the studie heereof, Maister *William Lambert*, Maister *Iohn Ioscelin*, Maister *Francis Tate* were once published. Otherwise it is to bee feared, that devouring *Time*, in few yeeres will vtterly swallow it, without hope of recoverie.

The alteration and innovation in our tongue as in all others, hath beene brought in by entrance of Strangers, as *Danes*, *Normans*, and others which have swarmed hither, by trafficke, for new words as well as for new wares, have alwaies come in by the tyranne *Time*, which altereth all vnder heaven, by *Vse*, which swayeth most, and hath an absolute command in words, and by *Pregnant wits*: specially since that learning after long banishment, was recalled in the time of King *Henry* the eight, it hath beene beautified and enriched out of other good tongues, partly by enfranchising and endenizing strange words, partly by refining and mollifying olde words, partly by implanting new wordes with artificiall composition, happily containing themselves within the bounds prescribed by *Horace*. So that our tong is (and I doubt not but hath beene) as copious, pithie, and significative, as any other tongue in *Europe*: and I hope we are not yet and shall not heereafter come to that which *Seneca* saw in his time, *When mens mindes beginne once to iniure themselves to dislike whatsoever is vsuall, is disdained. They affect noveltie in speech, they recall forworne and vncuth words, they forge new phrases, and that which is newest, is best liked; there is presumptuous and farre fetching of words. And some there are which thinke it a grace if their speech doe hover, and thereby hold the hearer in suspence*: you know what followeth.

Omitting this, pardon me and thinke me not overballanced with affection, if I thinke that our *English* tongue is (I will not say as sacred as the *Hebrew*, or as learned as the *Greeke*,) but as fluent as the *Latine*, as courteous as the *Spanish*, as courtlike as the *French*, and as amorous as the *Italian*, as some Italianated amorous have confessed. Neither hath any thing detracted more from the dignitie of our tongue, than our owne affection of forraine tongues, by admiring, praising, and studying them above measure: whereas the wise *Romans* thought no small part of their honour to consist in the honour of their language, esteeming it a dishonour to answer any forrainer in his owne language. As for a long time the English placed in the Borrough townes of *Ireland* and *Wales*, would admit neither Irish nor Welsh among them. And not long since for the honour of our native tongue, *Henry Fitz-Allan* Earle of *Arundell*, in his travaile into *Italie*, and the Lord *William Howard* of *Effingham*, in his government of *Calice*,[1] albeit they were not ignorant of other forraine tongues, would answer no strangers by word or writing, but onely in English. As in this consideration also before them Cardinall *Wolsey* in his ambassage into *France*, commaunded all his servaunts to vse no French, but meere English to the French, in all communication whatsoever.

As for the *Monosyllables* so rife in our tongue which were not so originally, although they are vnfitting for verses and measures, yet are they most fit for expressing briefly the first conceipts of the minde, or *Intentionalia* as they call them in schooles: so that we can set downe more matter in fewer lines, than any other language. Neither do we or the Welsh so curtall *Latine*, that we make all therein *Monosyllables*, as *Ioseph Scaliger* chargeth vs; who in the meane time forgetteth that his Frenchmen have put in their *Proviso* in the edict of *Pacification* in the *Grammaticall* warre, that they might not pronounce *Latine* distinctly, as the English common

[1] [*Calice* Calais.]

Lawyers obtained then a *Reservation* that they might write false *Latine*, and the Irish not to observe quantitie of syllables. I cannot yet but confesse that we have corruptly contracted most names both of men and places, if they were of more then two sillables, and thereby hath ensued no little obscuritie.

Whereas our tongue is mixed, it is no disgrace, whenas all the tongues of *Europe* doe participate interchangeably the one of the other, and in the learned tongues, there hath been like borrowing one from another. Yet is it false which *Gesner* affirmeth, that our tongue is the most mixt and corrupt of all other. For if it may please any to compare but the Lords Prayer in other languages, he shall finde as few *Latine* and borrowed forraine words in ours, as in any other whatsoever. Notwithstanding the diversitie of Nations which have swarmed hither, and the practise of the Normans, who as a monument of their Conquest, would have yoaked the English vnder their tongue, as they did vnder their command, by compelling them to teach their children in schooles nothing but French, by setting downe their lawes in the Norman-French, and enforcing them most rigorously to pleade and to be impleaded in that tongue onely, for the space of three hundred yeares, vntill King *Edward* the third enlarged them first from that bondage. Since which time, our language hath risen by little, and the proverbe proved vntrue, which so long had beene vsed, *Iacke would be a gentleman, if he could speake any French.*

Heerein is a notable argument of our Ancestors stedfastnes in esteeming and retaining their owne tongue. For as before the Conquest they misliked nothing more in King *Edward* the Confessor, than that he was Frenchified, & accounted the desire of forraine language, then to be a foretoken of the bringing in of forraine powers, which indeede happened. In like manner after the Conquest, notwithstanding those enforcements of the Normans in supplanting it, and the nature of men, which is most pliable with a curious iolitie to fashion & frame themselves according to the manners, attyre, and language of the Conquerours. Yet in all that long space of 300. yeares, they intermingled very few

French-Norman words, except some termes of law, hunting, hawking, and dicing, whenas wee within these 60. yeares, have incorporated so many Latine and French, as the third part of our tongue consisteth now in them. But like themselves, continue still those old Englishmen which were planted in *Ireland*, in *Fingall*, & the Country of *Weysford*, in the time of King *Henry* the second, who yet still continue their antient attyre and tongue, in somuch that an English gentleman not long since, sent thither in Commission among them, said that he would quickly vnderstand the Irish, when they spake the antient English. So that our Ancestors seemed in part as iealous of their native language, as those *Britans* which passed hence into *Armorica* in *France*, and marrying strange women there, did cut out their tongs, lest their children should corrupt their language with their mothers tongues, or as the *Germans* which have most of all Nations opposed themselves against all innovations in habite, and language.

Whereas the *Hebrew Rabbines* say, and that truly, that Nature hath given man five instruments for the pronouncing of all letters, the lips, the teeth, the tongue, the palate, and throate; I will not denie but some among vs do pronounce more fully, some flatly, some broadly, and no few mincingly, offending in defect, excesse, or change of letters, which is rather to be imputed to the persons and their education, than to the language. Whenas generally wee pronounce by the confession of strangers, as sweetely, smoothly, and moderately, as any of the Northerne Nations of the world, who are noted to soupe[1] their words out of the throat with fat and full spirits.

This variety of pronuntiation hath brought in some diversitie of Orthographie, and heere-vpon Sir *Iohn Price*, to the derogation of our tongue, and glorie of his *Welsh*, reporteth that a sentence spoken by him in *English*, & penned out of his mouth by foure good Secretaries, severally, for trial of our Orthography, was so set downe by them, that they all differed one from the other in many letters: whereas so many *Welsh* writing the same likewise

[1] [*soupe* utter forcibly.]

in their tongue varied not in any one letter at all. Well, I will not derogate from the good Knights credite; yet it hath beene seene where tenne English writing the same sentence, have all so concurred, that among them all there hath beene no other difference, than the adding, or omitting once or twice of our silent *E*, in the end of some wordes. As for the *Welsh*, I could never happen on two of that Nation together, that would acknowledge that they could write their owne language.

Sir *Thomas Smith* her Maiesties secretarie not long since, a man of great learning and iudgement, occasioned by som vncertainty of our Orthographie, though it seeme grounded vpon *Sound, Reason*, and *Custome*, laboured to reduce it to certaine heads; Seeing that whereas of Necessity there must be so many letters in every tongue, as there are simple and single sounds, that the Latine letters were not sufficient to expresse all our simple sounds. Therefore he wished that we should have A short, and A long, bicause *a* in 𝕸𝖆𝖓, and in *Mân* of horse hath different sounds; E long as in *Mên* moderate, and *e* short as in 𝕸𝖊𝖓, and an English 𝖊 as in 𝖜𝖊𝖊, 𝖙𝖍𝖊𝖊, 𝖍𝖊, 𝖒𝖊: I long, and I short, as in Bi, *per*, and Bî, *emere*: O short, and O long, as in smōk of a woman, and smôk of the fire: V long, as in Bût, *Ocrea*, and V short, as in Būt, *Sed*: and v or y *Greeke*, as slu, nu, tru. For consonants he would have C be never vsed but for Ch, as it was among the olde English, and K in all other words; for Th, he would have the *Saxon* letter *Thorne*, which was a D with a dash through the head, or þ; for I consonant the *Saxon* ʒ, as ʒet, not Ieat for Ieat-stone, ʒaẏ for Iay: Q, if he were king of the A, B, C, should be putte to the horne, and banished; and *Ku* in his place, as *Kuik*, not *quik*, *Kuarel*, not *Quarel*: Z; he would have vsed for the softer S, or eth, and es, as *dîz* for dieth, *lîz* for lies, and the same ſ inverted for *sh*, as ſal for *shall*, fleſ for *flesh*. Thus briefly I have set you downe his devise, which albeit *Sound* and *Reason* seemed to countenance, yet that Tyranne *Custome* hath so confronted, that it will never be admitted.

If it be any glorie which the *French* and *Dutch* do brag of, that many wordes in their tongues doe not differ from the *Greeke*,

WILLIAM CAMDEN (1551–1623)

I can shew you as many in the *English*; whereof I will give you a few for a taste, as they have offred themselves in reading; but withall, I trust you will not gather by consequence, that wee are descended from the *Græcians*. Who dooth not see an identitie in these wordes, as if the one descended from the other.

Καλέω, to call.	Ρᾶκος, a ragge.
Πάτος, a path.	Κλίμαξ, a climbing.
Λάπτω, to lappe.	Οὔθαρ, an vdder.
Ρανις, raine.	Ο″αροι, whoorish sporte.
Ραπίζειν, to rappe.	Κῦσαι, to kisse.
Λοῖσθος, last.	Α″γχεσθαι, to hang.
Ζέω, to seethe.	Ε″ρα, earth.
Θρασὺς, rash.	Κάραβος, a crabbe.
Νέος, new.	Φῶλος, a phoale.
Γράστις, grasse.	Λύχνος, a linke.
Ο″ρχατος, an Orchard.	Κόπτω, to cut.
Κρέκω, to creake.	Ραιειν, to raze out.
Αστὴρ, a starre.	Ω″χρα, oker.
Ο″λος, whole.	Μωκάω, to mocke.
Φαῦλος, foule.	Ε᾽λάσσων, lesse.
Θὴρ, a Dere.	Α᾽ξίνη, an axe.
Ρᾶβδος, a rodde.	Σκόπτειν, to scoffe.
Ραστώνη, rest.	Στρώνυμι, to strowe.
Μήνη, the Moone.	Χάρμη, a skirmish.
Μύλη, a mill.	Κυριακὴ, a Church.
Τίτθος, a teate.	Ποτήριον, a potte.
Σκάφη, a shippe.	Μυστάχες, Mustaches.
Στρόφος, a rope.	Θύρα, a doore.
Καλπάζειν, to galloppe.	Ο″λκας, a hulke.
Α″χος, ache.	Κακάω,[1] to you know what.

With many more if a man would be so idle to gather them with *Budæus*, *Baifius*, *Iunius*, *Pichardus*, and others.

Heereby may be seene the originall of some english words, and

[1] [Κακάω cf. English 'cack', to void excrement.]

34

the *Etymology* or reason whence many other are derived, beside them alreadie specified may as well be found in our tongue, as in the learned tongues, although hardly; for that heerein as in other tongues, the truth lieth hidden and is not easilie found, as both *Varro* and *Isidor* do acknowledge. But an indifferent man may iudge that our name of the most divine power, God, is better derived from Good, the chiefe attribute of God, than *Deus* from Δεος,[1] because God is to be feared. So *Winter* from Winde, *Sommer* from the Sonne, *Lent* from springing, because it falleth in the spring, for which our Progenitours the *Germans*, vse *Glent*. The feast of Christs Rising, *Easter*, from the old word *East*, which we now vse for the place of the rising of the *Sonne*, *Sayle* as the *Sea-haile*, *Windor* or *Windowe*, as a doore against the winde, *King* from *Conning*, for so our Great grandfathers called them, which one word imployeth two most important matters in a Governour, *Power* and *Skill*, and many other better answering in sound and sence, then those of the *Latines*, *Frater quasi ferè alter*, *Tempestas quasi Tempus pestis*, *Caput à capiendo*, *Digiti quia decentèr iuncti*, *Cura quia cor vrit*, *Peccare quasi pedem capere*.[2]

Dionysius a Greeke coyner of *Etymologyes* is commended by *Athenæus*, in his supper-gulls, table-talkers, or *Deipnosophistæ*, for making mowse-traps of *Musteria*: and verily if that be commendable, the Mint-masters of our *Etymologies*, deserve no lesse commendation, for they have merily forged *Mony* from *My-hony*, *Flatter* from flie-at-her, *Shovell* from shove-full, *mayd* as my ayd, *Mastiefe* as Mase-thiefe, *Staffe* as *Stay of*, *Beere*, *Be-heere*, *Symony See-mony*, *Stirrup*, a *Stayre-vp*, &c.

This merry playing with words too much vsed by some hath occasioned a great and high personage, to say, that as the *Italian* tongue is fit for courting, the *Spanish* for treating, the *French* for trafficke; so the *English* is most fit for trifling and toying. And so doth *Giraldus Cambrensis* seem to think whenas in his time he

---

[1] [Δεος fear.]
[2] [*Frater...capere* Brother, as if to say almost another; Tempest, as if to say destructive time; Head, from understanding; Fingers, because properly jointed; Care, because it burns the heart; To Sin, as if to say to stumble.]

saith, the *English* and *Welsh* delighted much in licking the letter and clapping together of Agnominations. But now will I conclude this trifling discourse with a true tale out of an antient Historian.

Of the effectuall power of words, great disputes have beene of great wits in all ages; the *Pithagoreans* extolled it, the impious Iewes ascribed all miracles to a name which was ingravened in the revestiarie of the Temple, watched by two brazen dogges, which one stale away and enseamed it in his thigh, as you may reade in *Osorius de Sapientia*, and the like in *Rabi Hamas Speculation*: and strange it is what *Samonicus Serenus* ascribed to the word ABRADACABRA, against agues. But there was one true English word of as great, if not greater force than them all, now out of all vse and will be thought for sound barbarous; but therefore of more officacie (as it pleaseth *Porphyrie*) and in signification it signifieth as it seemeth, no more then abiect, base minded, false harted, coward, or nidget. Yet it hath levied Armies, and subdued rebellious enemies; and that I may hold you no longer it is *Niding*. For when there was a daungerous rebellion against King *William Rufus*, and *Rochester* Castle then the most important & strongest fort of this Realm was stowtly kept against him, after that he had but proclaimed that his subiects should repaire thither to his Campe, vpon no other penaltie, but that whosoever refused to come, should be reputed a *Niding*: they swarmed to him immediatly from all sides in such numbers, that he had in few daies an infinite Armie, and the rebells therewith weere so terrified, that they forthwith yeelded. While I runne on in this course of English tongue, rather respecting matter then words, I forget that I may be charged by the minion refiners of English, neither to write State-English, Court-English, nor Secretarie-English, and verily I acknowledge it. Sufficient it is for me, if I have waded hither-vnto in the fourth kinde, which is plaine English, leaving to such as are compleat in all, to supply whatsoever remaineth.

5

BEN JONSON

(1572–1637)

Jonson also wrote an *English Grammar...for the Benefit of All Strangers, out of his Observation of the English Language now Spoken, and in Use*, like *Timber* published in the posthumous 1640 Folio; perhaps both were written when he was Professor of Rhetoric at Gresham College. In this excerpt he attempts to measure the role of linguistic propriety in literary style, basing his view on the examples and dictates of the ancients. His two basic criteria are suitability and the sanction of custom.

Timber: or, Discoveries

(An excerpt, before 1637)

It is not the passing through these Learnings that hurts us, but the dwelling and sticking about them. To descend to those extreame anxieties, and foolish cavils of *Grammarians*, is able to breake a wit in pieces; being a worke of manifold misery, and vainenesse, to bee *Elementarij senes*.[1] Yet even Letters are as it were the Banke of words, and restore themselves to an Author, as the pawnes of Language: But talking and Eloquence are not the same: to speake, and to speake well, are two things. A foole may talke, but a wise man speakes, and out of the observation, knowledge, and use of things. Many Writers perplexe their Readers, and Hearers with meere *Non-sense*. Their writings need sunshine. Pure and neat Language I love, yet plaine and customary. A barbarous Phrase hath often made mee out of love with a good sense; and doubtfull writing hath wrackt mee beyond my patience. The reason why a *Poet* is said, that hee ought to have all knowledges, is that hee should not be ignorant of the most, especially of those hee will

---

[1] [*Elementarij senes* old men studying rudiments (cf. Seneca, *Epist.* 36. 4).]

handle. And indeed when the attaining of them is possible, it were a sluggish, and base thing to despaire. For frequent imitation of any thing, becomes a habit quickly. If a man should prosecute[1] as much, as could be said of every thing; his worke would find no end.

Speech is the only benefit man hath to expresse his excellencie of mind above other creatures. It is the Instrument of *Society*. Therefore *Mercury*, who is the President of Language, is called *Deorum hominumque interpres*.[2] In all speech, words and sense, are as the body, and the soule. The sense is as the life and soule of Language, without which all words are dead. Sense is wrought out of experience, the knowledge of humane life, and actions, or of the liberall Arts, which the *Greeks* call'd Ε'γκυκλοπαιδείαν.[3] Words are the Peoples; yet there is a choise of them to be made. For *Verborum delectus, origo est eloquentiæ*.[4] They are to be chose according to the persons wee make speake, or the things wee speake of. Some are of the Campe, some of the Councell-board, some of the Shop, some of the Sheepe-coat, some of the Pulpit, some of the Barre,[5] &c. And herein is seene their Elegance, and Propriety, when wee use them fitly, and draw them forth to their just strength and nature, by way of Translation, or *Metaphore*. But in this Translation wee must only serve necessity (*Nam temerè nihil transfertur à prudenti*)[6] or commodity,[7] which is a kind of necessity; that is, when wee either absolutely want a word to expresse by, and that is necessity; or when wee have not so fit a word, and that is commodity. As when wee avoid losse by it, and escape obscenenesse, and gaine in the grace and property, which helpes significance. *Metaphors* farfet hinder to be understood, and affected, lose their grace. Or when the person fetcheth

---

[1] [*prosecute* pursue an undertaking with a view to completing it.]
[2] [*Deorum...interpres* the intermediary of gods and men (quoted by Vives, *De ratione dicendi*, as also the next two).]
[3] [Ε'γκυκλοπαιδείαν general education.]
[4] [*Verborum...eloquentiæ* The choice of words is the beginning of eloquence.]
[5] [*Campe...Barre* the language of military, government, trade, agriculture, religion, law.]
[6] [*Nam...prudenti* Metaphor is never hastily used by the prudent (quoted by Vives, *op. cit.*).] [7] [*commodity* convenience.]

his translations from a wrong place. As if a Privie-Counsellor should at the Table take his *Metaphore* from a Dicing-house, or Ordinary, or a Vintners Vault; or a Justice of Peace draw his similitudes from the *Mathematicks*; or a *Divine* from a Bawdy-house, or Tavernes; or a Gentleman of *Northampton-shire, Warwick-shire,* or the *Mid-land,* should fetch all his Illustrations to his countrey neighbours from shipping, and tell them of the maine *sheat,* and the Boulin.¹ *Metaphors* are thus many times deform'd, as in him that said, *Castratam morte Aphricani Rempublicam.*² And an other, *stercus curiæ Glauciam.*³ And *Canâ nive conspuit Alpes.*⁴ All attempts that are new in this kind, are dangerous; and some-what hard, before they be softned with use. A man coynes not a new word without some perill, and lesse fruit; for if it happen to be received, the praise is but moderate; if refus'd, the scorne is assur'd. Yet wee must adventure, for things at first, hard and rough, are by use made tender and gentle. It is an honest errour that is committed, following great *Chiefes.*

*Custome*⁵ is the most certaine Mistresse of Language, as the publicke stampe makes the current money. But wee must not be too frequent with the mint, every day coyning. Nor fetch words from the extreme and utmost ages; since the chiefe vertue of a style is perspicuitie, and nothing so vitious in it, as to need an Interpreter. Words borrow'd of Antiquity, doe lend a kind of Majesty to style, and are not without their delight sometimes. For they have the Authority of yeares, and out of their inter-mission doe win to themselves a kind of grace-like newnesse. But the eldest of the present, and newest of the past Language is the best. For what was the ancient Language, which some men so doate upon, but the ancient Custome? Yet when I name Cus-tome, I understand not the vulgar Custome: For that were a

---

¹ [*Boulin* bowline.]
² [*Castratam...Rempublicam* The state was emasculated by the death of Africanus (quoted by Quintilian, *Instit. Orat.* VIII. 6. 15–17, as also the next three).]
³ [*stercus...Glauciam* Glaucia, the dung of the senate house.]
⁴ [*Canâ...Alpes* He bespewed the Alps with white snow.]
⁵ [*Custome* usage.]

precept no lesse dangerous to Language, then life, if wee should speake or live after the manners of the vulgar: But that I call Custome of speech, which is the consent of the Learned; as Custome of life, which is the consent of the good. *Virgill* was most loving of Antiquity; yet how rarely doth hee insert *aquai*, and *pictai*!¹ *Lucretius* is scabrous and rough in these; hee seekes 'hem: As some doe *Chaucerismes* with us, which were better expung'd and banish'd. Some words are to be cull'd out for ornament and colour, as wee gather flowers to straw² houses, or make Garlands; but they are better when they grow to our style; as in a Meadow, where though the meere grasse and greennesse delights; yet the variety of flowers doth heighten and beautifie. Marry we must not play, or riot too much with them, as in *Paranomasies*:³ Nor use too swelling, or ill-sounding words; *Quæ per salebras, altaque saxa cadunt.*⁴ It is true, there is no sound but shall find some Lovers, as the bitter'st confections are gratefull to some palats. Our composition must bee more accurate in the beginning and end, then in the midst; and in the end more, then in the beginning; for through the midst the streame beares us. And this is attain'd by Custome more then care, or diligence. Wee must expresse readily, and fully, not profusely. There is difference betweene a liberall, and a prodigall hand. As it is a great point of Art, when our matter requires it, to enlarge, and veere out all sayle; so to take it in, and contract it, is of no lesse praise when the Argument doth aske it. Either of them hath their fitnesse in the place. A good man always profits by his endeavour, by his helpe; yea, when he is absent; nay when he is dead by his example and memory. So good Authors in their style: A strict and succinct style is that, where you can take away nothing without losse, and that losse to be manifest. The briefe style is that which expresseth much in little. The concise style,

---

¹ [*aquai...pictai* archaic inflections, *Aen.* VII. 464, IX. 26.]
² [*straw* strew, spread.]
³ [*Paranomasies* puns.]
⁴ [*Quæ...cadunt* which stumble along rough places, and steep rocks (Martial, *Epig.* XI. 90. 2).]

which expresseth not enough, but leaves somewhat to bee understood. The abrupt style, which hath many breaches, and doth not seeme to end, but fall. The congruent, and harmonious fitting of parts in a sentence, hath almost the fastning, and force of knitting, and connexion: As in stones well squar'd, which will rise strong a great way without mortar. Periods are beautifull; when they are not too long; for so they have their strength too, as in a Pike or Javelin. As wee must take the care that our words and sense bee cleare; so if the obscurity happen through the Hearers, or Readers want of understanding, I am not to answer for them; no more then for their not listning or marking; I must neither find them eares, nor mind. But a man cannot put a word so in sense, but some thing about it will illustrate it, if the Writer understand himselfe. For Order helpes much to Perspicuity, as Confusion hurts. *Rectitudo lucem adfert; obliquitas et circumductio offuscat.*[1] We should therefore speake what wee can, the neerest way, so as wee keepe our gate, not leape;[2] for too short may as well be not let into the memory, as too long not kept in. Whatsoever looseth the grace, and clearenesse, converts into a Riddle; the obscurity is mark'd, but not the valew. That perisheth, and is past by, like the Pearle in the Fable. Our style should be like a skeine of silke to be carried, and found by the right thred, not ravel'd, and perplex'd; then all is a knot, a heape. There are words, that doe as much raise a style, as others can depresse it. Superlation, and overmuchnesse amplifies. It may be above faith, but never above a meane. It was ridiculous in *Cestius*, when hee said of *Alexander*:

Fremit Oceanus, quasi indignetur, quòd terras relinquas;[3]

But propitiously from *Virgil*:

Credas innare reuulsas Cycladas.[4]

[1] [*Rectitudo...offuscat* Directness illuminates, obliquity and deviousness obscure (quoted by Vives, *De ratione dicendi*).]

[2] [*keepe...leape* maintain our pace, without jumps.]

[3] [*Fremit...relinquas* The ocean roars as if outraged that you leave the land (quoted by Marcus Seneca, *Suasoriae*, I. 11. 12, as also the following).]

[4] [*Credas...Cycladas* You would believe that the Cyclades islands floated uprooted (*Aen.* VIII, 691–2).]

Hee doth not say it was so, but seem'd to be so. Although it be somewhat incredible, that is excus'd before it be spoken. But there are *Hyperboles*, which will become one Language, that will by no meanes admit another. As *Eos esse* P. R. *exercitus, qui cœlum possint perrumpere*:[1] who would say this with us, but a mad man? Therefore wee must consider in every tongue what is us'd, what receiv'd. *Quintilian* warnes us, that in no kind of Translation, or *Metaphore*, or *Allegory*, wee make a turne from what wee began; As if wee fetch the originall of our *Metaphore* from sea, and billowes; wee end not in flames and ashes; It is a most fowle inconsequence. Neither must wee draw out our *Allegory* too long, lest either wee make our selves obscure, or fall into affectation, which is childish. But why doe men depart at all from the right, and naturall wayes of speaking? Sometimes for necessity, when wee are driven, or thinke it fitter to speake that in obscure words, or by circumstance, which utter'd plainely would offend the hearers. Or to avoid obscenenesse, or sometimes for pleasure, and variety; as Travailers turne out of the high way, drawne, either by the commodity of a foot-path, or the delicacy, or freshnesse of the fields. And all this is call'd ἐσχηματισμένη, or figur'd Language.

Language most shewes a man: speake that I may see thee. It springs out of the most retired, and inmost parts of us, and is the Image of the Parent of it, the mind. No glasse renders a mans forme, or likenesse, so true as his speech. Nay, it is likened to a man; and as we consider feature, and composition in a man; so words in Language: in the greatnesse, aptnesse, sound, structure, and harmony of it. Some men are tall, and bigge, so some Language is high and great. Then the words are chosen, their sound ample, the composition full, the absolution plenteous, and powr'd out, all grave, sinnewye and strong. Some are little, and Dwarfes: so of speech it is humble, and low, the words poore and flat; the members and *Periods*, thinne and weake without

---

[1] [*Eos...perrumpere* The armies of the Roman people are such that they can break through the skies (quoted by Vives, *De ratione dicendi*, as also the next three quotations).]

knitting, or number. The middle are of a just stature. There the Language is plaine, and pleasing: even without stopping, round without swelling; all well-torn'd, compos'd, elegant, and accurate. The vitious Language is vast, and gaping, swelling, and irregular; when it contends to be high, full of Rocke, Mountaine, and pointednesse: As it affects to be low, it is abject, and creeps, full of bogs, and holes. And according to their Subject, these stiles vary, and lose their names: For that which is high and lofty, declaring excellent matter, becomes vast and tumorous: Speaking of petty and inferiour things: so that which was even, and apt in a meane and plaine subject, will appeare most poore and humble in a high Argument. Would you not laugh, to meet a great Counsellor of state in a flat cap, with his trunck hose, and a hobby-horse Cloake, his Gloves under his girdle, and yond Haberdasher in a velvet Gowne, furr'd with sables? There is a certaine latitude in these things, by which wee find the degrees. The next thing to the stature, is the figure and feature in Language: that is, whether it be round, and streight,[1] which consists of short and succinct *Periods*, numerous, and polish'd, or square and firme; which is to have equall and strong parts, every where answerable, and weighed. The third is the skinne, and coat, which rests in the well-joyning, cementing, and coagmentation of words; when as it is smooth, gentle, and sweet; like a Table, upon which you may runne your finger without rubs, and your nayle cannot find a joynt; not horrid, rough, wrinckled, gaping, or chapt: After these the flesh, blood, and bones come in question. Wee say it is a fleshy style, when there is much *Periphrasis*, and circuit of words; and when with more then enough, it growes fat and corpulent; *Arvina orationis*,[2] full of suet and tallow. It hath blood, and juyce, when the words are proper and apt, their sound sweet, and the *Phrase* neat and pick'd. *Oratio uncta, & benè pasta.*[3] But where there is Redundancy, both the blood and juyce are faulty, and

---

[1] [*streight* of narrow compass.]
[2] [*Arvina orationis* the lard of speech.]
[3] [*Oratio...pasta* oiled and well-fed speech.]

vitious. *Redundat sanguine, quæ multò plus dicit, quàm necesse est.*[1]
Juyce in Language is somewhat lesse then blood; for if the words
be but becomming, and signifying, and the sense gentle, there is
Juyce: but where that wanteth, the Language is thinne, flagging,
poore, starv'd; scarce covering the bone, and shewes like stones
in a sack. Some men to avoid Redundancy, runne into that; and
while they strive to have no ill blood, or Juyce, they loose their
good. There be some styles againe, that have not lesse blood, but
lesse flesh, and corpulence. These are bony, and sinnewy: *Ossa
habent, et nervos.*[2]

It was well noted by the late Lord St. *Alban,*[3] that the study of
words is the first distemper of Learning: Vaine matter the second:
And a third distemper is deceit, or the likenesse of truth; Im-
posture held up by credulity. All these are the Cobwebs of
Learning, and to let them grow in us, is either sluttish or foolish.
Nothing is more ridiculous, then to make an Author a *Dictator*,
as the schooles have done *Aristotle*. The dammage is infinite,
knowledge receives by it. For to many things a man should owe
but a temporary beliefe, and a suspension of his owne Judgement,
not an absolute resignation of himselfe, or a perpetuall captivity.
Let *Aristotle*, and others have their dues; but if wee can make
farther Discoveries of truth and fitnesse then they, why are we
envied? Let us beware, while wee strive to adde, wee doe not
diminish, or deface; wee may improve, but not augment. By
discrediting falshood, Truth growes in request. Wee must not goe
about like men anguish'd, and perplex'd, for vitious affectation
of praise: but calmely study the separation of opinions, find the
errours have intervened, awake Antiquity, call former times into
question; but make no parties with the present, nor follow any
fierce undertakers, mingle no matter of doubtfull credit, with
the simplicity of truth, but gently stirre the mould about the root
of the Question, and avoid all digladiations,[4] facility of credit, or

---

[1] [*Redundat...est* That which says much more than is necessary has too much blood.]
[2] [*Ossa...nervos* They have bones and nerves.]
[3] [*Lord St. Alban* Francis Bacon.]
[4] [*digladiations* conflicts.]

superstitious simplicity; seeke the consonancy, and concatenation of Truth; stoope only to point of necessity; and what leads to convenience. Then make exact animadversion where style hath degenerated, where flourish'd, and thriv'd in choisenesse of Phrase, round and cleane composition of sentence, sweet falling of the clause, varying an illustration by tropes and figures, weight of Matter, worth of Subject, soundnesse of Argument, life of Invention, and depth of Judgement. This is *Monte potiri*, to get the hill. For no perfect Discovery can bee made upon a flat or a levell.

6

THOMAS HOBBES

(1588–1679)

Hobbes studies language in the course of his philosophical treatise on political man, regarding it as a link between past and present and a bond between individuals, that is, as a prerequisite to organized society. It is for him a necessity for learning and teaching the arts and sciences, including philosophy itself, and his carefully categorized discussion has the appearance of objectivity. His historical view, however, is based on Eden and Babel, and he describes language as a collection of items—'names'—not as a structure.

'Of Speech'

(Chapter IV from *Leviathan*, Book I, 1651)

The Invention of *Printing*, though ingenious, compared with the invention of *Letters*, is no great matter. But who was the first that found the use of Letters, is not known. He that first brought them into *Greece*, men say was *Cadmus*, the sonne of *Agenor*, King of Phænicia. A profitable Invention for continuing the memory of time past, and the conjunction of mankind, dispersed into so many, and distant regions of the Earth; and with all difficult, as proceeding from a watchfull observation of the divers motions of the Tongue, Palat, Lips, and other organs of Speech; whereby to make as many differences of characters, to remember them. But the most noble and profitable invention of all other, was that of SPEECH, consisting of *Names* or *Appellations*, and their Connexion; whereby men register their Thoughts; recall them when they are past; and also declare them one to another for mutuall utility and conversation; without which, there had been amongst men, neither Common-wealth, nor Society, nor Contract, nor Peace, no more than amongst Lyons, Bears, and Wolves. The first author of Speech was *God* himself, that instructed *Adam* how to name such creatures as he presented to his sight; For the Scripture goeth no further in this matter. But this was sufficient to direct him to adde more names, as the experience and use of the creatures should give him occasion; and to joyn them in such manner by degrees, as to make himself understood; and so by succession of time, so much language might be gotten, as he had found use for; though not so copious, as an Orator or Philosopher has need of. For I do not find any thing in the Scripture, out of which, directly or by consequence can be gathered, that *Adam* was taught the names of all Figures, Numbers, Measures, Colours, Sounds, Fancies, Relations; much less the names of Words and Speech, as *Generall, Speciall, Affirmative, Negative, Interrogative, Optative, Infinitive,* all which are usefull; and least of all, of *Entity, Intentionality, Quiddity,* and other insignificant words of the School.[1]

But all this language gotten, and augmented by *Adam* and his posterity, was again lost at the tower of *Babel,* when by the hand of God, every man was stricken for his rebellion, with an oblivion of his former language. And being hereby forced to disperse themselves into severall parts of the world, it must needs be, that the diversity of Tongues that now is, proceeded by degrees from them, in such manner, as need (the mother of all inventions) taught them; and in tract of time grew every where more copious.

The generall use of Speech, is to transferre our Mentall Discourse, into Verbal; or the Trayne of our Thoughts, into a Trayne of Words; and that for two commodities; whereof one is, the Registring of the Consequences of our Thoughts; which being apt to slip out of our memory, and put us to a new labour, may again be recalled, by such words as they were marked by. So that the first use of names, is to serve for *Markes,* or *Notes* of remembrance. Another is, when many use the same words, to signifie (by their connexion and order,) one to another, what they conceive, or think of each matter; and also what they desire, feare, or have any other passion for. And for this use they are called *Signes.* Speciall uses of Speech are these; First, to

[1] [*the School* the scholastic philosophers.]

Register, what by cogitation, wee find to be the cause of any thing, present or past; and what we find things present or past may produce, or effect: which in summe, is acquiring of Arts. Secondly, to shew to others that knowledge which we have attained; which is, to Counsell, and Teach one another. Thirdly, to make known to others our wills, and purposes, that we may have the mutuall help of one another. Fourthly, to please and delight our selves, and others, by playing with our words, for pleasure or ornament, innocently.

To these Uses, there are also foure correspondent Abuses. First, when men register their thoughts wrong, by the inconstancy of the signification of their words; by which they register for their conceptions, that which they never conceived; and so deceive themselves. Secondly, when they use words metaphorically; that is, in other sense than that they are ordained for; and thereby deceive others. Thirdly, when by words they declare that to be their will, which is not. Fourthly, when they use them to grieve one another: for seeing nature hath armed living creatures, some with teeth, some with horns, and some with hands, to grieve an enemy, it is but an abuse of Speech, to grieve him with the tongue, unlesse it be one whom wee are obliged to govern; and then it is not to grieve, but to correct and amend.

The manner how Speech serveth to the remembrance of the consequence of causes and effects, consisteth in the imposing of *Names*, and the *Connexion* of them.

Of Names, some are *Proper*, and singular to one onely thing; as *Peter, Iohn, This man, this Tree*: and some are *Common* to many things; as *Man, Horse, Tree*; every of which though but one Name, is nevertheless the name of divers particular things; in respect of all which together, it is called an *Universall*; there being nothing in the world Universall but Names; for the things named, are every one of them Individuall and Singular.

One Universall name is imposed on many things, for their similitude in some quality, or other accident: And wheras a Proper Name bringeth to mind one thing onely; Universals recall any one of those many.

And of Names Universall, some are of more, and some of lesse extent; the larger comprehending the lesse large: and some again of equall extent, comprehending each other reciprocally. As for example, the Name *Body* is of larger signification than the word *Man*, and comprehendeth it; and the names *Man* and *Rationall*, are of equall extent, comprehending mutually one another. But here wee must take notice, that by a Name is not always understood, as in Grammar, one onely Word; but sometimes by circumlocution many words together. For all these words, *Hee that in his actions observeth the Lawes of his Country*, make but one Name, equivalent to this one word, *Just*.

By this imposition of Names, some of larger, some of stricter signification, we turn the reckoning of the consequences of things imagined in the mind, into a reckoning of the consequences of Appellations. For example, a man that hath no use of Speech at all, (such, as is born and remains perfectly deafe and dumb,) if he set before his eyes a triangle, and by it two right angles, (such as are the corners of a square figure,) he may by meditation compare and find, that the three angles of that triangle, are equall to those two right angles that stand by it. But if another triangle be shewn him different in shape from the former, he cannot know without a new labour, whether the three angles of that also be equall to the same. But he that hath the use of words, when he observes, that such equality was consequent, not to the length of the sides, nor to any other particular thing in his triangle; but onely to this, that the sides were straight, and the angles three; and that that was all, for which he named it a Triangle; will boldly conclude Universally, that such equality of angles is in all triangles whatsoever; and register his invention in these generall termes, *Every triangle hath its three angles equall to two right angles*. And thus the consequence found in one particular, comes to be registred and remembred, as an Universall rule; and discharges our mentall reckoning, of time and place; and delivers us from all labour of the mind, saving the first; and makes that which was found true *here*, and *now*, to be true in *all times* and *places*.

But the use of words in registring our thoughts, is in nothing so evident as in Numbring. A naturall foole that could never learn by heart the order of numerall words, as *one*, *two*, and *three*, may observe every stroak of the Clock, and nod to it, or say one, one, one; but can never know what houre it strikes. And it seems, there was a time when those names of number were not in use; and men were fayn to apply their fingers of one or both hands, to those things they desired to keep account of; and that thence it proceeded, that now our numerall words are but ten, in any Nation, and in some but five, and then they begin again. And he that can tell ten, if he recite them out of order, will lose himselfe, and not know when he has done: Much lesse will he be able to adde, and substract, and performe all other operations of Arithmetique. So that without words, there is no possibility of reckoning of Numbers; much lesse of Magnitudes, of Swiftnesse, of Force, and other things, the reckonings whereof are necessary to the being, or well-being of man-kind.

When two Names are joyned together into a Consequence, or Affirmation; as thus, *A man is a living creature*; or thus, *if he be a man, he is a living creature*, If the later name *Living creature*, signifie all that the former name *Man* signifieth, then the affirmation, or consequence is *true*; otherwise *false*. For *True* and *False* are attributes of Speech, not of Things. And where Speech is not, there is neither *Truth* nor *Falshood*. *Errour* there may be, as when wee expect that which shall not be; or suspect what has not been: but in neither case can a man be charged with Untruth.

Seeing then that *truth* consisteth in the right ordering of names in our affirmations, a man that seeketh precise *truth*, had need to remember what every name he uses stands for; and to place it accordingly; or else he will find himselfe entangled in words, as a bird in limetwiggs; the more he struggles, the more belimed. And therefore in Geometry, (which is the onely Science that it hath pleased God hitherto to bestow on mankind,) men begin at settling the significations of their words; which settling of significations, they call *Definitions*; and place them in the beginning of their reckoning.

By this it appears how necessary it is for any man that aspires to true Knowledge, to examine the Definitions of former Authors; and either to correct them, where they are negligently set down; or to make them himselfe. For the errours of Definitions multiply themselves, according as the reckoning proceeds; and lead men into absurdities, which at last they see, but cannot avoyd, without reckoning anew from the beginning; in which lyes the foundation of their errours. From whence it happens, that they which trust to books, do as they that cast up many little summs into a greater, without considering whether those little summes were rightly cast up or not; and at last finding the errour visible, and not mistrusting their first grounds, know not which way to cleere themselves; but spend time in fluttering over their bookes; as birds that entring by the chimney, and finding themselves inclosed in a chamber, flutter at the false light of a glasse window, for want of wit to consider which way they came in. So that in the right Definition of Names, lyes the first use of Speech; which is the Acquisition of Science: And in wrong, or no Definitions, lyes the first abuse; from which proceed all false and senslesse Tenets; which make those men that take their instruction from the authority of books, and not from their own meditation, to be as much below the condition of ignorant men, as men endued with true Science are above it. For between true Science, and erroneous Doctrines, Ignorance is in the middle. Naturall sense and imagination, are not subject to absurdity. Nature it selfe cannot erre: and as men abound in copiousnesse of language; so they become more wise, or more mad than ordinary. Nor is it possible without Letters for any man to become either excellently wise, or (unless his memory be hurt by disease, or ill constitution of organs) excellently foolish. For words are wise mens counters, they do but reckon by them: but they are the mony of fooles, that value them by the authority of an *Aristotle*, a *Cicero*, or a *Thomas*, or any other Doctor whatsoever, if but a man.

Subject to Names, is whatsoever can enter into, or be considered in an account; and be added one to another to make a summe; or substracted one from another, and leave a remainder. The Latines called Accounts of mony *Rationes*, and accounting, *Ratiocinatio*: and that which we in bills or books of account call *Items*, they called *Nomina*; that is, *Names*: and thence it seems to proceed, that they extended the word *Ratio*, to the faculty of Reckoning in all other things. The Greeks have but one word λόγος, for both *Speech* and *Reason*; not that they thought there was no Speech without Reason; but no Reasoning without Speech: And the act of reasoning they called *Syllogisme*; which signifieth summing up of the consequences of one saying to another. And because the same things may enter into account for divers accidents; their names are (to shew that diversity) diversly wrested, and diversified. This diversity of names may be reduced to foure generall heads.

First, a thing may enter into account for *Matter*, or *Body*; as *living*, *sensible*, *rationall*, *hot*, *cold*, *moved*, *quiet*; with all which names the word *Matter*, or *Body* is understood; all such, being names of Matter.

Secondly, it may enter into account, or be considered, for some accident or quality, which we conceive to be in it; as for *being moved*, for *being so long*, for *being hot*, &c; and then, of the name of the thing it selfe, by a little change or wresting, wee make a name for that accident, which we consider; and for *living* put into the account *life*; for *moved*, *motion*; for *hot*, *heat*; for *long*, *length*, and the like: And all such Names, are the names of the accidents and properties, by which one Matter, and Body is distinguished from another. These are called *names Abstract*; because severed (not from Matter, but) from the account of Matter.

Thirdly, we bring into account, the Properties of our own bodies, whereby we make such distinction: as when any thing is *Seen* by us, we reckon not the thing it selfe; but the *sight*, the *Colour*, the *Idea* of it in the fancy: and when any thing is *heard*, wee reckon it not; but the *hearing*, or *sound* onely, which is our fancy or conception of it by the Eare: and such are names of fancies.

Fourthly, we bring into account, consider, and give names, to *Names* themselves, and to *Speeches*: For, *generall*, *universall*, *speciall*, *æquivocall*, are names of Names. And *Affirmation, Interrogation, Commandement, Narration, Syllogisme, Sermon, Oration,* and many other such, are names of Speeches. And this is all the variety of Names *Positive*; which are put to mark somewhat which is in Nature, or may be feigned by the mind of man, as Bodies that are, or may be conceived to be; or of bodies, the Properties that are, or may be feigned to be; or Words and Speech.

There be also other Names, called *Negative*; which are notes to signifie that a word is not the name of the thing in question; as these words *Nothing, no man, infinite, indocible, three want foure,* and the like; which are nevertheless of use in reckoning, or in correcting of reckoning; and call to mind our past cogitations, though they be not names of any thing; because they make us refuse to admit of Names not rightly used.

All other Names, are but insignificant sounds; and those of two sorts. One, when they are new, and yet their meaning not explained by Definition; whereof there have been aboundance coyned by Schoole-men, and pusled Philosophers.

Another, when men make a name of two Names, whose significations are contradictory and inconsistent; as this name, an *incorporeall body*, or (which is all one) an *incorporeall substance*, and a great number more. For whensoever any affirmation is false, the two names of which it is composed, put together and made one, signifie nothing at all. For example, if it be a false affirmation to say *a quadrangle is round*, the word *round quadrangle* signifies nothing; but is a meere sound. So likewise if it be false, to say that vertue can be powred,[1] or blown up and down; the words *In-powred vertue, In-blown vertue,* are as absurd and insignificant, as a *round quadrangle*. And therefore you shall hardly meet with a senslesse and insignificant word, that is not made up of some Latin or Greek names. A Frenchman seldome hears our Saviour called by the name of *Parole*, but by the name of *Verbe* often; yet *Verbe* and *Parole* differ no more, but that one is Latin, the other French.

[1] [*powred* poured.]

When a man upon the hearing of any Speech, hath those thoughts which the words of that Speech, and their connexion, were ordained and constituted to signifie; Then he is said to understand it: *Understanding* being nothing else, but conception caused by Speech. And therefore if Speech be peculiar to man (as for ought I know it is,) then is Understanding peculiar to him also. And therefore of absurd and false affirmations, in case they be universall, there can be no Understanding; though many think they understand, then, when they do but repeat the words softly, or con them in their mind.

What kinds of Speeches signifie the Appetites, Aversions, and Passions of mans mind; and of their use and abuse, I shall speak when I have spoken of the Passions.

The names of such things as affect us, that is, which please, and displease us, because all men be not alike affected with the same thing, nor the same man at all times, are in the common discourses of men, of *inconstant* signification. For seeing all names are imposed to signifie our conceptions; and all our affections are but conceptions; when we conceive the same things differently, we can hardly avoyd different naming of them. For though the nature of that we conceive, be the same; yet the diversity of our reception of it, in respect of different constitutions of body, and prejudices of opinion, gives every thing a tincture of our different passions. And therefore in reasoning, a man must take heed of words; which besides the signification of what we imagine of their nature, have a signification also of the nature, disposition, and interest of the speaker; such as are the names of Vertues, and Vices; For one man calleth *Wisdome*, what another calleth *feare*; and one *cruelty*, what another *justice*; one *prodigality*, what another *magnanimity*; and one *gravity*, what another *stupidicy*, &c. And therefore such names can never be true grounds of any ratiocination. No more can Metaphors, and Tropes of speech: but these are less dangerous, because they profess their inconstancy; which the other do not.

7

JOHN DRYDEN

(1631–1700)

Dryden was a member of the Royal Society's 'committee for improving the English language' and later Poet Laureate. Here he takes up Jonson's concern for the place of linguistic criteria in literary criticism, concentrating on Jonson himself. He uses the standards of the ancients to show that in language, as well as in wit and conversation, his own age exceeds in correctness the 'golden age' of Elizabethan and Jacobean drama. The essay was appended to the first edition of his play *The Conquest of Granada*, to the second part of which he had written the brief verse Epilogue he here defends.

'Defence of the Epilogue' (1672)

The promises of Authors, that they will write again, are in effect, a threatning of their Readers with some new impertinence, and they who perform not what they promise, will have their pardon on easy terms. 'Tis from this consideration that I could be glad to spare you the trouble which I am now giving you, of a Preface, if I were not oblig'd by many reasons to write somewhat concerning our present Playes, and those of our predecessors on the English stage. The truth is, I have so farr ingag'd my self in a bold *Epilogue* to this Play, wherein I have somewhat tax'd the former writing, that it was necessary for me either not to print it, or to show that I could defend it. Yet, I would so maintain my opinion of the present Age, as not to be wanting in my veneration for the past: I would ascribe to dead Authors their just praises, in those things wherein they have excell'd us: and in those wherein we contend with them for the preheminence, I would acknowledge our advantages to the Age, and claim no victory from our wit. This being what I have propos'd to my self, I hope I shall not be thought arrogant when I inquire into their Errors. For, we live in an Age, so Sceptical, that as it determines little, so it takes nothing from Antiquity on trust. and I profess to have no other ambition in this Essay, than that Poetry may not go backward, when all other Arts and Sciences are advancing. Whoever censures me for this inquiry, let him hear his Character from *Horace*:

> *Ingeniis non ille favet plauditque sepultis,*
> *Nostra sed impugnat; nos nostraque Lividus odit.*[1]

He favours not dead wits, but hates the living.

It was upbraided to that excellent Poet that he was an enemy to the writings of his Predecessor *Lucilius*, because he had said, *Lucilium lutulentum fluere*,[2] that he ran muddy: and that he ought to have retrench'd from his Satyrs many unnecessary verses. But *Horace* makes *Lucilius* himself to justifie him from the imputation of Envy, by telling you that he would have done the same had he liv'd in an age which was more refin'd.

> *Si foret hoc nostrum, fato, delapsus in ævum,*
> *Detraheret sibi multa, recideret omne quod ultra*
> *Perfectum traheretur: &c.*[3]

And, both in the whole course of that Satyr, and in his most admirable Epistle to *Augustus*, he makes it his business to prove that Antiquity alone is no plea for the excellency of a Poem: but, that one Age learning from another, the last (if we can suppose an equallity of wit in the writers,) has the advantage of knowing more, and better than the former. and this I think is the state of the question in dispute. It is therefore my part to make it clear, that the Language, Wit, and Conversation of our Age are improv'd and refin'd above the last: and then it will not be difficult, to inferr, that our Playes have receiv'd some part of those advantages.

---

[1] [*Ingeniis...odit* That man does not favour and applaud dead artists, but assails ours, and spitefully hates us and ours (Horace, *Epist.* II. I. 88–9).]

[2] [*Lucilium...fluere* Lucilius runs muddy (Horace, *Sat.* I. 10. 50).]

[3] [*Si...traheretur* If he had been reserved by fate for this our age, he would be erasing much, and cutting everything that exceeded the perfect (Horace, *Sat.* I. 10. 68–70).]

In the first place, therefore, it will be necessary to state, in general, what this refinement is of which we treat: and that I think will not be defin'd amiss: *An improvement of our Wit, Language, and Conversation. or, an alteration in them for the better.*

To begin with *Language*. That an Alteration is lately made in ours or since the Writers of the last Age (in which I comprehend *Shakespear, Fletcher* and *Jonson*) is manifest. Any man who reads those excellent Poets, and compares their language with what is now written, will see it almost in every line. But, that this is an *Improvement* of the Language, or an alteration for the better, will not so easily be granted. For many are of a contrary opinion, that the English tongue was then in the height of its perfection; that, from *Jonsons* time to ours, it has been in a continual declination; like that of the *Romans* from the Age of *Virgil* to *Statius*, and so downward to *Claudian*: of which, not onely *Petronius*, but *Quintilian* himself so much complains, under the person of *Secundus*, in his famous Dialogue *de causis corruptæ eloquentiæ*.[1]

But, to shew that our Language is improv'd; and that those people have not a just value for the Age in which they live, let us consider in what the refinement of a language principally consists: that is, *either in rejecting such old words or phrases which are ill sounding, or improper, or in admitting new, which are more proper, more sounding and more significant.*

The Reader will easily take notice, that when I speak of rejecting improper words and phrases I mention not such as are Antiquated by custome onely: and, as I may say, without any fault of theirs: for in this case the refinement can be but accidental: that is when the words and phrases which are rejected happen to be improper. Neither would I be understood (when I speak of impropriety in Language) either wholly to accuse the last Age, or to excuse the present; and least of all my self. For all writers have their imperfections and failings. but I may safely conclude in the general, that our improprieties are less frequent, and less gross than theirs.

[1] [*de...eloquentiæ* on the causes of corrupt speech (actually *De oratoribus*, of orators, by Quintilian or Tacitus).]

One Testimony of this is undeniable, that we are the first who have observ'd them. and, certainly, to observe errours is a great step to the correcting of them. But, malice and partiality set apart, let any man who understands English, read diligently the works of *Shakespear* and *Fletcher*; and I dare undertake that he will find, in every page either some *Solecism* of Speech, or some notorious flaw in Sence: and yet these men are reverenc'd when we are not forgiven. That their wit is great and many times their expressions noble, envy it self cannot deny.

> ————*Neque ego illis detrahere ausim*
> *Hærentem capiti, multa cum laude, coronam:*[1]

but the times were ignorant in which they liv'd. Poetry was then, if not in its infancy among us, at least not arriv'd to its vigor and maturity: witness the lameness of their Plots: many of which, especially those which they writ first, (for even that Age refin'd itself in some measure,) were made up of some ridiculous, incoherent story, which, in one Play many times took up the business of an Age. I suppose I need not name *Pericles Prince* of *Tyre*, nor the Historical Plays of *Shakespear*. Besides many of the rest as the *Winters Tale, Love's labour lost, Measure for Measure*, which were either grounded on impossibilities, or at least, so meanly written, that the Comedy neither caus'd your mirth, nor the serious part your concernment. If I would expatiate on this Subject, I could easily demonstrate that our admir'd *Fletcher*, who writ after him, neither understood correct Plotting, nor that which they call *the Decorum of the Stage*. I would not search in his worst Playes for examples: he who will consider his *Philaster*, his *Humorous Lieutenant*, his *Faithful Shepheardess*; and many others which I could name, will find them much below the applause which is now given them. he will see *Philaster* wounding his Mistriss, and afterwards his Boy, to save himself: Not to mention the Clown who enters immediately, and not only has the advantage

[1] [*Neque...coronam* Nor would I dare to tear away the wreath which with great glory clings to their head (Horace, *Sat.* I. 10. 48–9, reading *illi*).]

of the Combat against the Heroe, but diverts you from your serious concernment, with his ridiculous and absurd Raillery. In his *Humorous Lieutenant* you find his *Demetrius* and *Leoncius* staying in the midst of a routed Army to hear the cold mirth of the *Lieutenant*: and *Demetrius* afterwards appearing with a Pistol in his hand, in the next Age to *Alexander* the Great. And for his *Shepheard*, he falls twice into the former indecency of wounding Women. but these absurdities, which those Poets committed, may more properly be call'd the Ages fault than theirs. for, besides the want of Education and Learning, (which was their particular unhappiness) they wanted the benefit of converse. but of that, I shall speak hereafter, in a place more proper for it. Their Audiences knew no better: and therefore were satisfy'd with what they brought. Those who call theirs the *Golden Age of Poetry*, have only this reason for it, that they were then content with Acorns, before they knew the use of Bread: or that Ἅλις δρυός[1] was become a Proverb. They had many who admir'd them, and few who blam'd them. and, certainly, a severe Critique is the greatest help to a good Wit. he does the Office of a Friend, while he designs that of an Enemy: and his malice keeps a Poet within those bounds, which the Luxuriancy of his Fancy would tempt him to overleap.

But it is not their Plots which I meant, principally to tax: I was speaking of their Sence and Language. and I dare almost challenge any man to show me a page together, which is correct in both. As for *Ben. Johnson*, I am loath to name him, because he is a most Judicious Writer; yet he very often falls into these errors. And I once more beg the Readers pardon, for accusing him or them. Onely let him consider that I live in an age where my least faults are severely censur'd: and that I have no way left to extenuate my failings but my showing as great in those whom we admire.

Cædimus, inque vicem præbemus crura sagittis.[2]

[1] [Ἅλις δρυός enough of acorns, i.e. now for some better food (quoted by Cicero, *Ad Atticum*, II. 19).]

[2] [*Cædimus...sagittis* We alternately strike, and expose our legs to arrows (Persius, *Sat.* 4. 42).]

I cast my eyes but by chance on *Catiline*; and in the three or four first pages, found enough to conclude that *Johnson* writ not correctly.

> ——————————*Let the long hid seeds*
> *Of treason, in thee, now shoot forth in deeds*
> *Ranker than horrour.*

In reading some bombast speeches of *Macbeth*, which are not to be understood, he us'd to say that it was horrour. and I am much afraid that this is so.

> *Thy parricide, late on thy onely Son,*
> *After his mother, to make empty way*
> *For thy last wicked Nuptials, worse than they*
> *That blaze that act of thy incestuous life,*
> *Which gain'd thee at once a daughter and a wife.*

The Sence is here extreamly perplex'd: and I doubt the word *They* is false Grammar.

> ——————————*And be free*
> *Not Heaven itself from thy impiety.*

A *Synchœsis*, or ill placing of words, of which *Tully* so much complains in Oratory.

> *The Waves, and Dens of beasts cou'd not receive*
> *The bodies that those Souls were frighted from.*

The Preposition in the end of the sentence; a common fault with him, and which I have but lately observ'd in my own writings.

> *What all the several ills that visit earth,*
> *Plague, famine, fire, could not reach unto,*
> *The Sword nor surfeits, let thy fury do.*

Here are both the former faults: for, besides that the Preposition *unto*, is plac'd last in the verse, and at the half period, and is redundant, there is the former *Synchœsis*, in the words (*The Sword nor Surfeits*) which in construction ought to have been plac'd before the other.

Catiline sayes of *Cethegus*, that for his sake he would

> *Go on upon the Gods; kiss Lightning, wrest*
> *The Engine from the Cyclops, and give fire*
> *At face of a full clowd, and stand his ire.*

To *go on upon*, is onely to go on twice. to give fire at face of a full cloud, was not understood in his own time: (and stand his *ire*) besides the antiquated word *ire* there is the Article His, which makes false construction: and Giving fire at the face of a cloud, is a perfect image of shooting, however it came to be known in those daies to *Catiline*.

> ————————*others there are*
> *Whom Envy to the State draws and pulls on,*
> *For Contumelies receiv'd; and such are sure ones.*

Ones in the plural Number: but that is frequent with him; for he sayes, not long after.

> *Cæsar and* Crassus*; if they be ill men,*
> *Are Mighty ones.*
> *Such Men they do not succour more the cause, &c.*

They redundant.

> *Though Heav'n should speak with all his wrath at once;*
> *We should stand upright and unfear'd.*

His is ill Syntax with Heaven: and by Unfear'd he means Unaffraid. words of a quite contrary signification.

> *The Ports are open,*

He perpetually uses Ports for Gates: which is an affected error in him, to introduce *Latine* by the loss of the *English* Idiom: as in the Translation of *Tully*'s Speeches he usually does.

Well placing of Words for the sweetness of pronunciation was not known till Mr. *Waller* introduc'd it: and therefore 'tis not to be wonder'd if *Ben. Johnson* has many such lines as these

> *But being bred up in his father's needy fortunes, Brought up in's sister's*
> *Prostitution, &c.*

But meaness of expression one would think not to be his error in a Tragedy, which ought to be more high and sounding than any other kind of Poetry. and yet amongst many others in *Catiline* I find these four lines together:

> *So* Asia, *thou art cruelly even*
> *With us, for all the blows thee given:*
> *When we, whose Vertues conquer'd thee,*
> *Thus, by thy Vices, ruin'd be.*

Be there is false *English*, for *are*: though the Rhyme hides it.

But I am willing to close the Book, partly out of veneration to the Author, partly out of weariness to pursue an argument which is so fruitful in so small a compass. And what correctness, after this, can be expected from *Shakespear* or from *Fletcher*, who wanted that Learning and Care which *Johnson* had? I will therefore spare my own trouble of inquiring into their faults: who had they liv'd now, had doubtless written more correctly. I suppose it will be enough for me to affirm (as I think I safely may) that these and the like errors which I tax'd in the most correct of the last Age, are such, into which we doe not ordinarily fall. I think few of our present Writers would have left behind them such a line as this,

> *Contain your Spirit in more stricter bounds.*

But that gross way of two Comparatives was then, ordinary: and therefore more pardonable in *Johnson*.

As for the other part of refining, which consists in receiving new Words and Phrases, I shall not insist much on it. 'Tis obvious that we have admitted many: some of which we wanted, and, therefore our Language is the richer for them: as it would be by importation of Bullion: others are rather Ornamental than Necessary; yet by their admission, the Language is become more courtly: and our thoughts are better drest. These are to be found scatter'd in the Writers of our Age: and it is not my business to collect them. They who have lately written with most care, have, I believe, taken the Rule of *Horace* for their guide; that is, not to be too hasty in receiving of Words: but rather to stay till Custome has made them familiar to us,

> Quem penes, arbitrium est, & jus & norma loquendi.[1]

For I cannot approve of their way of refining, who corrupt our *English* Idiom by mixing it too much with *French*: that is a Sophistication of Language, not an improvement of it: a turning *English* into *French*, rather than a refining of *English* by *French*. We meet daily with those Fopps, who value themselves on their Travelling, and pretend they cannot express their meaning in *English*, because they would put off to us some *French* Phrase of the last Edition: without considering that, for ought they know, we have a better of our own; but these are not the men who are to refine us: their Tallent is to prescribe Fashions, not Words: at best they are onely serviceable to a Writer, so as *Ennius* was to *Virgil*. He may *Aurum ex stercore colligere*[2] for 'tis hard if, amongst many insignificant Phrases, there happen not something worth preserving: though they themselves, like *Indians*, know not the value of their own Commodity.

There is yet another way of improving Language, which Poets especially have practic'd in all Ages: that is by applying receiv'd words to a new Signification. and this I believe, is meant by *Horace*, in that Precept which is so variously constru'd by Expositors:

> Dixeris Egregié, notum si callida verbum,
> Reddiderit junctura novum.[3]

And, in this way, he himself had a particular happiness: using all the Tropes, and particularly Metaphors, with that grace which is observable in his Odes: where the Beauty of Expression is often greater than that of thought. as in that one example, amongst an infinite number of others; *Et vultus nimium lubricus aspici*.[4]

---

[1] [*Quem...loquendi* to whom belongs the rule, the law, and the government of speech (Horace, *Ars poet.* 72).]

[2] [*Aurum...colligere* pick up gold from the dung (proverbial).]

[3] [*Dixeris...novum* You will speak well, if a well-chosen setting gives new force to a familiar word (Horace, *Ars poet.* 47–8).]

[4] [*Et...aspici* and a face too dangerous to behold (Horace, *Odes*, I. 19. 8).]

And therefore though he innovated little, he may justly be call'd a great Refiner of the *Roman* Tongue. This choice of words, and height'ning of their natural signification, was observ'd in him by the Writers of the following Ages: for *Petronius* says of him, *& Horatii curiosa fœlicitas.*[1] By this graffing, as I may call it, on old words, has our Tongue been Beautified by the three fore mention'd Poets, *Shakespear, Fletcher* and *Johnson*: whose Excellencies I can never enough admire. and in this, they have been follow'd especially by Sir *John Suckling* and Mr. *Waller*, who refin'd upon them. neither have they, who now succeed them, been wanting in their endeavours to adorn our Mother Tongue: but it is not so lawful for me to praise my living Contemporaries, as to admire my dead Predecessors.

I should now speak of the Refinement of Wit: but I have been so large on the former Subject that I am forc'd to contract my self in this. I will therefore onely observe to you, that the wit of the last Age, was yet more incorrect than their language. *Shakespear*, who many times has written better than any Poet, in any Language, is yet so far from writing Wit always, or expressing that Wit according to the Dignity of the Subject, that he writes in many places, below the dullest Writer of ours, or of any precedent Age. Never did any Author precipitate himself from such heights of thought to so low expressions, as he often does. He is the very *Janus* of Poets; he wears, almost every where two faces: and you have scarce begun to admire the one, e're you despise the other. Neither is the Luxuriance of *Fletcher*, (which his friends have tax'd in him,) a less fault than the carelessness of *Shakespear*. He does not well always, and, when he does, he is a true *Englishman*; he knows not when to give over. If he wakes in one Scene he commonly slumbers in another: And if he pleases you in the first three Acts, he is frequently so tir'd with his labor, that he goes heavily in the fourth and, sinks under his burden in the fifth.

For *Ben. Johnson*, the most judicious of Poets, he always writ

---

[1] [*Horatii...fœlicitas* the studied felicity of Horace (Petronius, *Satyricon*, 118).]

properly; and as the Character requir'd: and I will not contest farther with my Friends who call that Wit. It being very certain, that even folly it self, well represented, is Wit in a larger signification: and that there is Fancy, as well as Judgement in it; though not so much or noble: because all Poetry being imitation, that of Folly is a lower exercise of Fancy, though perhaps as difficult as the other: for 'tis a kind of looking downward in the Poet; and representing that part of Mankind which is below him.

In these low Characters of Vice and Folly, lay the excellency of that inimitable Writer: who, when at any time, he aim'd at Wit, in the stricter sence, that is, Sharpness of Conceit, was forc'd either to borrow from the Ancients, as, to my knowledge he did very much from *Plautus*: or, when he trusted himself alone, often fell into meanness of expression. Nay, he was not free from the lowest and most groveling kind of Wit, which we call clenches; of which, *Every Man in his Humour*, is infinitely full. and, which is worse, the wittiest persons in the *Drama* speak them. His other Comedies are not exempted from them: will you give me leave to name some few? *Asper*, in which Character he personates himself, (and he neither was, nor thought himself a fool.) exclaiming against the ignorant Judges of the Age, speaks thus.

> *How monstrous and detested is't, to see*
> *A fellow, that has neither Art nor Brain,*
> *Sit like an* Aristarchus, *or* Stark-Ass,
> *Taking Mens Lines, with a* Tobacco-Face,
> *In Snuffe, &c.*

And presently after

I mar'le whose wit 'twas to put a Prologue in yond Sackbut's *mouth? they might well think he would be out of Tune, and yet you'd play upon him too.*

Will you have another of the same stamp?

   O, I cannot abide these limbs of Sattin, *or rather* Satan.

But, it may be you will object that this was *Asper, Macilente*, or, *Carlo Buffone*: you shall, therefore, hear him speak in his own person: and, that, in the two last lines, or sting of an Epigram; 'tis Inscrib'd to *Fine Grand*: who, he says, was indebted to him for many things, which he reckons there: and concludes thus;

> *Forty things more*, dear Grand, *which you know true*,
> *For which, or pay me quickly, or I'le pay you.*

This was then the mode of wit, the vice of the Age and not *Ben. Johnson*'s. for you see, a little before him, that admirable wit, Sir *Philip Sidney*, perpetually playing with his words. In his time, I believe, it ascended first into the Pulpit: where (if you will give me leave to clench too) it yet finds the benefit of its Clergy. for they are commonly the first corrupters of Eloquence, and the last reform'd from vicious Oratory: as a famous *Italian* has observ'd before me, in his Treatise of the Corruption of the *Italian Tongue*; which he principally ascribes to Priests and preaching Friars.

But, to conclude with what brevity I can; I will only add this in the defence of our present Writers, that if they reach not some excellencies of *Ben. Jonson*; (which no Age, I am confident, ever shall) yet, at least, they are above that meanness of thought which I have tax'd, and which is frequent in him.

That the wit of this Age is much more Courtly, may easily be prov'd by viewing the Characters of Gentlemen which were written in the last. First, for *Jonson*, *True-Wit* in the *Silent Woman*, was his Master-piece. and *True-wit* was a Scholar-like kind of man, a Gentleman with an allay[1] of Pedantry: a man who seems mortifi'd to the world, by much reading. The best of his discourse, is drawn, not from the knowledge of the Town, but Books. and, in short, he would be a fine Gentleman, in an University. *Shakespear* show'd the best of his skill in his *Mercutio*, and he said himself, that he was forc'd to kill him in the third Act, to prevent being kill'd by him. But, for my part, I cannot find he was so dangerous a person: I see nothing in him but what was so exceeding harmless, that he might have liv'd to the end of the Play, and dy'd in his bed, without offence to any man.

---

[1] [*allay* alloy, admixture.]

Fletcher's Don John is our onely Bug-bear: and yet, I may affirm, without suspition of flattery, that he now speaks better, and that his Character is maintain'd with much more vigour in the fourth and fifth Acts than it was by *Fletcher* in the three former. I have alwayes acknowledg'd the wit of our Predecessors, with all the veneration which becomes me, but, I am sure, their wit was not that of Gentlemen, there was ever somewhat that was ill-bred and Clownish in it: and which confest the conversation of the Authors.

And this leads me to the last and greatest advantage of our writing, which proceeds from conversation. In the Age, wherein those Poets liv'd, there was less of gallantry than in ours; neither did they keep the best company of theirs. Their fortune has been much like that of *Epicurus*, in the retirement of his Gardens: to live almost unknown, and to be celebrated after their decease. I cannot find that any of them were conversant in Courts, except *Ben. Jonson*: and his *genius* lay not so much that way, as to make an improvement by it. greatness was not, then, so easy of access, nor conversation so free as now it is. I cannot, therefore, conceive it any insolence to affirm, that, by the knowledge, and pattern of their wit, who writ before us, and by the advantage of our own conversation, the discourse and Raillery of our *Comedies* excell what has been written by them. and this will be deny'd by none, but some few old fellows who value themselves on their acquaintance with the *Black-Friars*:[1] who, because they saw their Playes, would pretend a right to judge ours. The memory of these grave Gentlemen is their only Plea for being Wits. they can tell a story of *Ben. Jonson*, and perhaps have had fancy enough to give a supper in *Apollo* that they might be call'd his Sons: and because they were drawn in to be laught at in those times, they think themselves now sufficiently intitled to laugh at ours. Learning I never saw in any of them, and wit no more than they could remember. In short, they were unlucky to have been bred in an unpolish'd Age, and more unlucky to live to a refin'd one. They have lasted beyond their own, and are cast behind ours: and not

[1] [*Black-Friars* a theatre.]

contented to have known little at the age of twenty, they boast of their ignorance at threescore.

Now if any ask me, whence it is that our conversation is so much refin'd? I must freely, and without flattery, ascribe it to the Court: and, in it, particularly to the King; whose example gives a law to it. His own mis-fortunes and the Nations, afforded him an opportunity, which is rarely allow'd to Sovereign Princes, I mean of travelling, and being conversant in the most polish'd Courts of *Europe*; and, thereby, of cultivating a Spirit, which was form'd by Nature, to receive the impressions of a gallant and generous education. At his return, he found a Nation lost as much in Barbarism as in Rebellion. and as the excellency of his Nature forgave the one, so the excellency of his manners reform'd the other. the desire of imitating so great a pattern, first waken'd the dull and heavy spirits of the *English*, from their natural re-serv'dness: loosen'd them, from their stiff forms of conversation; and made them easy and plyant to each other in discourse. Thus, insensibly, our way of living became more free: and the fire of the English wit, which was before stifled under a constrain'd melancholy way of breeding, began first to display its force: by mixing the solidity of our Nation, with the air and gayety of our neighbours. This being granted to be true, it would be a wonder, if the Poets, whose work is imitation, should be the onely persons in three Kingdoms, who should not receive advantage by it: or, if they should not more easily imitate the wit and conversation of the present age, than of the past.

Let us therefore admire the beauties and the heights of *Shake-spear*, without falling after him into a carelessness and (as I may call it) a Lethargy of thought, for whole Scenes together. Let us imitate, as we are able, the quickness and easiness of *Fletcher*, without proposing him as a pattern to us, either in the redundancy of his matter, or the incorrectness of his language. Let us admire his wit and sharpness of conceit; but, let us at the same time acknowledge that it was seldome so fix'd, and made proper to his characters, as that the same things might not be spoken by any person in the Play. let us applaud his Scenes of Love; but, let us confess that he understood not either greatness or perfect honour in the parts of any of his women. In fine, let us allow, that he had somuch fancy, as when he pleas'd he could write wit: but that he wanted so much Judgment as seldome to have written humour; or describ'd a pleasant folly. Let us ascribe to *Jonson* the height and accuracy of Judgment, in the ordering of his Plots, his choice of characters, and maintaining what he had chosen, to the end. but let us not think him a perfect pattern of imitation; except it be in humour: for Love, which is the foundation of all *Comedies* in other Languages, is scarcely mention'd in any of his Playes. and for humour it self, the Poets of this Age will be more wary than to imitate the meanness of his persons. Gentlemen will now be entertain'd with the follies of each other: and though they allow *Cob* and *Tib*[1] to speak properly, yet they are not much pleas'd with their Tankard or with their Raggs: And, surely, their conversation can be no jest to them on the *Theatre*, when they would avoid it in the street.

To conclude all, let us render to our Predecessors what is their due, without confineing our selves to a servile imitation of all they writ: and, without assuming to our selves the Title of better Poets, let us ascribe to the gallantry and civility of our age the advantage which we have above them; and to our knowledge of the customs and manners of it, the happiness we have to please beyond them.

[1] [*Cob and Tib* low-life characters in Jonson's *Every Man in his Humour.*]

8

SIR THOMAS BROWNE
(1605–1682)

Browne considers the heritage of the world's languages, attempting to reconcile what he knows of them with Scriptural history. He takes into account the main causes of linguistic change: time, dispersion, and conquest. He goes further than Camden in supposing a common original for the European (and, wrongly, the Hebrew) languages, and he pays particular attention to Saxon and its Germanic cognates. In old texts and in dialect words of his own day he finds evidence for the history of the language he speaks and writes, and he concludes with a brief etymological study.

'Of Languages, and Particularly of the Saxon Tongue'

(Tract VIII from *Certain Miscellany Tracts*, before 1682)

SIR,

The last Discourse we had of the Saxon Tongue recalled to my mind some forgotten considerations. Though the Earth were widely peopled before the Flood, (as many learned men conceive) yet whether after a large dispersion, and the space of sixteen hundred years, men maintained so uniform a Language in all parts, as to be strictly of one Tongue, and readily to understand each other, may very well be doubted. For though the World preserved in the Family of *Noah* before the confusion of Tongues might be said to be of one Lip, yet even permitted to themselves their humours, inventions, necessities, and new objects, without the miracle of Confusion at first, in so long a tract of time, there had probably been a Babel.[1] For whether *America* were first

[1] [*For...a Babel* For although the world preserved in the family of Noah might, before the confusion of languages at the tower of Babel, be said to have spoken one language; yet even so, if they indulged their individual personalities and interests, there would have been a consequent splitting up of their language without the necessity of a Babel.]

peopled by one or several Nations, yet cannot that number of different planting Nations, answer the multiplicity of their present different Languages, of no affinity unto each other; and even in their Northern Nations and incommunicating Angles, their Languages are widely differing. A native Interpreter brought from *California* proved of no use unto the Spaniards upon the neighbour Shore. From *Chiapa*, to *Guatemala, San Salvador, Honduras*, there are at least eighteen several Languages; and so numerous are they both in the Peruvian and Mexican Regions, that the great Princes are fain to have one common Language, which besides their vernaculous and Mother Tongues, may serve for commerce between them.

And since the confusion of Tongues at first fell onely upon those which were present in *Sinaar* at the work of *Babel*, whether the primitive Language from *Noah* were onely preserved in the Family of *Heber*, and not also in divers others, which might be absent at the same, whether all came away and many might not be left behind in their first Plantations about the foot of the Hills, whereabout the Ark rested and *Noah* became an Husbandman, is not absurdly doubted.

For so the primitive Tongue might in time branch out into several parts of *Europe* and *Asia*, and thereby the first or Hebrew Tongue which seems to be ingredient into so many Languages, might have larger originals and grounds of its communication and traduction than from the Family of *Abraham*, the Country of *Canaan* and words contained in the Bible which come short of the full of[1] that Language. And this would become more probable from the Septuagint or Greek Chronology strenuously asserted by *Vossius*; for making five hundred years between the Deluge and the days of *Peleg*, there ariseth a large latitude of multiplication and dispersion of People into several parts, before the descent of that Body which followed *Nimrod* unto *Sinaar* from the East.

They who derive the bulk of European Tongues from the

---

[1] [*come short of the full of* fall short of.]

Scythian and the Greek, though they may speak probably in many points, yet must needs allow vast difference or corruptions from so few originals, which however might be tolerably made out in the old Saxon, yet hath time much confounded the clearer derivations. And as the knowledge thereof now stands in reference unto our selves, I find many words totally lost, divers of harsh sound disused or refined in the pronunciation, and many words we have also in common use not to be found in that Tongue, or venially derivable from any other from whence we have largely borrowed, and yet so much still remaineth with us that it maketh the gross of our Language.

The religious obligation unto the Hebrew Language hath so notably continued the same, that it might still be understood by *Abraham*, whereas by the *Mazorite* Points[1] and Chaldee Character[2] the old Letter stands so transformed, that if *Moses* were alive again, he must be taught to reade his own Law.

The Chinoys, who live at the bounds of the Earth, who have admitted little communication, and suffered successive incursions from one Nation, may possibly give account of a very ancient Language; but consisting of many Nations and Tongues; confusion, admixtion and corruption in length of time might probably so have crept in as without the virtue of a common Character, and lasting Letter of things, they could never probably make out those strange memorials which they pretend, while they still make use of the Works of their great *Confutius* many hundred years before Christ, and in a series ascend as high as *Poncuus*, who is conceived our *Noah*.

The present Welch, and remnant of the old Britanes, hold so much of that ancient Language, that they make a shift to understand the Poems of *Merlin, Enerin, Telesin*, a thousand years ago, whereas the Herulian *Pater Noster*, set down by *Wolfgangus Lazius*, is not without much criticism made out, and but in some words; and the present Parisians can hardly hack out those few lines of

---

[1] [*Mazorite Points* vowel points inserted by the Masorete commentators.]
[2] [*Chaldee Character* a misnomer for Aramaic, a post-Mosaic form of Hebrew writing.]

the League between *Charles* and *Lewis*, the Sons of *Ludovicus Pius*, yet remaining in old French.

The Spaniards, in their corruptive traduction and Romance, have so happily retained the terminations from the Latin, that notwithstanding the Gothick and Moorish intrusion of words, they are able to make a Discourse completely consisting of Grammatical Latin and Spanish, wherein the Italians and French will be very much to seek.

The learned *Casaubon* conceiveth that a Dialogue might be composed in Saxon onely of such words as are derivable from the Greek, which surely might be effected, and so as the learned might not uneasily find it out. *Verstegan* made no doubt that he could contrive a Letter which might be understood by the English, Dutch and East Frislander, which, as the present confusion standeth, might have proved no very clear Piece, and hardly to be hammer'd out: yet so much of the Saxon still remaineth in our English, as may admit an orderly discourse and series of good sense, such as not onely the present English, but *Ælfric*, *Bede* and *Alured* might understand after so many hundred years.

Nations that live promiscuously, under the Power and Laws of Conquest, do seldom escape the loss of their Language with their Liberties, wherein the Romans were so strict that the Grecians were fain to conform in their judicial Processes; which made the Jews loose more in seventy years dispersion in the Provinces of *Babylon*, than in many hundred in their distinct habitation in *Ægypt*; and the English which dwelt dispersedly to loose their Language in *Ireland*, whereas more tolerable reliques there are thereof in *Fingall*, where they were closely and almost solely planted; and the Moors which were most huddled together and united about *Granada*, have yet left their *Arvirage* among the Granadian Spaniards.

But shut up in Angles and inaccessible corners, divided by Laws and Manners, they often continue long with little mixture, which hath afforded that lasting life unto the Cantabrian and British Tongue, wherein the Britanes are remarkable, who, having lived four hundred years together with the Romans, retained so much of the British as it may be esteemed a Language; which either they resolutely maintained in their cohabitation with them in Britane, or retiring after in the time of the Saxons into Countries and parts less civiliz'd and conversant with the Romans, they found the People distinct, the Language more intire, and so fell into it again.

But surely no Languages have been so straitly lock'd up as not to admit of commixture. The Irish, although they retain a kind of a Saxon Character, yet have admitted many words of Latin and English. In the Welch are found many words from Latin, some from Greek and Saxon. In what parity and incommixture the Language of that People stood which were casually discovered in the heart of *Spain*, between the Mountains of *Castile*, no longer ago than in the time of Duke *D' Alva*, we have not met with a good account any farther than that their words were Basquish or Cantabrian: but the present Basquensa one of the minor Mother Tongues of *Europe*, is not without commixture of Latin and Castilian, while we meet with *Santifica, tentationeten, Glaria, puissanca*, and four more in the short Form of the Lord's Prayer, set down by *Paulus Merula*: but although in this brief Form we may find such commixture, yet the bulk of their Language seems more distinct, consisting of words of no affinity unto others, of numerals totally different, of differing Grammatical Rule, as may be observed in the Dictionary and short *Basquensa* Grammar, composed by *Raphael Nicoleta*, a Priest of *Bilboa*.

And if they use the auxiliary Verbs of *Equin* and *Ysan*, answerable unto *Hazer* and *Ser*, to Have, and Be, in the Spanish, which Forms came in with the Northern Nations into the Italian, Spanish and French, and if that Form were used by them before, and crept not in from imitation of their neighbours, it may shew some ancienter traduction from Northern Nations, or else must seem very strange; since the Southern Nations had it not of old, and I know not whether any such mode be found in the Languages of any part of *America*.

The Romans, who made the great commixture and alteration of Languages in the World, effected the same, not onely by their proper Language, but those also of their military Forces, employed in several Provinces, as holding a standing *Militia* in all Countries, and commonly of strange Nations; so while the cohorts and Forces of the Britanes were quartered in *Ægypt*, *Armenia*, *Spain*, *Illyria*, &c. the Stablæsians and Dalmatians here, the Gauls, Spaniards and Germans in other Countries, and other Nations in theirs, they could not but leave many words behind them, and carry away many with them, which might make that in many words of very distinct Nations some may still remain of very unknown and doubtfull Genealogy.

And if, as the learned *Buxtorfius* contendeth, the Scythian Language as the Mother Tongue runs through the Nations of *Europe*, and even as far as *Persia*, the community in many words between so many Nations, hath a more reasonable original traduction, and were rather derivable from the common Tongue diffused through them all, than from any particular Nation, which hath also borrowed and holdeth but at second hand.

The Saxons settling over all *England*, maintained an uniform Language, onely diversified in Dialect, Idioms, and minor differences, according to their different Nations which came in to the common Conquest, which may yet be a cause of the variation in the speech and words of several parts of *England*, where different Nations most abode or settled, and having expelled the Britanes, their Wars were chiefly among themselves, with little action with foreign Nations untill the union of the Heptarchy under *Egbert*; after which time although the Danes infested this Land and scarce left any part free, yet their incursions made more havock in Buildings, Churches and Cities, than the Language of the Country, because their Language was in effect the same, and such as whereby they might easily understand one another.

And if the Normans, which came into *Neustria* or *Normandy* with *Rollo* the Dane, had preserved their Language in their new acquists, the succeeding Conquest of *England*, by Duke *William* of his race, had not begot among us such notable alterations; but having lost their Language in their abode in *Normandy* before they adventured upon *England*, they confounded the English with their French, and made the grand mutation, which was successively encreased by our possessions in *Normandy*, *Guien* and *Aquitain*, by our long Wars in *France*, by frequent resort of the French, who to the number of some thousands came over with *Isabel* Queen to *Edward* the Second, and the several Matches of *England* with the Daughters of *France* before and since that time.

But this commixture, though sufficient to confuse, proved not of ability to abolish the Saxon words; for from the French we have borrowed many Substantives, Adjectives and some Verbs, but the great Body of Numerals, auxiliary Verbs, Articles, Pronouns, Adverbs, Conjunctions and Prepositions, which are the distinguishing and lasting part of a Language, remain with us from the Saxon, which, having suffered no great alteration for many hundred years, may probably still remain, though the English swell with the inmates of Italian, French and Latin. An Example whereof may be observ'd in this following,

ENGLISH I

The first and formost step to all good Works is the dread and fear of the Lord of Heaven and Earth, which thorough the Holy Ghost enlightneth the blindness of our sinfull hearts to tread the ways of wisedom, and leads our feet into the Land of Blessing.

SAXON I

The erst and fyrmost stæp to eal gode Weorka is the dræd and feurt of the Lauord of Heofan and Eorth, whilc thurh the Heilig Gast onlihtneth the blindnesse of ure sinfull heorte to træd the wæg of wisdome, and thone læd ure fet into the Land of Blessung.

ENGLISH II

For to forget his Law is the Door, the Gate and Key to let in all unrighteousness, making our Eyes, Ears and Mouths to answer the lust of Sin, our Brains dull to good Thoughts, our Lips dumb to his Praise, our Ears deaf to his Gospel, and our Eyes dim to behold his Wonders, which witness against us that we have not well learned the word of God, that we are the Children of wrath, unworthy of the love and manifold gifts of God, greedily following after the ways of the Devil and witchcraft of the World, doing nothing to free and keep our selves from the burning fire of Hell, till we be buried in Sin and swallowed in Death, not to arise again in any hope of Christ's Kingdom.

SAXON II

For to fuorgytan his Laga is the Dure, the Gat and Cæg to let in eal unrightwisnysse, makend ure Eyge, Eore and Muth to answare the lust of Sin, ure Brœgan dolc to gode Theoht, ure Lippan dumb to his Preys, ure Earen deaf to his Gospel, and ure Eyge dim to behealden his Wundra, whilc ge witnysse ongen us that wee œf noht wel gelæred the weord of God, that wee are the Cilda of ured, unwyrthe of the lufe and mænigfeald gift of God, grediglice felygend æfter the wægen of the Deoful and wiccraft of the Weorld, doend nothing to fry and cæp ure saula from the byrnend fyr of Hell, till we be geburied in Synne and swolgen in Death not to arise agen in ænig hope of Christes Kynedome.

ENGLISH III

Which draw from above the bitter doom of the Almighty of Hunger, Sword, Sickness, and brings more sad plagues than those of Hail, Storms, Thunder, Bloud, Frogs, swarms of Gnats and Grashoppers, which ate the Corn, Grass and Leaves of the Trees in *Ægypt*.

SAXON III

Whilc drag from buf the bitter dome of the Almagan of Hunger, Sweorde, Seoknesse, and bring mere sad plag, thone they of Hagal, Storme, Thunner, Blode, Frog, swearme of Gnæt and Gærsupper, whilc eaten the Corn, Gærs and Leaf of the Treowen in *Ægypt.*

ENGLISH IV

If we reade his Book and holy Writ, these among many others, we shall find to be the tokens of his hate, which gathered together might mind us of his will, and teach us when his wrath beginneth, which sometimes comes in open strength and full sail, oft steals like a Thief in the night, like Shafts shot from a Bow at midnight, before we think upon them.

SAXON IV

Gyf we ræd his Boc and heilig Gewrit, these gemong mænig othern, we sceall findan the tacna of his hatung whilc gegatherod together miht gemind us of his willan, and teac us whone his ured onginneth, whilc sometima come in open strength and fill seyle, oft stæl gelyc a Theof in the niht, gelyc Sceaft scoten fram a Boge at midneoht, beforan we thinck uppen them.

ENGLISH V

And though they were a deal less, and rather short than beyond our sins, yet do we not a whit withstand or forbear them, we are wedded to, not weary of our misdeeds, we seldom look upward, and are not ashamed under sin, we cleanse not our selves from the blackness and deep hue of our guilt; we want tears and sorrow, we weep not, fast not, we crave not forgiveness from the mildness, sweetness and goodness of God, and with all livelihood and sted-fastness to our uttermost will hunt after the evil of guile, pride, cursing, swearing, drunkenness, overeating, uncleanness, all idle lust of the flesh, yes many uncouth and nameless sins, hid in our inmost Breast and Bosomes, which stand betwixt our forgiveness, and keep God and Man asunder.

SAXON V

And theow they wære a dæl lesse, and reither scort thone begond oure sinnan, get do we naht a whit withstand and forbeare them, we eare bewudded to, noht werig of ure agen misdeed, we seldon loc upweard, and ear not ofschæmod under sinne, we cleans noht ure selvan from the blacnesse and dæp hue of ure guilt; we wan teare and sara, we weope noht, fæst noht, we craf noht foregyfnesse fram the mildnesse, sweetnesse and goodnesse of God, and mit eal lifelyhood and stedfastnesse to ure uttermost witt hunt æfter the ufel of guile, pride, cursung, swearung, druncennesse, overeat, uncleannesse and eal idle lust of the flæsc, yis mænig uncuth and nameleas sinnan, hid in ure inmæst Brist and Bosome, whilc stand betwixt ure foregyfnesse, and cæp God and Man asynder.

ENGLISH VI

Thus are we far beneath and also worse than the rest of God's Works; for the Sun and Moon, the King and Queen of Stars, Snow, Ice, Rain, Frost, Dew, Mist, Wind, fourfooted and creeping things, Fishes and feathered Birds, and Fowls either of Sea or Land do all hold the Laws of his will.

SAXON VI

Thus eare we far beneoth and ealso wyrse thone the rest of Gods Weorka; for the Sun and Mone, the Cyng and Cquen of Stearran, Snaw, Ise, Ren, Frost, Deaw, Miste, Wind, feower fet and crypend dinga, Fix yefetherod Brid, and Fælan auther in Sæ or Land do eal heold the Lag of his willan.

Thus have you seen in few words how near the Saxon and English meet.

Now of this account the French will be able to make nothing; the modern Danes and Germans, though from several words they may conjecture at the meaning, yet will they be much to seek in the orderly sense and continued construction thereof, whether the Danes can continue such a series of sense out of their present Language and the old Runick, as to be intelligible unto present and ancient times, some doubt may well be made; and if the present French would attempt a Discourse in words common unto their present Tongue and the old *Romana Rustica* spoken in Elder times, or in the old Language of the Francks, which came to be in use some successions after *Pharamond*, it might prove a Work of some trouble to effect.

It were not impossible to make an Original reduction of many words of no general reception in *England* but of common use in *Norfolk*, or peculiar to the East Angle Countries; as, *Bawnd, Bunny, Thurck, Enemmis, Sammodithee, Mawther, Kedge, Seele, Straft, Clever, Matchly, Dere, Nicked, Stingy, Noneare, Feft, Thepes, Gosgood, Kamp, Sibrit, Fangast, Sap, Cothish, Thokish, Bide owe, Paxwax*: of these and some others of no easie originals, when time will permit, the resolution may be attempted; which to effect, the Danish Language new and more ancient may prove of good advantage: which Nation remained here fifty years upon agreement, and have left many Families in it, and the Language of these parts had surely been more commixed and perplex, if the Fleet of *Hugo de Bones* had not been cast away, wherein threescore thousand Souldiers out of *Britany* and *Flanders* were to be wafted over, and were by King *John*'s appointment to have a settled habitation in the Counties of *Norfolk* and *Suffolk*.

But beside your laudable endeavours in the Saxon, you are not like to repent you of your studies in the other European and Western Languages, for therein are delivered many excellent Historical, Moral and Philosophical Discourses, wherein men merely versed in the learned Languages are often at a loss: but although you are so well accomplished in the French, you will not surely conceive that you are master of all the Languages in *France*, for to omit the Briton, Britonant or old British, yet retained in some part of *Britany*, I shall onely propose this unto your construction.

Chavalisco d' aquestes Boemes chems an freitado lou cap cun taules Jargonades, ero necy chi voluiget bouta sin tens embè aquelles. Anin à lous occells, che dizen tat prou ben en ein voz L' ome nosap comochodochi yen ay jes de plazer, d' ausir la mitat de paraulles en el mon.

This is a part of that Language which *Scaliger* nameth *Idiotismus Tectosagicus*, or *Langue d' oc*, counterdistinguishing it unto the *Idiotismus Francicus*, or *Langue d'ouy*, not understood in a petty corner or between a few Mountains, but in parts of early civility, in *Languedoc*, *Provence* and *Catalonia*, which put together will make little less than *England*.

Without some knowledge herein you cannot exactly understand the Works of *Rablais*: by this the French themselves are fain to make out that preserved relique of old French, containing the League between *Charles* and *Lewis* the Sons of *Ludovicus Pius*. Hereby may tolerably be understood the several Tracts written in the Catalonian Tongue; and in this is published the Tract of Falconry written by *Theodosius* and *Symmachus*: in this is yet conserved the Poem *Vilhuardine* concerning the French expedition in the Holy War, and the taking of *Constantinople*, among the Works of *Marius Æquicola* an Italian Poet. You may find, in this Language, a pleasant Dialogue of Love: this, about an hundred years ago, was in high esteem, when many Italian Wits flocked into *Provence*; and the famous *Petrarcha* wrote many of his Poems in *Vaucluse* in that Country.

For the word [*Dread*] in the Royal Title [*Dread Sovereign*] of which you desire to know the meaning, I return answer unto your question briefly thus.

Most men do vulgarly understand this word *Dread* after the common and English acception, as implying *Fear, Awe* or *Dread.*

Others may think to expound it from the French word *Droit* or *Droyt.* For, whereas in elder times, the *Presidents* and *Supremes* of Courts were termed *Sovereigns,* men might conceive this a distinctive Title and proper unto the King as eminently and by right the Sovereign.

A third exposition may be made from some Saxon Original, particularly from *Driht, Domine,* or *Drihten, Dominus,* in the Saxon Language, the word for *Dominus* throughout the Saxon Psalms, and used in the expression of the year of our Lord in the Decretal Epistle of Pope *Agatho* unto *Athelred* King of the Mercians, *Anno,* 680.

Verstegan would have this term *Drihten* appropriate unto God. Yet, in the Constitutions of *Withred* King of *Kent,* we find the same word used for a Lord or Master, *Si in vesperâ præcedente solem servus ex mandato Domini aliquod opus servile egerit, Dominus (Drihten) 80 solidis luito.*[1] However therefore, though *Driht, Domine,* might be most eminently applied unto the Lord of Heaven, yet might it be also transferred unto Potentates and Gods on Earth, unto whom fealty is given or due, according unto the Feudist term *Ligeus à Ligando*[2] unto whom they were bound in fealty. And therefore from *Driht, Domine, Dread Sovereign,* may, probably, owe its Original.

I have not time to enlarge upon this Subject: 'Pray let this pass, as it is, for a Letter and not for a Treatise. I am

Yours, &c.

---

[1] [*Si . . . luito* If on the evening preceding Sunday a servant should do any servile work on the command of the master, the master must pay eighty shillings.]

[2] [*Ligeus à Ligando* 'liege' comes from 'binding'.]

9

JOHN LOCKE

(1632–1704)

Starting with the notion of language as a God-given medium for human communication, Locke explores the relationship between ideas and words, and between experience and ideas, in order to ascertain the precise role of language in human understanding. He agrees with Hobbes that language serves both memory and conversation by investing experience with convenient signs, and that names are the signs; but as an empiricist, he insists on the arbitrary connection between idea and word, and the danger of overlooking the nature of the connection.

'Of Words or Language in general' and 'Of the Signification of Words'

(Chapters i and ii from *An Essay Concerning Humane Understanding*, Book III, 1690)

i

§.1. God having designed Man for a sociable Creature, made him not only with an inclination, and under a necessity to have fellowship with those of his own kind; but furnished him also with Language, which was to be the great Instrument, and common Tye of Society. *Man* therefore had by Nature his Organs so fashioned, as to be *fit to frame articulate Sounds*, which we call Words. But this was not enough to produce Language; for Parrots, and several other Birds, will be taught to make articulate Sounds distinct enough, which yet, by no means, are capable of Language.

§.2. Besides articulate Sounds therefore, it was farther necessary, that he should be *able to use these Sounds, as signs of internal Conceptions*; and to make them stand as marks for the *Ideas* within his own Mind, whereby they might be made known to others, and the Thoughts of Mens Minds be conveyed from one to another.

§.3. But neither was this sufficient to make Words so useful as they ought to be. It is not enough for the perfection of Language, that Sounds can be made signs of *Ideas*, unless those *signs* can be so made use of, as *to comprehend several particular Things*: For the multiplication of Words would have perplexed their Use, had every particular thing need of a distinct name to be signified by.

§.4. *Words* then are made to be signs of our *Ideas*, and *are general or particular, as the Ideas they stand for are general or particular*. But besides these Names which stand for *Ideas*, there be others which Men have found and make use of, not to signifie any *Idea*, but the want or absence of some *Ideas*, simple or complex, or all *Ideas* together; such as are the Latin words, *Nihil*, and in English, *Ignorance* and *Barrenness*. All which negative or privative Words, cannot be said properly to belong to, or signifie no *Ideas*: for then they would be perfectly insignificant Sounds; but they relate to positive *Ideas*, and signifie their absence.

§.5. It may also lead us a little towards the Original of all our Notions and Knowledge, if we remark, how great a dependence our *Words* have on common sensible *Ideas*; and how those which are made use of, to stand for Actions and Notions quite removed from sense, *have their Original*, and are transferred *from obvious sensible Ideas*; *v. g.* to *Imagine, Apprehend, Comprehend, Adhere, Conceive, Instill, Disgust, Disturbance, Tranquillity*, &c. are all Words taken from the Operations of sensible Things, and applied to certain Modes of Thinking. *Spirit*, in its primary signification, is Breath; *Angel*, a Messenger: And I doubt not, but if we could trace them to their Originals, we should find, in all Languages, the names, which stand for Things that fall not under our Senses, to have had their first rise from sensible *Ideas*. By which we may give some kind of guess, what kind of Notions they were, and whence derived, which filled their Minds, who were the first Beginners of Languages; and how Nature, even in the naming of

Things, unawares suggested to Men the Originals and Principles of all their Knowledge: whilst, to give Names, that might make known to others any Operations they felt in themselves, or any other *Ideas*, that came not under their Senses, they were fain to borrow Words from ordinary known *Ideas* of Sensation, by that means to make others the more easily to conceive those Operations they experimented in themselves, which made no outward sensible appearances; and then when they had got known and agreed Names, to signifie those internal Operations of their own Minds, they were sufficiently furnished to make known by Words, all their other *Ideas*; since they could consist of nothing, but either of outward sensible Perceptions, or of the inward Operations of their Minds about them; we having, as has been proved, no *Ideas* at all, but what originally come either from sensible Objects without, or what we feel within our selves, from the inward Workings of our own Spirits, which we are conscious to our selves of within.

§.6. But to understand better the use and force of Language, as subservient to Instruction and Knowledge, it will be convenient to consider,

First, To what it is that Names, in the use of Language, are immediately applied.

Secondly, Since all (except proper) Names are general, and so stand not particularly for this or that single Thing; but for sorts and ranks of Things, it will be necessary to consider, in the next place, what the Sorts and Kinds, or, if you rather like the Latin Names, *what the Species and Genera of Things are*, wherein they consist, and how they come to be made. These being (as they ought) well looked into, we shall the better come to find the right use of Words; the natural Advantages and Defects of Language; and the remedies that ought to be used, to avoid the inconveniencies of obscurity or uncertainty in the signification of Words: without which, it is impossible to discourse with any clearness, or order, concerning Knowledge: Which being conversant about Propositions, and those most commonly universal ones, has greater connexion with Words, than perhaps is suspected.

These Considerations therefore, shall be the matter of the following Chapters.

ii

§. 1. Man, though he have great variety of Thoughts, and such, from which others, as well as himself, might receive Profit and Delight; yet they are all within his own Breast, invisible, and hidden from others, nor can of themselves be made appear. The Comfort therefore, and Advantage of Society, not being to be had without Communication of Thoughts, it was necessary, that Man should find out some external sensible Signs, whereby those invisible *Ideas*, which possess his Mind in so great variety, might be made known to others: For which purpose, nothing was so fit, either for Plenty or Quickness, as those articulate Sounds, which with so much Ease and Variety, he found himself able to make. Thus we may conceive how *Words*, which were by Nature so well adapted to that purpose, come to be made use of by Men, as *the Signs of* their *Ideas*; not by any natural connection, that there is between particular articulate Sounds, and certain *Ideas*, for then there would be but one Language amongst all Men; but by a voluntary Imposition, whereby such a Word is made arbitrarily the Mark of such an *Idea*. The use then of Words, is to be sensible Marks of *Ideas*; and the *Ideas* they stand for, are their proper and immediate Signification.

§. 2. The use Men have of these Marks, being either to record their own *Ideas* for the Assistence of their own Memory; or as it were, to bring them out, and lay them before the view of others. *Words in their primary and immediate Signification, stand for nothing, but the* Ideas *in the Mind of him that uses them*, how imperfectly soever, or carelesly those *Ideas* are collected from the Things, which they are supposed to represent. When a Man speaks to another, it is, that he may be understood; and the end of the Speech is, that those Sounds, as Marks, may make known his *Ideas* to the Hearer. That then which Words are the Marks of, are the *Ideas* of the Speaker: Nor can any one apply them, as

Saussure is not concerned with the *réponse* of the hearer (Blomfield) but with the 'langage' = the abstract system of communication - *parole*. Semiotics. Structural Linguistics.

OF THE SIGNIFICATION OF WORDS

Marks immediately to any thing else, but the *Ideas* that he himself hath: For this would be to make them Signs of his own Conception, and yet apply them to other *Ideas*; which would be to make them Signs, and not Signs of his *Ideas* at the same time; and so in Effect, to have no Signification at all. Words being voluntary Signs, they cannot be voluntary Signs imposed by him on Things he knows not. That would be to make them Signs of nothing, Sounds without Signification. A Man cannot make his Words the Signs either of Qualities in Things, or of Conceptions in the Mind of another, whereof he has none in his own. Till he has some *Ideas* of his own, he cannot suppose them to correspond with the Conceptions of another Man; nor can he use any Signs for them: For it would be the Signs of he knows not what, which is in Truth to be the Sign of nothing. But when he represents to himself other Men's *Ideas*, by some of his own, if he consent to give them the same Names, that other Men do, 'tis still to his own *Ideas*; to *Ideas* that he has, and not to *Ideas* that he has not.

§. 3. This is so necessary in the use of Language, that in this respect, the Knowing, and the Ignorant; the Learned, and Unlearned, use the *Words* they speak (with any meaning) all alike. They, *in every Man's Mouth, stand for the* Ideas *he has*, and which he would express by them. A Child having taken notice of nothing in the Metal he hears called Gold, but the bright shining Yellow-Colour, he applies the Word Gold only to his own *Idea* of that Colour, and nothing else; and therefore calls the same Colour in a Peacock's Tail, Gold. Another that hath better observed, adds to shining Yellow, great Weight: And then the Sound Gold, when he uses it, stands for a complex *Idea* of a shining Yellow, and very weighty Substance. Another adds to those Qualities, Fusibility: And then the Word Gold to him signifies, a Body, bright, yellow, fusible, and very heavy. Another adds Malleability. Each of these uses equally the Word Gold, when they have Occasion to express the *Idea*, they have apply'd it to. But it is evident, that each can apply it only to his own *Idea*; nor can he make it stand, as a Sign of such a complex *Idea*, as he has not.

§.4. But though Words, as they are used by Men, can properly and immediately signifie nothing but the *Ideas*, that are in their Minds; yet they in their Thoughts, give them a secret reference to two other Things.

First, They suppose their Words to be Marks of the Ideas *in the Minds also of other Men, with whom they communicate*: For else they should talk in vain, and could not be understood, if the Sounds they applied to one *Idea*, were such, as by the Hearer, were apply'd to another, which is to speak two Languages. But in this, Men stand not usually to examine, whether the *Idea* they, and he they discourse with, be the same: But think it enough, that they use the Word, as they imagine, in the common Acceptation of that Language; in which case, they suppose that the *Idea*, they make it a Sign of, is precisely the same, to which the Understanding Men of that Country apply that Name.

§.5. *Secondly*, Because *Men* would not be thought to talk *barely* of their own Imaginations, but of Things as really they are; therefore they *often suppose their Words to stand also for the Reality of Things*. But this relating more particularly to Substances, and their Names, as, perhaps, the former does to simple *Ideas* and Modes, we shall speak of these two different ways of applying Words more at large, when we come to treat of the Names of mixed Modes, and Substances, in particular: Though give me leave here to say, that it is a perverting the use of Words, and brings unavoidable Obscurity and Confusion into their Signification, whenever we make them stand for any thing, but those *Ideas* we have in our own Minds.

§.6. Concerning Words also, this is farther to be considered. *First*, That they being immediately the Signs of Men's *Ideas*; and by that means, the Instruments whereby Men communicate their Conceptions, and express to one another those Thoughts and Imaginations, they have within their own Breasts, *there comes by constant use*, to be such *a Connexion between certain Sounds, and the* Ideas *they stand for*, that the Names heard, almost as readily excite certain *Ideas*; as if the Objects themselves, which are apt to produce them did actually affect the Senses. Which is manifestly so in all obvious sensible Qualities; and in all Substances, that frequently, and familiarly occurr to us.

§. 7. *Secondly*, That though the proper and immediate Signification of Words, are *Ideas* in the Mind of the Speaker; yet because by familiar use from our Cradles, we come to learn certain articulate Sounds very perfectly, and have them readily on our Tongues, and Memories, but yet are not always careful to examine, or settle their Significations perfectly, it *often* happens, that *Men*, even when they would apply themselves to an attentive Consideration, do *set their Thoughts more on Words than Things*. Nay, because Words are many of them learn'd, before the *Ideas* are known for which they stand: Therefore some, not only Children, but Men, speak several Words, no otherwise than Parrots do, only because they have learn'd them, and have been accustomed to those Sounds. But so far as Words are of Use and Signification, so far is there a constant connexion between the Sound and the *Idea*; and a Designation, that the one stand for the other: without which Application of them, they are nothing, but so much insignificant Noise.

§. 8. *Words* by long and familiar use, as has been said, come to excite in Men certain *Ideas* so constantly and readily, that they are apt to suppose a natural connexion between them. But that they *signifie* only Men's peculiar *Ideas*, and that *by a perfectly arbitrary Imposition*, is evident, in that they often fail to excite in others (even that use the same Language) the same *Ideas* we take them to be the Signs of: And every Man has so inviolable a Liberty, to make Words stand for what *Ideas* he pleases, that no one hath the Power to make others have the same *Ideas* in their Minds, that he has, when they use the same Words, that he does. And therefore the great *Augustus* himself, in the Possession of that Power, which ruled the World, acknowledged he could not make a new Latin Word: which was as much as to say, that he could not arbitrarily appoint, what *Idea* any Sound should be a Sign of, in the Mouths and common Language of his Subjects. 'Tis true, common use, by a tacit Consent, appropriates certain Sounds to certain *Ideas* in all Languages; which so far limits the signification of that Sound, that unless a Man applies it to the same *Idea*, he cannot speak properly. And it is also true, that unless a Man's Words excite the same *Ideas* in the Hearer, which he makes them stand for in speaking, he cannot speak intelligibly. But whatever be the consequences of his use of any Words, different either from the Publick, or that Person to whom he addresses them: This is certain, their signification in his use of them, is limited to his *Ideas*, and they can be Signs of nothing else.

DANIEL DEFOE

(1660?–1731)

Two hundred years after Caxton, Defoe voices anew the doubts of literary men
that English can, unregulated, bear comparison with the achievements of other
tongues, particularly French. He had already, with Lord Roscommon, attempted
the formation of an academy on the French model, and he here outlines the
composition and programme of his proposed body. In an excursus, he deplores
the spread of swearing as an impediment to conversation, and considers in this
connection the conflicting authority of custom and reason, concluding in
favour of reason. The authority of the English academy should, he says, oppose
swearing. The excerpt breaks off at the point where he turns his attention to
other matters.

'Of Academies'

(From *An Essay upon Projects*, 1697)

We have in *England* fewer of these[1] than in any part of the World,
at least where Learning is in so much esteem. But to make amends,
the two great Seminaries we have, are without comparison the
Greatest, I won't say the *Best* in the World; and tho' much might
be said here concerning Universities in general, and Foreign Academies in particular, I content my self with noting that part in
which we seem defective. The *French*, who justly value themselves
upon erecting the most Celebrated Academy of *Europe*, owe the
Lustre of it very much to the great Encouragement the Kings of
France have given to it. And one of the Members making a Speech
at his Entrance, tells you, *That 'tis not the least of the Glories of their
Invincible Monarch, to have engross'd all the Learning of the World in
that Sublime Body*.

The peculiar Study of the Academy of *Paris*, has been to Refine
and Correct their own Language; which they have done to that

---

[1] [*fewer of these* i.e. academies.]

happy degree, that we see it now spoken in all the Courts of *Christendom*, as the Language allow'd to be most universal.

I had the Honour once to be a Member of a small Society, who seem'd to offer at this Noble Design in *England*. But the Greatness of the Work, and the Modesty of the Gentlemen concern'd, prevail'd with them to desist an Enterprize which appear'd too great for Private Hands to undertake. We want indeed a *Richlieu* to commence such a Work: For I am persuaded, were there such a *Genius* in our Kingdom to lead the way, there wou'd not want Capacities who cou'd carry on the Work to a Glory equal to all that has gone before them. The *English* Tongue is a Subject not at all less worthy the Labour of such a Society than the *French*, and capable of a much greater Perfection. The Learned among the *French* will own, That the Comprehensiveness of Expression is a Glory in which the *English* Tongue not only Equals but Excels its Neighbours; *Rapin*, St. *Evremont*, and the most Eminent *French* Authors have acknowledg'd it: And my Lord *Roscommon*, who is allow'd to be a good Judge of *English*, because he wrote it as exactly as any ever did, expresses what I mean, in these Lines;

> '*For who did ever in* French *Authors see*
> *The Comprehensive* English *Energy?*
> *The weighty* Bullion *of one* Sterling *Line,*
> *Drawn to* French *Wire* *wou'd through whole Pages shine.*

And if our Neighbours will yield us, as their greatest Critick has done, the Preference for Sublimity and Nobleness of Stile, we will willingly quit all Pretensions to their Insignificant Gaiety.'

'Tis great pity that a Subject so Noble shou'd not have some as Noble to attempt it: And for a Method, what greater can be set before us, than the Academy of *Paris*? Which, to give the *French* their due, stands foremost among all the Great Attempts in the Learned Part of the World.

The present King of *England*, of whom we have seen the whole World writing *Panegyricks* and *Encomiums*, and whom his Enemies,

when their Interest does not silence them, are apt to say more of
than our selves; as in the War he has given surprizing Instances of
a Greatness of Spirit more than common; so in Peace, I dare say,
with Submission, he shall never have an Opportunity to illustrate
his Memory more, than by such a Foundation: By which he shall
have Opportunity to darken the Glory of the *French* King in
Peace, as he has by his daring Attempts in the War.

Nothing but Pride loves to be flatter'd, and that only as 'tis a
Vice which blinds us to our own Imperfections. I think Princes
as particularly unhappy in having their Good Actions magnify'd,
as their Evil Actions cover'd: But King *William*, who has already
won Praise by the Steps of dangerous Virtue, seems reserv'd for
some Actions which are above the Touch of Flattery, whose
Praise is in themselves.

And such wou'd this be: And because I am speaking of a Work
which seems to be proper only for the Hand of the King himself,
I shall not presume to carry on this Chapter to the Model, as I
have done in other Subjects. Only thus far;

That a Society be erected by the King himself, *if his Majesty
thought fit*, and composed of none but Persons of the first Figure
in Learning; and 'twere to be wish'd our Gentry were so much
Lovers of Learning, that Birth might always be join'd with
Capacity.

The Work of this Society shou'd be to encourage Polite Learning, to polish and refine the *English* Tongue, and advance the so
much neglected Faculty of Correct Language, to establish Purity
and Propriety of Stile, and to purge it from all the Irregular
Additions that Ignorance and Affectation have introduc'd; and
all those Innovations in Speech, if I may call them such, which
some Dogmatic Writers have the Confidence to foster upon their
Native Language, as if their Authority were sufficient to make
their own Fancy legitimate.

By such a Society I dare say the true Glory of our *English* Stile
wou'd appear; and among all the Learned Part of the World, be

esteem'd, as it really is, the Noblest and most Comprehensive of all the Vulgar[1] Languages in the World.

Into this Society should be admitted none but Persons Eminent for Learning, and yet none, or but very few, whose Business or Trade was Learning: For I may be allow'd, I suppose, to say, We have seen many great Scholars, meer Learned Men, and Graduates in the last Degree of Study, whose *English* has been far from Polite, full of Stiffness and Affectation, hard Words, and long unusual Coupling of *Syllables* and Sentences, which sound harsh and untuneable to the Ear, and shock the Reader both in Expression and Understanding.

In short, There should be room in this Society for neither *Clergyman*, *Physician*, or *Lawyer*. Not that I wou'd put an Affront upon the Learning of any of those Honourable Employments, much less upon their Persons: But if I do think that their several Professions do naturally and severally prescribe Habits of Speech to them peculiar to their Practice, and prejudicial to the Study I speak of, I believe I do them no wrong. Nor do I deny but there may be, and now are among some of all those Professions, Men of Stile and Language, great Masters of *English*, whom few men will undertake to Correct; and where such do at any time appear, their extraordinary Merit shou'd find them a Place in this Society; but it shou'd be rare, and upon very extraordinary Occasions, that such be admitted.

I wou'd therefore have this Society wholly compos'd of Gentlemen; whereof Twelve to be of the Nobility, if possible, and Twelve Private Gentlemen, and a Class of Twelve to be left open for meer Merit, let it be found in who or what sort it would, which should lye as the Crown of their Study, who have done something eminent to deserve it. The Voice of this Society should be sufficient Authority for the Usage of Words, and sufficient also to expose the Innovations of other mens Fancies; they shou'd preside with a Sort of Judicature over the Learning of the Age, and have liberty to Correct and Censure the Exorbitance of Writers, especially of

---

[1] [*Vulgar* vernacular.]

Translators. The Reputation of this Society wou'd be enough to make them the allow'd Judges of Stile and Language; and no Author wou'd have the Impudence to Coin without their Authority. *Custom*, which is now our best Authority for Words, wou'd always have its Original here, and not be allow'd without it. There shou'd be no more occasion to search for Derivations and Constructions, and 'twou'd be as Criminal then to *Coin Words*, *as Money*.

The Exercises of this Society wou'd be Lectures on the *English* Tongue, Essays on the Nature, Original, Usage, Authorities and Differences of Words, on the Propriety, Purity, and *Cadence of Stile*, and of the Politeness and *Manner* in Writing; Reflections upon Irregular Usages, and Corrections of Erroneous Customs in Words; and in short, every thing that wou'd appear necessary to the bringing our *English* Tongue to a due Perfection, and our Gentlemen to a Capacity of Writing like themselves; to banish Pride and Pedantry, and silence the Impudence and Impertinence of Young Authors, whose Ambition is to be known, tho' it be by their Folly.

I ask leave here for a Thought or two about that Inundation Custom has made upon our Language and Discourse by *Familiar Swearing*; and I place it here, because Custom has so far prevail'd in this foolish Vice, that a man's Discourse is hardly agreeable without it; and some have taken upon them to say, *It is pity it shou'd not be lawful, 'tis such a Grace in a man's Speech, and adds so much Vigour to his Language.*

I desire to be understood right, and that by Swearing I mean all those Cursory Oaths, Curses, Execrations, Imprecations, Asseverations, and by whatsoever other Names they are distinguish'd, which are us'd in Vehemence of Discourse, in the Mouths almost of all men more or less, of what sort soever.

I am not about to argue any thing of their being sinful and unlawful, as forbid by Divine Rules; *let the Parson alone to tell you that*, who has, no question, said as much to as little purpose in this Case as in any other: But I am of the opinion, that there is nothing so Impertinent, so Insignificant, so Sensless and Foolish, as our vulgar way of Discourse, when mix'd with Oaths and Curses; and I wou'd only recommend a little Consideration to our Gentlemen, who have Sense and Wit enough, and wou'd be asham'd to speak Nonsense in other things, but value themselves upon their Parts;[1] I wou'd but ask them to put into Writing the Common-Places of their Discourse, and read them over again, and examine the *English*, the *Cadence*, the *Grammar* of them; then let them turn them into *Latin*, or translate them into any other Language, and but see what a *Jargon* and Confusion of Speech they make together.

Swearing, that Lewdness of the Tongue, that Scum and Excrement of the Mouth, is of all Vices the most foolish and sensless; it makes a man's Conversation *unpleasant*, his Discourse *fruitless*, and his Language *Nonsense*.

It makes Conversation *unpleasant*, at least to those who do not use the same foolish way of Discourse; and indeed, is an Affront to all the Company who swear not as he does; for if I swear and Curse in Company, I either presume all the Company likes it, or affront them who do not.

Then 'tis *fruitless*; for no man is believ'd a jot the more for all the Asseverations, *Damnings* and Swearings he makes: Those who are us'd to it themselves, do not believe a man the more, because they know they are so customary, that they signify little to bind a man's Intention; and they who practise them not, have so mean an opinion of those that do, as makes them think they deserve no belief.

Then, they are the Spoilers and Destroyers of a man's Discourse, and turn it into perfect *Nonsense*; and to make it out, I must descend a little to Particulars, and desire the Reader a little to foul his Mouth with the Bruitish, Sordid, Sensless Expressions, which some Gentlemen call Polite *English*, and speaking with a Grace.

Some part of them indeed, tho' they are foolish enough, as Effects of a mad, inconsiderate Rage, are yet *English*; as when a

[1] [*Parts* talents.]

man swears he will do this or that, and it may be adds, *God damn him he will*; that is, *God damn him if he don't*: This, tho' it be horrid in another sense, yet may be read in writing, and is *English*: But what Language is this?

Jack, *God damn me* Jack, *How do'st do, thou little dear Son of a Whore? How hast thou done this long time, by God?* —And then they kiss; and the t'other, as lewd as himself, goes on;

Dear Tom, *I am glad to see thee with all my heart, let me dye. Come, let us go take a Bottle, we must not part so; prithee let's go and be drunk by God.*—

This is some of our new florid Language, and the Graces and Delicacies of Stile, which if it were put into *Latin*, I wou'd fain know which is the principal Verb.

But for a little further remembrance of this Impertinence, go among the Gamesters, and there nothing is more frequent than, *God damn the Dice*, or *God damn the Bowls*.

Among the Sportsmen 'tis, *God damn the Hounds*, when they are at a Fault, or *God damn the Horse*, if he bau'ks a Leap: They call men *Sons of Bitches*, and *Dogs*, *Sons of Whores*: And innumerable Instances may be given of the like Gallantry of Language, grown now so much a *Custom*.

'Tis true, Custom is allow'd to be our best Authority for Words, and 'tis fit it should be so; but Reason must be the Judge of Sense in Language, and Custom can never prevail over it. *Words*, indeed, like Ceremonies in Religion, may be submitted to the Magistrate; but *Sense*, like the Essentials, is positive, unalterable, and cannot be submitted to any Jurisdiction; 'tis a Law to it self, 'tis ever the same, even an Act of Parliament cannot alter it.

Words, and even Usages in Stile, may be alter'd by Custom, and Proprieties in Speech differ according to the several Dialects of the Countrey, and according to the different manner in which several Languages do severally express themselves.

But there is a direct Signification of Words, or a *Cadence in Expression*, which we call speaking *Sense*; this, like Truth, is sullen and the same, ever was and will be so, in what manner, and in what Language soever 'tis express'd. *Words* without it, are only Noise, which any Brute can make as well as we, and Birds much better; for *Words* without *Sense* make but dull Musick. Thus a man may speak in *Words*, but perfectly unintelligible as to *Meaning*; he may *talk* a great deal, but *say* nothing. But 'tis the proper Position of *Words*, adapted to their Significations, which makes them intelligible, and conveys the Meaning of the Speaker to the Understanding of the Hearer; the contrary to which we call *Nonsense*; and there is a superfluous crowding in of insignificant Words, more than are needful to express the thing intended, and this is *Impertinence*; and that again carry'd to an extreme, is *ridiculous*.

Thus when our Discourse is interlin'd with needless Oaths, Curses, and long *Parentheses* of Imprecations, and with some of very indirect signification, they become very *Impertinent*; and these being run to the extravagant degree instanc'd in before, become perfectly *ridiculous* and *Nonsense*; and without forming it into an Argument, it appears to be *Nonsense* by the Contradictoriness; and it appears *Impertinent*, by the Insignificancy of the Expression.

After all, how little it becomes a Gentleman to debauch his Mouth with Foul Language, I refer to themselves in a few Particulars.

This Vicious Custom has prevail'd upon Good Manners too far; but yet there are some degrees to which it is not yet arriv'd.

As first, The worst Slaves to this Folly will neither teach it *to*, nor approve of it *in* their Children: Some of the most careless will indeed negatively teach it, by not reproving them for it; but sure no man ever order'd his Children to be taught to curse or swear.

2. The Grace of Swearing has not obtain'd to be a Mode yet among the Women; *God damn ye*, does not sit well upon a Female Tongue; it seems to be a Masculine Vice, which the Women are not arriv'd to yet; and I wou'd only desire those Gentlemen who practice it themselves, to hear a Woman swear: It has no Musick

at all there, I am sure; and just as little does it become any Gentleman, if he wou'd suffer himself to be judg'd by all the Laws of Sense or Good Manners in the world.

'Tis a sensless, foolish, ridiculous Practice; 'tis a Mean to no manner of End; 'tis Words spoken which signify nothing; 'tis Folly acted for the sake of Folly, which is a thing even the Devil himself don't practice: The Devil does evil, we say, but it is for some design, either to seduce others, or, as some Divines say, from a Principle of Enmity to his Maker: Men Steal for Gain, and Murther to gratify their Avarice or Revenge; Whoredoms and Ravishments, Adulteries and Sodomy, are committed to please a vicious Appetite, and have always alluring Objects; and generally all Vices have some previous Cause, and some visible Tendency; but this, of all Vicious Practices, seems the most Nonsensical and Ridiculous; there is neither Pleasure nor Profit; no Design pursued, no Lust gratified, but is a mere Frenzy of the Tongue, a Vomit of the Brain, which works by putting a Contrary upon the Course of Nature.

Again, other Vices men find some Reason or other to give for, or Excuses to palliate; men plead Want, to extenuate Theft; and strong Provocations, to excuse Murthers; *and many a lame Excuse they will bring for Whoring*; but this sordid Habit, even those that practise it will own to be a Crime, and make no Excuse for it; and the most I cou'd ever hear a man say for it, was, That *he cou'd not help it.*

Besides, as 'tis an inexcusable Impertinence, so 'tis a Breach upon Good Manners and Conversation, for a man to impose the Clamour of his Oaths upon the Company he converses with; if there be any one person in the Company that does not approve the way, 'tis an imposing upon him with a freedom beyond Civility; as if a man shou'd *Fart* before a Justice, or *talk Bawdy* before the Queen, or the like.

To suppress this, Laws, Acts of Parliaments, and Proclamations, are Bawbles[1] and Banters, the Laughter of the Lewd Party, and

---

[1] [*Bawbles* jests.]

never had, as I cou'd perceive, any Influence upon the Practice; nor are any of our Magistrates fond or forward of putting them in execution.

It must be Example, not Penalties, must sink this Crime; and if the Gentlemen of *England* wou'd once drop it as a Mode, the Vice is so foolish and ridiculous in it self, 'twou'd soon grow odious and out of fashion.

This Work such an Academy might begin; and I believe nothing wou'd so soon explode the Practice, as the Publick Discouragement of it by such a Society. Where all our Customs and Habits both in Speech and Behaviour, shou'd receive an Authority. All the Disputes about Precedency of Wit, with the Manners, Customs, and Usages of the Theatre wou'd be decided here; Plays shou'd pass here before they were Acted, and the Criticks might give their Censures, and damn at their pleasure; nothing wou'd ever dye which once receiv'd Life at this Original: The Two Theatres might end their Jangle, and dispute for Priority no more; Wit and Real Worth shou'd decide the Controversy, and here shou'd be the *Infallible Judge.*

> The Strife wou'd then be only to do well,
> And he alone be crown'd who did excell.
> Ye call'd them Whigs, who from the Church with-
> drew,
> But now we have our Stage-Dissenters too;
> Who scruple Ceremonies of Pit and Box,
> And very few are Sound and Orthodox:
> But love Disorder so, and are so nice,
> They hate Conformity, tho' 'tis in Vice.
> Some are for Patent-Hierarchy; and some,
> Like the old Gauls, seek out for Elbow-room;
> Their Arbitrary Governors disown,
> And build a Conventicle-Stage o' their own.
> Phanatick Beaus make up the gawdy Show,
> And Wit alone appears Incognito.

Wit and Religion suffer equal Fate;
Neglect of both attends the warm Debate.
For while the Parties strive and countermine,
Wit will as well as Piety decline.

Next to this, which I esteem as the most Noble and most Useful Proposal in this Book, I proceed to Academies for Military Studies; and because I design rather to express my meaning, than make a large Book, I bring them all into one Chapter.

II

JOSEPH ADDISON

(1672–1719)

Addison begins by characterizing English as laudably compact in speech and writing, particularly through the abundance of its monosyllables. But he deplores a recent tendency to abbreviate further in the reduction of inflectional endings, and in mere slang and stylistic elisions. The prevailing uncertainty in matters like the use of relative pronouns convinces him the time has come for an English academy. The essay reflects the conversations about language which Swift said he held with Addison as early as 1710.

Spectator 135

Saturday, August 4, 1711

Est brevitate opus, ut currat Sententia[1]—Hor.

I have somewhere read of an eminent Person who us'd in his private Offices of Devotion, to give Thanks to Heaven that he was Born a *Frenchman*: For my own part I look upon it as a peculiar Blessing that I was Born an *Englishman*. Among many other Reasons, I think my self very happy in my Country, as the *Language* of it is wonderfully adapted to a Man that is sparing of his Words, and an Enemy to Loquacity.

As I have frequently reflected on my good Fortune in this Particular, I shall communicate to the Publick my Speculations upon the *English* Tongue, not doubting but they will be acceptable to all my curious Readers.

The *English* delight in Silence more than any other *European* Nation, if the Remarks which are made on us by Foreigners are true. Our Discourse is not kept up in Conversation, but falls into more Pauses and Intervals than in our Neighbouring Countries;

---

[1] [*Est...Sententia* Brevity is needed, so that the sense may run on (Horace, *Sat.* I. 10. 9).]

as it is observ'd, that the matter of our Writings is thrown much closer together, and lies in a narrower Compass than is usual in the Works of Foreign Authors. For, to favour our Natural Taciturnity, when we are obliged to utter our Thoughts, we do it in the shortest way we are able, and give as quick a Birth to our Conceptions as possible.

This Humour shows it self in several Remarks that we may make upon the *English* Language. As first of all by its abounding in Monosyllables, which gives us an Opportunity of delivering our Thoughts in few Sounds. This indeed takes off from the Elegance of our Tongue, but at the same time expresses our Ideas in the readiest manner, and consequently answers the first Design of Speech better than the multitude of Syllables, that makes the Words of other Languages more Tunable and Sonorous. The Sounds of our *English* Words are commonly like those of String Musick, short and transient, that rise and perish upon a single touch; those of other Languages are like the Notes of Wind Instruments, sweet and swelling, and lengthen'd out into variety of Modulation.

In the next place we may observe, that where the Words are not Monosyllables, we often make them so, as much as lies in our Power, by our Rapidity of Pronunciation; as it generally happens in most of our long Words which are deriv'd from the *Latin*, where we contract the length of the Syllables that gives them a grave and solemn Air in their own Language, to make them more proper for Dispatch, and more conformable to the Genius of our Tongue. This we may find in a multitude of Words, as *Liberty*, *Conspiracy*, *Theatre*, *Orator*, &c.

The same natural Aversion to Loquacity has of late Years made a very considerable Alteration in our Language, by closing in one Syllable the Termination of our Præterperfect Tense, as in the Words *drown'd*, *walk'd*, *arriv'd*, for *drowned*, *walked*, *arrived*, which has very much disfigured the Tongue, and turn'd a tenth part of our smoothest Words into so many Clusters of Consonants. This is the more remarkable, because the want of Vowels in our

Language has been the general Complaint of our politest
Authors, who nevertheless are the Men that have made these
Retrenchments, and consequently very much increased our former
Scarcity.

This Reflection on the Words that end in *ed*, I have heard in
Conversation from one of the greatest Genius's this Age has produced. I think we may add to the foregoing Observation, the
Change that has happen'd in our Language, by the Abbreviation
of several Words that are terminated in *eth*, by substituting an *s* in
the room of the last Syllable, as in *drowns, walks, arrives*, and innumerable other Words, which in the Pronunciation of our Forefathers were *drowneth, walketh, arriveth*. This has wonderfully
multiplied a Letter which was before too frequent in the *English*
Tongue, and added to that *hissing* in our Language, which is
taken so much notice of by Foreigners; but at the same time
humours our Taciturnity, and eases us of many superfluous Syllables.

I might here observe, that the same single Letter on many
occasions does the Office of a whole Word, and represents the
His and *Her* of our Forefathers. There is no doubt but the Ear of
a Foreigner, which is the best Judge in this Case, would very much
disapprove of such Innovations, which indeed we do our selves
in some measure, by retaining the old Termination in Writing,
and in all the Solemn Offices of our Religion.

As in the Instances I have given we have epitomized many of
our particular Words to the Detriment of our Tongue, so on
other Occasions we have drawn two Words into one, which has
likewise very much untuned our Language, and clogged it with
Consonants, as *mayn't, can't, sha'n't, wo'n't*, and the like, for *may
not, can not, shall not, will not*, &c.

It is perhaps this Humour of speaking no more than we needs
must, which has so miserably curtailed some of our Words, that
in familiar Writings and Conversations they sometimes lose all
but their first Syllables, as in *Mob. rep. pos. incog.* and the like;
and as all ridiculous Words make their first Entry into a Language

by familiar Phrases, I dare not answer for them that they will not in time be looked upon as a part of our Tongue. We see some of our Poets that have been so indiscreet as to imitate *Hudibras*'s Doggrel Expressions in their serious Compositions, by throwing out the signs of our Substantives, which are essential to the *English* Language. Nay this Humour of shortning our Language had once run so far that some of our celebrated Authors, among whom we may reckon Sir *Roger L' Estrange* in particular, began to prune their Words of all superfluous Letters, as they termed them, in order to adjust the Spelling to the Pronunciation, which would have lost all our Etymologies, and have quite destroyed our Tongue.

We may here likewise observe that our Proper Names, when familiarized in *English*, generally dwindle to Monosyllables, whereas in other Modern Languages they receive a softer Turn on this occasion, by the Addition of a new Syllable. *Nick* in *Italian* is *Nicolini, Jack* in *French Janot*, and so of the rest.

There is another Particular in our Language which is a great Instance of our Frugality of Words, and that is the suppressing of several Particles, which must be produced in other Tongues to make a Sentence intelligible: This often perplexes the best Writers, when they find the Relatives, *Who, which* or *that*, at their Mercy whether it may have Admission or not, and will never be decided till we have something like an Academy, that by the best Authorities and Rules drawn from the Analogy of Languages shall settle all Controversies between Grammar and Idiom.

I have only considered our Language as it shows the Genius and natural Temper of the *English*, which is modest, thoughtful and sincere, and which perhaps may recommend the People, though it has spoiled the Tongue. We might perhaps carry the same Thought into other Languages, and deduce a great part of what is peculiar to them from the Genius of the People that speak them. It is certain the light talkative Humour of the *French* has not a little infected their Tongue, as might be shown by many

Instances; as the Genius of the *Italians*, which is so much addicted to Musick and Ceremony, has moulded all their Words and Phrases to those particular Uses. The Stateliness and Gravity of the *Spaniard* shews it self to Perfection in the Solemnity of their Language; and the blunt honest Humour of the *Germans* sounds better in the Roughness of the *High Dutch*,[1] than it would in a Politer Tongue.

[1] [*High Dutch Hochdeutsch*, i.e. German.]

12

JONATHAN SWIFT
(1667–1745)

Swift traces the reasons for the decline in the Latin language, and shows from
Greek that such decline is not inevitable. The golden age of English, he goes on,
was the Elizabethan, Jacobean and Caroline, since when politics and fashion
have increasingly corrupted it. In his own day jargon, poetic licence, phonetic
spelling and slang have encouraged the worst propensities of the language. He
proposes that his dedicatee establish an academy to rectify and fix English, lest
future ages be unable to read of the glories of Queen Anne and the Earl of
Oxford, and literary genius perish in an unpropitious climate. The hopes of the
proposal were destroyed by the fall of the Tory ministry in 1714, but later
writers regarded it as the classic statement of its point of view.

'A Proposal for Correcting, Improving and Ascertaining the English Tongue' (1712)

To the Most Honourable
ROBERT
Earl of OXFORD, &c.

MY LORD,

What I had the Honour of mentioning to Your LORDSHIP some
time ago in Conversation, was not a new Thought, just then
started by Accident or Occasion, but the Result of long Reflection;
and I have been confirmed in my Sentiments by the Opinion of
some very judicious Persons, with whom I consulted. They all
agreed, That nothing would be of greater Use towards the Improvement of Knowledge and Politeness,[1] than some effectual
Method for *Correcting*, *Enlarging* and *Ascertaining* our Language;
and they think it a Work very possible to be compassed, under

[1] [*Politeness* civilization.]

107

the Protection of a Prince, the Countenance and Encouragement of a Ministry, and the Care of proper Persons chosen for such an Undertaking. I was glad to find Your LORDSHIP's Answer in so different a Style, from what hath been commonly made use of on the like Occasions, for some Years past, *that all such Thoughts must be deferred to a Time of Peace*: A Topick which some have carried so far, that they would not have us, by any means, think of preserving our Civil or Religious Constitution, because we were engaged in a War abroad. It will be among the distinguishing Marks of your Ministry, My LORD, that you had a Genius above all such Regards, and that no reasonable Proposal for the Honour, the Advantage, or the Ornament of Your Country, however foreign to Your more immediate Office, was ever neglected by You. I confess, the Merit of this Candor and Condescension is very much lessened, because Your LORDSHIP hardly leaves us room to offer our good Wishes, removing all our Difficulties, and supplying our Wants, faster than the most visionary Projector[1] can adjust his Schemes. And therefore, My LORD, the Design of this Paper is not so much to offer You *Ways and Means*, as to complain of a *Grievance*, the redressing of which is to be Your own Work, as much as that of paying the *Nation*'s *Debts*, or opening a Trade into the *South Sea*; and though not of such immediate Benefit as either of these, or any other of Your glorious Actions, yet perhaps, in future Ages, not less to Your Honour.

My LORD; I do here, in the Name of all the Learned and Polite Persons of the Nation, complain to Your LORDSHIP, as *First Minister*, that our Language is extremely imperfect; that its daily Improvements are by no means in proportion to its daily Corruptions; that the Pretenders to polish and refine it, have chiefly multiplied Abuses and Absurdities; and, that in many Instances, it offends against every Part of Grammar. But lest Your LORDSHIP should think my Censure too severe, I shall take leave to be more particular.

[1] [*Projector* planner of (sometimes fantastic) projects; cf. the title of Defoe's essay, and Swift's *Gulliver's Travels*, III, iv–vi.]

I believe Your LORDSHIP will agree with me in the Reason, Why our Language is less Refined than those of *Italy*, *Spain*, or *France*. 'Tis plain that the *Latin* Tongue, in its Purity, was never in this Island; towards the Conquest of which few or no Attempts were made till the Time of *Claudius*; neither was that Language ever so vulgar in *Britain*, as it is known to have been in *Gaul* and *Spain*. Further, we find, that the *Roman* Legions here, were at length all recalled to help their Country against the *Goths*, and other barbarous Invaders. Mean time, the *Britains*, left to shift for themselves, and daily harassed by cruel Inroads from the *Picts*, were forced to call in the *Saxons* for their Defence; who, consequently, reduced the greatest Part of the Island to their own Power, drove the *Britains* into the most remote and mountainous Parts, and the rest of the Country, in Customs, Religion and Language, became wholly *Saxon*. This I take to be the Reason, why there are more *Latin* Words remaining in the *British* Tongue, than in the old *Saxon*; which, excepting some few Variations in the Orthography, is the same, in most original Words, with our present *English*, as well as with the German, and other *Northern* Dialects.

Edward the *Confessor* having lived long in *France*, appears to be the first who introduced any mixture of the *French* Tongue with the *Saxon*; the Court affecting what the Prince was fond of, and others taking it up for a Fashion, as it is now with us. *William* the *Conqueror* proceeded much further; bringing over with him vast numbers of that Nation; scattering them in every Monastery; giving them great Quantities of Land, directing all Pleadings to be in that Language, and endeavouring to make it universal in the Kingdom. This, at least, is the Opinion generally received: But Your LORDSHIP hath fully convinced me, that the *French* Tongue made yet a greater Progress here under *Harry* the *Second*, who had large Territories on that Continent, both from his Father and his Wife, made frequent Journies and Expeditions there, and was always attended with a number of his Countrymen, Retainers at his Court. For some Centuries after, there was a constant Intercourse between *France* and *England*, by the Dominions we possessed there, and the Conquests we made; so that our Language, between two and three hundred Years ago, seems to have had a greater mixture with *French*, than at present; many Words having been afterwards rejected, and some since the time of *Spencer*; although we have still retained not a few, which have been long antiquated in *France*. I could produce several Instances of both kinds, if it were of any Use or Entertainment.

To examine into the several Circumstances by which the Language of a Country may be altered, would force me to enter into a wide Field. I shall only observe, That the *Latin*, the *French*, and the *English*, seem to have undergone the same Fortune. The first, from the Days of *Romulus* to those of *Julius Cæsar*, suffered perpetual Changes, and by what we meet in those Authors who occasionally speak on that Subject, as well as from certain Fragments of old Laws, it is manifest, that the *Latin*, Three hundred Years before *Tully*, was as unintelligible in his Time, as the *English* and *French* of the same Period are now; and these two have changed as much since *William the Conqueror*, (which is but little less than Seven hundred Years) as the *Latin* appears to have done in the like Term. Whether our Language or the *French* will decline as fast as the *Roman* did, is a Question that would perhaps admit more Debate than it is worth. There were many Reasons for the Corruptions of the last: As, the Change of their Government into a Tyranny, which ruined the Study of Eloquence, there being no further Use or Encouragement for popular Orators: Their giving not only the Freedom of the City, but Capacity for Employments, to several Towns in *Gaul*, *Spain*, and *Germany*, and other distant Parts, as far as *Asia*; which brought a great Number of forein Pretenders into *Rome*: The slavish Disposition of the Senate and People, by which the Wit and Eloquence of the Age were wholly turned into Panegyrick, the most barren of all Subjects: The great Corruption of Manners, and Introduction of forein Luxury, with forein Terms to express it; with several others that might be assigned: Not to mention those Invasions from the *Goths* and *Vandals*, which are too obvious to insist on.

The *Roman* Language arrived at great Perfection before it began to decay: And the *French* for these last Fifty Years hath been polishing as much as it will bear, and appears to be declining by the natural Inconstancy of that People, and the Affectation of some late Authors to introduce and multiply *Cant* Words, which is the most ruinous Corruption in any Language. *La Bruyere*, a late celebrated Writer among them, makes use of many hundred new Terms, which are not to be found in any of the common Dictionaries before his Time. But the *English* Tongue is not arrived to such a Degree of Perfection, as to make us apprehend any Thoughts of its Decay; and if it were once refined to a certain Standard, perhaps there might be Ways found out to fix it for ever; or at least till we are invaded and made a Conquest by some other State; and even then our best Writings might probably be preserved with Care, and grow into Esteem, and the Authors have a Chance for Immortality.

But without such great Revolutions as these, (to which we are, I think, less subject than Kingdoms upon the Continent) I see no absolute Necessity why any Language should be perpetually changing; for we find many Examples to the contrary. From *Homer* to *Plutarch* are above a Thousand Years; so long at least the Purity of the *Greek* Tongue may be allow'd to last, and we know not how far before. The *Grecians* spread their Colonies round all the Coasts of *Asia Minor*, even to the *Northern* Parts, lying towards the *Euxine*; in every Island of the *Ægean Sea*, and several others in the *Mediterranean*; where the Language was preserved entire for many Ages, after they themselves became Colonies to *Rome*, and till they were over-run by the barbarous Nations, upon the Fall of that Empire. The *Chinese* have Books in their Language above two Thousand Years old, neither have the frequent Conquests of the *Tartars* been able to alter it. The *German*, *Spanish*, and *Italian*, have admitted few or no Changes for some Ages past. The other Languages of *Europe* I know nothing of, neither is there any occasion to consider them.

Having taken this compass, I return to those Considerations

upon our own Language, which I would humbly offer Your LORDSHIP. The Period wherein the *English* Tongue received most Improvement, I take to commence with the beginning of Queen *Elizabeth*'s Reign, and to conclude with the Great Rebellion in Forty Two. 'Tis true, there was a very ill Taste both of Style and Wit, which prevailed under King *James* the First, but that seems to have been corrected in the first Years of his Successor, who among many other Qualifications of an excellent Prince, was a great Patron of Learning. From the Civil War to this present Time, I am apt to doubt whether the Corruptions in our Language have not at least equalled the Refinements of it; and these Corruptions very few of the best Authors in our Age have wholly escaped. During the Usurpation, such an Infusion of Enthusiastick Jargon[1] prevailed in every Writing, as was not shook off in many Years after. To this succeeded that Licentiousness which entered with the *Restoration*, and from infecting our Religion and Morals, fell to corrupt our Language; which last was not like to be much improved by those who at that Time made up the Court of King *Charles* the Second; either such who had followed Him in His Banishment, or who had been altogether conversant in the Dialect of those *Fanatick Times*; or young Men, who had been educated in the same Company; so that the *Court*, which used to be the Standard of Propriety and Correctness of Speech, was then, and, I think, hath ever since continued the worst School in *England* for that Accomplishment; and so will remain, till better Care be taken in the Education of our young Nobility, that they may set out into the World with some Foundation of Literature, in order to qualify them for Patterns of Politeness. The Consequence of this Defect, upon our Language, may appear from the Plays, and other Compositions, written for Entertainment within Fifty Years past; filled with a Succession of affected Phrases, and new, conceited Words, either borrowed from the current Style of the Court, or from those who, under the Character of Men of Wit

---

[1] [*Enthusiastick Jargon* the exalted language of bigoted sectarians claiming private inspiration.]

and Pleasure, pretended to give the Law. Many of these Refinements have already been long antiquated, and are now hardly intelligible; which is no wonder, when they were the Product only of Ignorance and Caprice.

I have never known this great Town without one or more *Dunces* of Figure,[1] who had Credit enough to give Rise to some new Word, and propagate it in most Conversations, though it had neither Humor, nor Significancy. If it struck the present Taste, it was soon transferred into the Plays and current Scribbles of the Week, and became an Addition to our Language; while the Men of Wit and Learning, instead of early obviating such Corruptions, were too often seduced to imitate and comply with them.

There is another Sett of Men who have contributed very much to the spoiling of the *English* Tongue; I mean the Poets, from the Time of the Restoration. These Gentlemen, although they could not be insensible how much our Language was already overstocked with Monosyllables; yet, to save Time and Pains, introduced that barbarous Custom of abbreviating Words, to fit them to the Measure of their Verses; and this they have frequently done, so very injudiciously, as to form such harsh unharmonious Sounds, that none but a *Northern* Ear could endure: They have joined the most obdurate Consonants without one intervening Vowel, only to shorten a Syllable: And their Taste in time became so depraved, that what was at first a Poetical Licence not to be justified, they made their Choice, alledging, that the Words pronounced at length, sounded faint and languid. This was a Pretence to take up the same Custom in Prose; so that most of the Books we see now a-days, are full of those Manglings and Abbreviations. Instances of this Abuse are innumerable: What does Your LORDSHIP think of the Words, *Drudg'd, Disturb'd, Rebuk't, Fledg'd,* and a thousand others, every where to be met in Prose as well as Verse? Where, by leaving out a Vowel to save a Syllable, we form so jarring a Sound, and so difficult to utter, that I have often wondred how it could ever obtain.

[1] [*of Figure* of mark, of importance.]

Another Cause (and perhaps borrowed from the former) which hath contributed not a little to the maiming of our Language, is a foolish Opinion, advanced of late Years, that we ought to spell exactly as we speak; which beside the obvious Inconvenience of utterly destroying our Etymology, would be a thing we should never see an End of. Not only the several Towns and Countries of *England*, have a different way of Pronouncing, but even here in *London*, they clip their Words after one Manner about the Court, another in the City, and a third in the Suburbs; and in a few Years, it is probable, will all differ from themselves, as Fancy or Fashion shall direct: All which reduced to Writing would entirely confound Orthography. Yet many People are so fond of this Conceit, that it is sometimes a difficult matter to read modern Books and Pamphlets; where the Words are so curtailed, and varied from their original Spelling, that whoever hath been used to plain *English*, will hardly know them by sight.

Several young Men at the Universities, terribly possessed with the fear of Pedantry, run into a worse Extream, and think all Politeness to consist in reading the daily Trash sent down to them from hence: This they call *knowing the World*, and *reading Men and Manners*. Thus furnished they come up to Town, reckon all their Errors for Accomplishments, borrow the newest Sett of Phrases, and if they take a Pen into their Hands, all the odd Words they have picked up in a Coffee-House, or a Gaming Ordinary, are produced as Flowers of Style; and the Orthography refined to the utmost. To this we owe those monstrous Productions, which under the Names of *Trips*, *Spies*, *Amusements*, and other conceited Appellations, have over-run us for some Years past. To this we owe that strange Race of Wits, who tell us, they Write to the *Humour of the Age*: And I wish I could say, these quaint Fopperies were wholly absent from graver Subjects. In short, I would undertake to shew Your LORDSHIP several Pieces, where the Beauties of this kind are so predominant, that with all your Skill in Languages, you could never be able either to read or understand them.

But I am very much mistaken, if many of these false Refinements among us, do not arise from a Principle which would quite destroy their Credit, if it were well understood and considered. For I am afraid, My LORD, that with all the real good Qualities of our Country, we are naturally not very Polite. This perpetual Disposition to shorten our Words, by retrenching the Vowels, is nothing else but a tendency to lapse into the Barbarity of those *Northern* Nations from whom we are descended, and whose Languages labour all under the same Defect. For it is worthy our Observation, that the *Spaniards*, the *French*, and the *Italians*, although derived from the same *Northern* Ancestors with our selves, are, with the utmost Difficulty, taught to pronounce our Words, which the *Suedes* and *Danes*, as well as the *Germans* and the *Dutch*, attain to with Ease, because our Syllables resemble theirs in the Roughness and Frequency of Consonants. Now, as we struggle with an ill Climate to improve the nobler kinds of Fruit, are at the Expence of Walls to receive and reverberate the faint Rays of the Sun, and fence against the *Northern* Blasts; we sometimes by the help of a good Soil equal the Productions of warmer Countries, who have no need to be at so much Cost or Care. It is the same thing with respect to the politer Arts among us; and the same Defect of Heat which gives a Fierceness to our Natures, may contribute to that Roughness of our Language, which bears some Analogy to the harsh Fruit of colder Countries. For I do not reckon that we want a *Genius* more than the rest of our Neighbours: But Your LORDSHIP will be of my Opinion, that we ought to struggle with these natural Disadvantages as much as we can, and be careful whom we employ, whenever we design to correct them, which is a Work that has hitherto been assumed by the least qualified Hands. So that if the Choice had been left to me, I would rather have trusted the Refinement of our Language, as far as it relates to Sound, to the Judgment of the Women, than of illiterate Court-Fops, half-witted-Poets, and University-Boys. For, it is plain that Women in their manner of corrupting Words, do naturally discard the Consonants, as we do the Vowels. What

I am going to tell Your LORDSHIP, appears very trifling; that more than once, where some of both Sexes were in Company, I have persuaded two or three of each, to take a Pen, and write down a number of Letters joyned together, just as it came into their Heads, and upon reading this Gibberish we have found that which the Men had writ, by the frequent encountring of rough Consonants, to sound like *High-Dutch*; and the other by the Women, like *Italian*, abounding in Vowels and Liquids. Now, though I would by no means give Ladies the Trouble of advising us in the Reformation of our Language; yet I cannot help thinking, that since they have been left out of all Meetings, except Parties at Play, or where worse Designs are carried on, our Conversation hath very much degenerated.

In order to reform our Language, I conceive, My LORD, that a free judicious Choice should be made of such Persons, as are generally allowed to be best qualified for such a Work, without any regard to Quality, Party, or Profession. These, to a certain Number at least, should assemble at some appointed Time and Place, and fix on Rules by which they design to proceed. What Methods they will take, is not for me to prescribe. Your LORDSHIP, and other Persons in great Employment, might please to be of the Number; and I am afraid, such a Society would want Your Instruction and Example, as much as Your Protection: For, I have, not without a little Envy, observed of late, the Style of some great Ministers very much to exceed that of any other Productions.

The Persons who are to undertake this Work, will have the Example of the *French* before them, to imitate where these have proceeded right, and to avoid their Mistakes. Beside the Grammarpart, wherein we are allowed to be very defective, they will observe many gross Improprieties, which however authorised by Practice, and grown familiar, ought to be discarded. They will find many Words that deserve to be utterly thrown out of our Language, many more to be corrected; and perhaps not a few, long since antiquated, which ought to be restored, on account of their Energy and Sound.

But what I have most at Heart is, that some Method should be thought on for *ascertaining* and *fixing* our Language for ever, after such Alterations are made in it as shall be thought requisite. For I am of Opinion, that it is better a Language should not be wholly perfect, than that it should be perpetually changing; and we must give over at one Time, or at length infallibly change for the worse: As the *Romans* did, when they began to quit their *Simplicity* of Style for affected Refinements; such as we meet in *Tacitus* and other Authors, which ended by degrees in many Barbarities, even before the *Goths* had invaded *Italy*.

The Fame of our Writers is usually confined to these two Islands, and it is hard it should be limited in *Time*, as much as *Place*, by the perpetual Variations of our Speech. It is Your LORDSHIP's Observation, that if it were not for the *Bible* and *Common Prayer Book* in the vulgar Tongue, we should hardly be able to understand any Thing that was written among us an hundred Years ago: Which is certainly true: For those Books being perpetually read in Churches, have proved a kind of Standard for Language, especially to the common People. And I doubt whether the Alterations since introduced, have added much to the Beauty or Strength of the *English* Tongue, though they have taken off a great deal from that *Simplicity*, which is one of the greatest Perfections in any Language. You, My LORD, who are so conversant in the Sacred Writings, and so great a Judge of them in their Originals, will agree, that no Translation our Country ever yet produced, hath come up to that of the *Old* and *New Testament*: And by the many beautiful Passages, which I have often had the Honor to hear Your LORDSHIP cite from thence, I am persuaded that the Translators of the Bible were Masters of an *English* Style much fitter for that Work, than any we see in our present Writings, which I take to be owing to the *Simplicity* that runs through the whole. Then, as to the greatest part of our *Liturgy*, compiled long before the Translation of the *Bible* now in use, and little altered since; there seem to be in it as great strains of true sublime Eloquence, as are any where to be found in our

Language; which every Man of good Taste will observe in the *Communion-Service*, that of *Burial*, and other Parts.

But where I say, that I would have our Language, after it is duly correct, always to last; I do not mean that it should never be enlarged: Provided, that no Word which a Society shall give a Sanction to, be afterwards antiquated and exploded, they may have liberty to receive whatever new ones they shall find occasion for: Because then the old Books will yet be always valuable, according to their intrinsick Worth, and not thrown aside on account of unintelligible Words and Phrases, which appear harsh and uncouth, only because they are out of Fashion. Had the *Roman* Tongue continued vulgar in that City till this Time; it would have been absolutely necessary from the mighty Changes that have been made in Law and Religion; from the many Terms of Art required in Trade and in War; from the new Inventions that have happened in the World: From the vast spreading of Navigation and Commerce, with many other obvious Circumstances, to have made great Additions to that Language; yet the Ancients would still have been read, and understood with Pleasure and Ease. The *Greek* Tongue received many Enlargements between the Time of *Homer*, and that of *Plutarch*, yet the former Author was probably as well understood in *Trajan*'s Time, as the latter. What *Horace* says of *Words going off and perishing like Leaves, and new ones coming in their Place*, is a Misfortune he laments, rather than a Thing he approves; But I can not see why this should be absolutely necessary, or if it were, what would have become of his *Monumentum ære perennius*.[1]

Writing by Memory only, as I do at present, I would gladly keep within my Depth; and therefore shall not enter into further Particulars. Neither do I pretend more than to shew the Usefulness of this Design, and to make some general Observations, leaving the rest to that Society, which I hope will owe its Institution and Patronage to Your LORDSHIP. Besides, I would willingly

---

[1] [*Monumentum...perennius* a monument more enduring than brass (Horace, *Odes*, III. 30. 1).]

avoid Repetition, having about a Year ago, communicated to the
Publick, much of what I had to offer upon this Subject, by the
Hands of an ingenious¹ Gentleman, who for a long Time did
thrice a Week divert or instruct the Kingdom by his Papers; and
is supposed to pursue the same Design at present, under the Title
of *Spectator*. This Author, who hath tried the Force and Compass
of our Language with so much Success, agrees entirely with me
in most of my Sentiments relating to it; so do the greatest part
of the Men of Wit and Learning, whom I have had the Happiness
to converse with; and therefore I imagine that such a Society
would be pretty unanimous in the main Points.

Your LORDSHIP must allow, that such a Work as this, brought
to Perfection, would very much contribute to the Glory of Her
MAJESTY's Reign; which ought to be recorded in Words more
durable than Brass, and such as our Posterity may read a thousand
Years hence, with Pleasure as well as Admiration. I have always
disapproved that false Compliment to Princes, that the most
lasting Monument they can have, is the Hearts of their Subjects.
It is indeed their greatest present Felicity to reign in their Subjects
Hearts; but these are too perishable to preserve their Memories,
which can only be done by the Pens of able and faithful Historians.
And I take it to be Your LORDSHIP's Duty, as *Prime Minister*, to
give order for inspecting our Language, and rendring it fit to
record the History of so great and good a Princess. Besides, My
LORD, as disinterested as You appear to the World, I am convinced,
that no Man is more in the Power of a prevailing favorite Passion
than Your Self; I mean that Desire of true and lasting Honor,
which you have born along with You through every Stage of
Your Life. To this You have often sacrificed Your Interest, Your
Ease and Your Health: For preserving and encreasing this, you
have exposed Your Person to secret Treachery, and open Violence.
There is not perhaps an Example in History of any Minister, who
in so short a time hath performed so many great Things, and
overcome so many great Difficulties. Now, tho' I am fully con-

---

¹ [*ingenious* of great talent; the reference is to Addison's essay, above.]

vinced, that You fear God, honor Your QUEEN, and love Your Country, as much as any of Your Fellow-Subjects; yet I must believe that the Desire of Fame hath been no inconsiderable Motive to quicken You in the Pursuit of those Actions which will best deserve it. But at the same time, I must be so plain as to tell Your LORDSHIP, that if You will not take some Care to settle our Language, and put it into a state of Continuance, I cannot promise that Your Memory shall be preserved above an hundred Years, further than by imperfect Tradition.

As barbarous and ignorant as we were in former Centuries, there was more effectual Care taken by our Ancestors, to preserve the Memory of Times and Persons, than we find in this Age of Learning and Politeness, as we are pleased to call it. The rude *Latin* of the *Monks* is still very intelligible; whereas, had their Records been delivered down only in the vulgar Tongue, so barren and so barbarous, so subject to continual succeeding Changes, they could not now be understood, unless by Antiquaries who made it their Study to expound them. And we must at this Day have been content with such poor Abstracts of our *English* Story, as laborious Men of low Genius would think fit to give us; And even these in the next Age would be likewise swallowed up in succeeding Collections. If Things go on at this rate, all I can promise Your LORDSHIP is, that about two hundred Years hence, some painful Compiler, who will be at the Trouble of studying Old Language, may inform the World, that in the Reign of QUEEN ANNE, ROBERT Earl of OXFORD, a very wise and excellent Man, was made *High Treasurer*, and saved his Country, which in those Days was almost ruined by a *Foreign War*, and a *Domestick Faction*. Thus much he may be able to pick out, and willing to transfer into his new History; but the rest of Your Character, which I or any other Writer may now value our selves by drawing, and the particular Account of the great Things done under Your Ministry, for which You are already so celebrated in most Parts of *Europe*, will probably be dropt, on account of the antiquated Style, and Manner they are delivered in.

How then shall any Man who hath a Genius for History, equal to the best of the Antients, be able to undertake such a Work with Spirit and Chearfulness, when he considers, that he will be read with Pleasure but a very few Years, and in an Age or two shall hardly be understood without an Interpreter? This is like employing an excellent Statuary to work upon mouldring Stone. Those who apply their Studies to preserve the Memory of others, will always have some Concern for their own. And I believe it is for this Reason, that so few Writers among us, of any Distinction, have turned their Thoughts to such a discouraging Employment: For the best *English* Historian must lie under this Mortification, that when his Style grows antiquated, he will be only considered as a tedious Relator of Facts; and perhaps consulted in his turn, among other neglected Authors, to furnish Materials for some future Collector.

I doubt, Your LORDSHIP is but ill entertained with a few scattered Thoughts, upon a Subject that deserves to be treated with Ability and Care: However, I must beg leave to add a few Words more, perhaps not altogether foreign to the same Matter. I know not whether that which I am going to say, may pass for Caution, Advice, or Reproach, any of which will be justly thought very improper from one in my Station, to one in Yours. However, I must venture to affirm, that if Genius and Learning be not encouraged under Your LORDSHIP's Administration, you are the most inexcusable Person alive. All Your other Virtues, My LORD, will be defective without this; Your Affability, Candor, and good Nature; that perpetual agreeableness of Conversation, so disengaged in the midst of such a Weight of Business and Opposition; Even Your Justice, Prudence, and Magnanimity, will shine less bright without it. Your LORDSHIP is universally allowed to possess a very large Portion in most Parts of Literature; and to this You owe the cultivating those many Virtues, which otherwise would have been less adorned, or in lower Perfection. Neither can You acquit your self of these Obligations, without letting the Arts, in their turn, share Your Influence and Protection: Besides, who knows, but some *true Genius* may happen to arise under Your Ministry, *exortus ut ætherius Sol.*[1] Every Age might perhaps produce one or two of these to adorn it, if they were not sunk under the Censure and Obloquy of plodding, servile, imitating Pedants. I do not mean by a true Genius, any bold Writer who breaks through the Rules of Decency to distinguish himself by the singularity of Opinions; but one, who upon a deserving Subject, is able to open new Scenes, and discover a Vein of true and noble thinking, which never entered into any Imagination before: Every Stroke of whose Pen, is worth all the Paper blotted by Hundreds of others in the compass of their Lives. I know, My LORD, Your Friends will offer in Your Defence, that in Your private Capacity, You never refus'd Your Purse and Credit to the Service and Support of learned or ingenious Men; and that ever since You have been in publick Employment, You have constantly bestowed Your Favours to the most deserving Persons. But I desire Your LORDSHIP not to be deceived: We never will admit of these Excuses, nor will allow Your private Liberality, as great as it is, to attone for Your excessive publick Thrift. But here again, I am afraid most good Subjects will interpose in Your Defence, by alledging the desperate Condition You found the Nation in, and the Necessity there was for so able and faithful a Steward, to retrieve it, if possible, by the utmost Frugality. We grant all this, My LORD; but then, it ought likewise to be considered, that You have already saved several Millions to the Publick, and that what we ask, is too inconsiderable to break into any Rules of the strictest good Husbandry. The *French King* bestows about half a dozen Pensions to learned Men in several Parts of *Europe*, and perhaps a dozen in his own Kingdom; which, in the whole, do probably not amount to half the Income of many a private Commoner in *England*; yet have more contributed to the Glory of that Prince, than any Million he hath otherwise employed. For Learning, like all true Merit, is easily satisfied, whilst the False and Counterfeit is perpetually craving, and never thinks it

[1] [*exortus...Sol* arisen like the heavenly sun (Lucretius, III, 1044).]

hath enough. The smallest Favour given by a Great PRINCE, as a Mark of Esteem, to reward the Endowments of the Mind, never fails to be returned with Praise and Gratitude, and loudly celebrated to the World. I have known some Years ago, several Pensions given to particular Persons, (how deservedly I shall not enquire) any one of which, if divided into smaller Parcels, and distributed by the Crown, to those who might, upon occasion, distinguish themselves by some extraordinary Production of Wit or Learning, would be amply sufficient to answer the End. Or if any such Persons were above Money, (as every great *Genius* certainly is, with very moderate Conveniencies of Life) a Medal, or some Mark of Distinction, would do full as well.

But I forget my Province, and find my self turning Projector before I am aware; although it be one of the last Characters under which I should desire to appear before Your LORDSHIP, especially when I have the Ambition of aspiring to that of being, with the greatest Respect and Truth,

My LORD,

Your LORDSHIP'S

most Obedient, most Obliged,

and most Humble Servant,

London,   J. SWIFT.

Feb. 22.

1711,12.

13

PHILIP DORMER STANHOPE, LORD CHESTERFIELD

(1694–1773)

Chesterfield had been approached by Johnson as a possible patron of the *Dictionary* as early as 1746, and the *Plan* he mentions was dedicated to him; but he gave little support until this letter, and another on 5 December, appeared. Here he harks back to Swift's *Proposal*, and notes that the dictionaries of the French and Italian Academies are a reproach to the English, whose language, for all the glories of its literature, still lacks the regulation of an authoritative grammar and dictionary, the mark of a truly 'classical' tongue. He declares himself ready, to this end, to submit entirely to the authority of Dr Johnson.

Letter to *The World* (28 November 1754)

I heard the other day with great pleasure from my worthy friend Mr. Dodsley, that Mr. Johnson's English dictionary, with a grammar and history of our language prefixed, will be published this winter, in two large volumes in folio.

I had long lamented that we had no lawful standard of our language set up, for those to repair to, who might chuse to speak and write it grammatically and correctly: and I have as long wished that either some one person of distinguished abilities would undertake the work singly, or that a certain number of gentlemen would form themselves, or be formed by the government, into a society for that purpose. The late ingenious doctor Swift proposed a plan of this nature to his friend (as he thought him) the lord treasurer Oxford, but without success; precision and perspicuity not being in general the favourite objects of ministers, and perhaps still less so of that minister than of any other.

Many people have imagined that so extensive a work would have been best performed by a number of persons, who should have taken their several departments, of examining, sifting, winnowing (I borrow this image from the Italian *crusca*) purifying, and finally fixing our language, by incorporating their respective funds into one joint stock. But whether this opinion be true or false, I think the public in general, and the republic of letters in particular, greatly obliged to Mr. Johnson, for having undertaken and executed so great and desireable a work. Perfection is not to be expected from man; but if we are to judge by the various works of Mr. Johnson, already published, we have good reason to believe that he will bring this as near to perfection as any one man could do. The plan of it, which he published some years ago, seems to me to be a proof of it. Nothing can be more rationally imagined, or more accurately and elegantly expressed. I therefore recommend the previous perusal of it to all those who intend to buy the dictionary, and who, I suppose, are all those who can afford it.

The celebrated dictionaries of the Florentine and French academies owe their present size and perfection to very small beginnings. Some private gentlemen at Florence, and some at Paris, had met at each others houses to talk over and consider their respective languages; upon which they published some short essays, which essays were the embrio's of those perfect productions, that now do so much honour to the two nations. Even Spain, which seems not to be the soil where, of late at least, letters have either prospered or been cultivated, has produced a dictionary, and a good one too, of the Spanish language, in six large volumes in folio.

I cannot help thinking it a sort of disgrace to our nation, that hitherto we have had no such standard of our language; our dictionaries at present being more properly what our neighbours the Dutch and the Germans call theirs, WORD-BOOKS, than dictionaries in the superior sense of that title. All words, good and bad, are there jumbled indiscriminately together, insomuch that the injudicious reader may speak and write as inelegantly, improperly and vulgarly as he pleases, by and with the authority of one or other of our WORD-BOOKS.

It must be owned that our language is at present in a state of anarchy; and hitherto, perhaps, it may not have been the worse for it. During our free and open trade, many words and expressions have been imported, adopted and naturalized from other languages, which have greatly enriched our own. Let it still preserve what real strength and beauty it may have borrowed from others, but let it not, like the Tarpeian maid, be overwhelmed and crushed by unnecessary foreign ornaments. The time for discrimination seems to be now come. Toleration, adoption and naturalization have run their lengths. Good order and authority are now necessary. But where shall we find them, and at the same time, the obedience due to them? We must have recourse to the old Roman expedient in times of confusion, and chuse a dictator. Upon this principle I give my vote for Mr. Johnson to fill that great and arduous post. And I hereby declare that I make a total surrender of all my rights and privileges in the English language, as a freeborn British subject, to the said Mr. Johnson, during the term of his dictatorship. Nay more; I will not only obey him, like an old Roman, as my dictator, but, like a modern Roman, I will implicitly believe in him as my pope, and hold him to be infallible while in the chair; but no longer. More than this he cannot well require; for I presume that obedience can never be expected when there is neither terror to enforce, nor interest to invite it.

I confess that I have so much honest English pride, or perhaps, prejudice about me, as to think myself more considerable for whatever contributes to the honour, the advantage, or the ornament of my native country. I have therefore a sensible pleasure in reflecting upon the rapid progress which our language has lately made, and still continues to make, all over Europe. It is frequently spoken, and almost universally understood, in Holland; it is kindly entertained as a relation in the most civilized parts of Germany; and it is studied as a learned language, though yet little spoke, by all those in France and Italy, who either have, or pretend to have, any learning.

The spreading the French language over most parts of Europe, to the degree of making it almost a universal one, was always reckoned among the glories of the reign of Lewis the fourteenth. But be it remembered that the success of his arms first opened the way to it, though at the same time it must be owned, that a great number of most excellent authors who flourished in his time, added strength and velocity to it's progress. Whereas our language has made it's way singly by it's own weight and merit, under the conduct of those great leaders, Shakespear, Bacon, Milton, Locke, Newton, Swift, Pope, Addison, &c. A nobler sort of conquest, and a far more glorious triumph, since graced by none but willing captives!

These authors, though for the most part but indifferently translated into foreign languages, gave other nations a sample of the British genius. The copies, imperfect as they were, pleased, and excited a general desire of seeing the originals; and both our authors and our language soon became classical.

But a grammar, a dictionary, and a history of our language through it's several stages were still wanting at home, and importunately called for from abroad. Mr. Johnson's labours will now, and, I dare say, very fully, supply that want, and greatly contribute to the farther spreading of our language in other countries. Learners were discouraged by finding no standard to resort to, and consequently thought it incapable of any. They will now be undeceived and encouraged.

There are many hints and considerations relative to our language, which I should have taken the liberty of suggesting to Mr. Johnson, had I not been convinced that they have equally occurred to him: but there is one, and a very material one it is, to which perhaps he may not have given all the necessary attention. I mean the genteeler part of our language, which owes both it's rise and progress to my fair countrywomen, whose natural turn is more to the copiousness, than to the correctness of diction. I would not advise him to be rash enough to proscribe any of those happy redundancies and luxuriancies of expression, with which they have enriched our language. They willingly inflict fetters, but very unwillingly submit to wear them. In this case his task will be so difficult, that I design as a common friend, to propose in some future paper the means which appear to me the most likely to reconcile matters.

P. S. I hope that none of my courteous readers will upon this occasion be so uncourteous, as to suspect me of being a hired and interested puff of this work; for I most solemnly protest, that neither Mr. Johnson, nor any person employed by him, nor any bookseller or booksellers concerned in the success of it, have ever offered me the usual compliment of a pair of gloves or a bottle of wine; nor has even Mr. Dodsley, though my publisher, and, as I am informed, deeply interested in the sale of this dictionary, so much as invited me to take a bit of mutton with him.

14

SAMUEL JOHNSON

(1709–1784)

In the first part of his Preface, Dr Johnson considers how, and how far, he has managed in 'settling the orthography, displaying the analogy, regulating the structures, and ascertaining the significations of English words'. He goes on to recall his original ambition to fix the language, and to ask whether such an ambition can ever succeed. Given the causes of change—commerce, the arts and sciences, society, translation and the study of languages—he concludes that complete success is impossible, but even partial success worthwhile. The text is from the fourth edition of 1773.

Preface to *A Dictionary of the English Language* (1755)

It is the fate of those who toil at the lower employments of life, to be rather driven by the fear of evil, than attracted by the prospect of good; to be exposed to censure, without hope of praise; to be disgraced by miscarriage, or punished for neglect, where success would have been without applause, and diligence without reward.

Among these unhappy mortals is the writer of dictionaries; whom mankind have considered, not as the pupil, but the slave of science, the pionier[1] of literature, doomed only to remove rubbish and clear obstructions from the paths through which Learning and Genius press forward to conquest and glory, without bestowing a smile on the humble drudge that facilitates their progress. Every other authour may aspire to praise; the lexicographer can only hope to escape reproach, and even this negative recompense has been yet granted to very few.

I have, notwithstanding this discouragement, attempted a dic-

[1] [*pionier* pioneer in the military sense, a digger of foundations.]

tionary of the *English* language, which, while it was employed in the cultivation of every species of literature, has itself been hitherto neglected; suffered to spread, under the direction of chance, into wild exuberance; resigned to the tyranny of time and fashion; and exposed to the corruptions of ignorance, and caprices of innovation.

When I took the first survey of my undertaking, I found our speech copious without order, and energetick without rules: wherever I turned my view, there was perplexity to be disentangled, and confusion to be regulated; choice was to be made out of boundless variety, without any established principle of selection; adulterations were to be detected, without a settled test of purity; and modes of expression to be rejected or received, without the suffrages of any writers of classical reputation or acknowledged authority.

Having therefore no assistance but from general grammar, I applied myself to the perusal of our writers; and noting whatever might be of use to ascertain or illustrate any word or phrase, accumulated in time the materials of a dictionary, which, by degrees, I reduced to method, establishing to myself, in the progress of the work, such rules as experience and analogy suggested to me; experience, which practice and observation were continually increasing; and analogy, which, though in some words obscure, was evident in others.

In adjusting the ORTHOGRAPHY, which has been to this time unsettled and fortuitous, I found it necessary to distinguish those irregularities that are inherent in our tongue, and perhaps coeval with it, from others which the ignorance or negligence of later writers has produced. Every language has its anomalies, which, though inconvenient, and in themselves once unnecessary, must be tolerated among the imperfections of human things, and which require only to be registered, that they may not be increased, and ascertained, that they may not be confounded: but every language has likewise its improprieties and absurdities, which it is the duty of the lexicographer to correct or proscribe.

As language was at its beginning merely oral, all words of necessary or common use were spoken before they were written; and while they were unfixed by any visible signs, must have been spoken with great diversity, as we now observe those who cannot read to catch sounds imperfectly, and utter them negligently. When this wild and barbarous jargon was first reduced to an alphabet, every penman endeavoured to express, as he could, the sounds which he was accustomed to pronounce or to receive, and vitiated in writing such words as were already vitiated in speech. The powers of the letters, when they were applied to a new language, must have been vague and unsettled, and therefore different hands would exhibit the same sound by different combinations.

From this uncertain pronunciation arise in a great part the various dialects of the same country, which will always be observed to grow fewer, and less different, as books are multiplied; and from this arbitrary representation of sounds by letters, proceeds that diversity of spelling observable in the *Saxon* remains, and I suppose in the first books of every nation, which perplexes or destroys analogy, and produces anomalous formations, that, being once incorporated, can never be afterward dismissed or reformed.

Of this kind are the derivatives *length* from *long*, *strength* from *strong*, *darling* from *dear*, *breadth* from *broad*, from *dry*, *drought*, and from *high*, *height*, which *Milton*, in zeal for analogy, writes *highth*; *Quid te exempta juvat spinis de pluribus una*;[1] to change all would be too much, and to change one is nothing.

This uncertainty is most frequent in the vowels, which are so capriciously pronounced, and so differently modified, by accident or affectation, not only in every province, but in every mouth, that to them, as is well known to etymologists, little regard is to be shewn in the deduction of one language from another.

Such defects are not errours in orthography, but spots of barbarity impressed so deep in the *English* language, that criticism

[1] [*Quid...una* What good to you is one thorn removed from many? (Horace, *Epist.* II. 2. 212).]

can never wash them away: these, therefore, must be permitted to remain untouched; but many words have likewise been altered by accident, or depraved by ignorance, as the pronunciation of the vulgar has been weakly followed; and some still continue to be variously written, as authours differ in their care or skill: of these it was proper to enquire the true orthography, which I have always considered as depending on their derivation, and have therefore referred them to their original languages: thus I write *enchant*, *enchantment*, *enchanter*, after the *French*, and *incantation* after the *Latin*; thus *entire* is chosen rather than *intire*, because it passed to us not from the *Latin integer*, but from the *French entier*.

Of many words it is difficult to say whether they were immediately received from the *Latin* or the *French*, since at the time when we had dominions in *France*, we had *Latin* service in our churches. It is, however, my opinion, that the *French* generally supplied us; for we have few *Latin* words, among the terms of domestick use, which are not *French*; but many *French*, which are very remote from *Latin*.

Even in words of which the derivation is apparent, I have been often obliged to sacrifice uniformity to custom; thus I write, in compliance with a numberless majority, *convey* and *inveigh*, *deceit* and *receipt*, *fancy* and *phantom*; sometimes the derivative varies from the primitive, as *explain* and *explanation*, *repeat* and *repetition*.

Some combinations of letters having the same power are used indifferently without any discoverable reason of choice, as in *choak*, *choke*; *soap*, *sope*; *fewel*, *fuel*, and many others; which I have sometimes inserted twice, that those who search for them under either form, may not search in vain.

In examining the orthography of any doubtful word, the mode of spelling by which it is inserted in the series of the dictionary, is to be considered as that to which I give, perhaps not often rashly, the preference. I have left, in the examples, to every authour his own practice unmolested, that the reader may balance suffrages, and judge between us: but this question is not always to be determined by reputed or by real learning; some men, intent upon greater things, have thought little on sounds and derivations; some, knowing in the ancient tongues, have neglected those in which our words are commonly to be sought. Thus *Hammond* writes *fecibleness* for *feasibleness*, because I suppose he imagined it derived immediately from the *Latin*; and some words, such as *dependant, dependent*; *dependance, dependence*, vary their final syllable, as one or another language is present to the writer.

In this part of the work, where caprice has long wantoned without controul, and vanity sought praise by petty reformation, I have endeavoured to proceed with a scholar's reverence for antiquity, and a grammarian's regard to the genius of our tongue. I have attempted few alterations, and among those few, perhaps the greater part is from the modern to the ancient practice; and I hope I may be allowed to recommend to those, whose thoughts have been perhaps employed too anxiously on verbal singularities, not to disturb, upon narrow views, or for minute propriety, the orthography of their fathers. It has been asserted, that for the law to be *known*, is of more importance than to be *right*. Change, says *Hooker*, is not made without inconvenience, even from worse to better. There is in constancy and stability a general and lasting advantage, which will always overbalance the slow improvements of gradual correction. Much less ought our written language to comply with the corruptions of oral utterance, or copy that which every variation of time or place makes different from itself, and imitate those changes, which will again be changed, while imitation is employed in observing them.

This recommendation of steadiness and uniformity does not proceed from an opinion, that particular combinations of letters have much influence on human happiness; or that truth may not be successfully taught by modes of spelling fanciful and erroneous: I am not yet so lost in lexicography, as to forget that *words are the daughters of earth, and that things are the sons of heaven*. Language is only the instrument of science, and words are but the signs of ideas: I wish, however, that the instrument might be less apt to decay, and that signs might be permanent, like the things which they denote.

In settling the orthography, I have not wholly neglected the pronunciation, which I have directed, by printing an accent upon the acute or elevated syllable. It will sometimes be found, that the accent is placed by the authour quoted, on a different syllable from that marked in the alphabetical series; it is then to be understood, that custom has varied, or that the authour has, in my opinion, pronounced wrong. Short directions are sometimes given where the sound of letters is irregular; and if they are sometimes omitted, defect in such minute observations will be more easily excused, than superfluity.

In the investigation both of the orthography and signification of words, their ETYMOLOGY was necessarily to be considered, and they were therefore to be divided into primitives and derivatives. A primitive word, is that which can be traced no further to any *English* root; thus *circumspect, circumvent, circumstance, delude, concave*, and *complicate*, though compounds in the *Latin*, are to us primitives. Derivatives, are all those that can be referred to any word in *English* of greater simplicity.

The derivatives I have referred to their primitives, with an accuracy sometimes needless; for who does not see that *remoteness* comes from *remote, lovely* from *love, concavity* from *concave*, and *demonstrative* from *demonstrate*? but this grammatical exuberance the scheme of my work did not allow me to repress. It is of great importance in examining the general fabrick of a language, to trace one word from another, by noting the usual modes of derivation and inflection; and uniformity must be preserved in systematical works, though sometimes at the expence of particular propriety.

Among other derivatives I have been careful to insert and elucidate the anomalous plurals of nouns and preterites of verbs, which in the *Teutonick* dialects are very frequent, and though familiar to those who have always used them, interrupt and embarrass the learners of our language.

The two languages from which our primitives have been de-

rived are the *Roman* and *Teutonick*: under the *Roman* I comprehend
the *French* and provincial tongues; and under the *Teutonick* range
the *Saxon*, *German*, and all their kindred dialects. Most of our
polysyllables are *Roman*, and our words of one syllable are very
often *Teutonick*.

In assigning the *Roman* original, it has perhaps sometimes happened that I have mentioned only the *Latin*, when the word was
borrowed from the *French*; and considering myself as employed
only in the illustration of my own language, I have not been very
careful to observe whether the *Latin* word be pure or barbarous,
or the *French* elegant or obsolete.

For the *Teutonick* etymologies I am commonly indebted to
Junius and *Skinner*, the only names which I have forborn to quote
when I copied their books; not that I might appropriate their
labours or usurp their honours, but that I might spare a perpetual
repetition by one general acknowledgment. Of these, whom I
ought not to mention but with the reverence due to instructors
and benefactors, *Junius* appears to have excelled in extent of
learning, and *Skinner* in rectitude of understanding. *Junius* was
accurately skilled in all the northern languages, *Skinner* probably
examined the ancient and remoter dialects only by occasional inspection into dictionaries; but the learning of *Junius* is often of
no other use than to show him a track by which he may deviate
from his purpose, to which *Skinner* always presses forward by the
shortest way. *Skinner* is often ignorant, but never ridiculous: *Junius*
is always full of knowledge; but his variety distracts his judgment,
and his learning is very frequently disgraced by his absurdities.

The votaries of the northern muses will not perhaps easily
restrain their indignation, when they find the name of *Junius*
thus degraded by a disadvantageous comparison; but whatever
reverence is due to his diligence, or his attainments, it can be no
criminal degree of censoriousness to charge that etymologist with
want of judgment, who can seriously derive *dream* from *drama*,
because *life is a drama, and a drama is a dream*; and who declares
with a tone of defiance, that no man can fail to derive *moan* from

μόνος, *monos, single* or *solitary,* who considers that grief naturally loves to be *alone.*¹

¹ That I may not appear to have spoken too irreverently of *Junius,* I have here subjoined a few Specimens of his etymological extravagance.

· BANISH, *relegare, ex banno vel territorio exigere, in exilium agere.* G. *bannir.* It. *bandire, bandeggiare.* H. *bandir.* B. bannen. Ævi medii scriptores bannire dicebant. V. Spelm. in Bannum & in Banleuga. Quoniam verò regionum urbiumque limites arduis plerumque montibus, altis fluminibus, longis denique flexuosisque angustissimarum viarum amfractibus includebantur, fieri potest id genus limites *ban* dici ab eo quod Βαννάται & Βάννατροι Tarentinis olim, sicuti tradit Hesychius, vocabantur αἱ λοξοὶ καὶ μὴ ἰθυτενεῖς ὁδοί, 'obliquæ ac minimè in rectum tendentes viæ.' Ac fortasse quoque huc facit quod Βανοὺς, eodem Hesychio teste, dicebant ὄρη στρογγύλα, montes arduos.

EMPTY, emtie, *vacuus, inanis.* A. S. Æmtig. Nescio an sint ab ἐμέω vel ἐμετιάω. Vomo, evomo, vomitu evacuo. Videtur interim etymologiam hanc non obscurè firmare codex Rush. Mat. xii. 44. ubi antiquè scriptum invenimus gemoeted hit emetig. 'Invenit eam vacantem.'

HILL, *mons, collis.* A. S. hyll. Quod videri potest abscissum ex κολώνη vel κολωνὸς. Collis, tumulus, locus in plano editior. Hom. Il. b. v. 811, ἔστι δέ τις προπάροιθε πόλεος αἰπεῖα κολώνη. Ubi authori brevium scholiorum κολώνη exp. τόπος εἰς ὕψος ἀνήκων, γεώλοφος ἐξοχή.

NAP, *to take a nap. Dormire, condormiscere.* Cym. heppian. A. S. hnæppan. Quod postremum videri potest desumptum ex κνέφας, obscuritas, tenebræ: nihil enim æqué solet conciliare somnum, quàm caliginosa profundæ noctis obscuritas.

STAMMERER, Balbus, blæsus. Goth. STAMMS. A. S. stamer, stamur. D. stam. B. stameler. Su. stamma. Isl. stamr. Sunt a στωμυλεῖν vel στωμύλλειν, nimiâ loquacitate alios offendere; quod impeditè loquentes libentissimè garrire soleant; vel quòd aliis nimii semper videantur, etiam parcissimè loquentes.

[*Banish...* ¹*oquentes* to banish, to expel from an area of jurisdiction or country, to send into exile. French *bannir,* Italian *bandire, bandeggiare,* Spanish *bandir,* Belgian *bannen.* The medieval writers said *bannire.* See Spelman under *Bannum* and *Banleuga.* Because the boundaries of regions and cities were mostly made up of stern mountains, deep rivers, and lastly of the long and tortuous winding of the narrowest routes, it may be that boundaries of that kind are called *ban* from the fact that, as Hesychius reports, 'crooked ways, very little tending straight' were called *Bannatai* and *Bannatroi* by the Tarentines. And perhaps too it is from this, as the same Hesychius says, that they called high mountains *banous.*

empty, void. Anglo-Saxon *æmtig.* I do not know whether it is from *emeo* ['vomit'] or from *emetiao* ['feel sick']. To give forth, to cast out, to disgorge in vomit. Anyhow the Rushworth MS. seems to confirm this etymology clearly: Matt. xii. 44, where we find anciently written *gemoeted hit emetig,* 'he found it empty'.

mount, hill. Anglo-Saxon *hyl¹.* Which seems to be shortened from *kolone* ['mount'] or *kolonos* ['hill']. Hill, eminence, a higher place in a plain. Homer, *Iliad,* II. 811: 'Now there is before the city a steep mound', where the authors of the short commentaries explain, '*kolone,* a place rising to a height, a hilly mound'.

to sleep, to fall asleep. Welsh *heppian,* Anglo-Saxon *hnæppan.* Which latter seems to be taken from *knephas,* darkness, shadows; for nothing brings sleep so much as the black darkness of a deep night.

stammering, lisping. Gothic *stamms,* Anglo-Saxon *stamer, stamur,* Danish *stam,* Belgian *stameler,* Swedish *stamma,* Icelandic *stamr.* They are from *stomylein* or *stomyllein,* 'to offend others by too much loquacity'. Because those who talk with a hindrance usually chatter most freely, or because they always seem excessive to others, even when they speak most sparingly.]

Our knowledge of the northern literature is so scanty, that of words undoubtedly *Teutonick* the original is not always to be found in any ancient language; and I have therefore inserted *Dutch* or *German* substitutes, which I consider not as radical but parallel, not as the parents, but sisters of the *English*.

The words which are represented as thus related by descent or cognation, do not always agree in sense; for it is incident to words, as to their authours, to degenerate from their ancestors, and to change their manners when they change their country. It is sufficient, in etymological enquiries, if the senses of kindred words be found such as may easily pass into each other, or such as may both be referred to one general idea.

The etymology, so far as it is yet known, was easily found in the volumes where it is particularly and professedly delivered; and, by proper attention to the rules of derivation, the orthography was soon adjusted. But to COLLECT the WORDS of our language was a task of greater difficulty: the deficiency of dictionaries was immediately apparent; and when they were exhausted, what was yet wanting must be sought by fortuitous and unguided excursions into books, and gleaned as industry should find, or chance should offer it, in the boundless chaos of a living speech. My search, however, has been either skilful or lucky; for I have much augmented the vocabulary.

As my design was a dictionary, common or appellative, I have omitted all words which have relation to proper names; such as *Arian*, *Socinian*, *Calvinist*, *Benedictine*, *Mahometan*; but have retained those of a more general nature, as *Heathen*, *Pagan*.

Of the terms of art I have received such as could be found either in books of science or technical dictionaries; and have often inserted, from philosophical writers, words which are supported perhaps only by a single authority, and which being not admitted into general use, stand yet as candidates or probationers, and must depend for their adoption on the suffrage of futurity.

The words which our authours have introduced by their knowledge of foreign languages, or ignorance of their own, by vanity or wantonness, by compliance with fashion or lust of innovation, I have registred as they occurred, though commonly only to censure them, and warn others against the folly of naturalizing useless foreigners to the injury of the natives.

I have not rejected any by design, merely because they were unnecessary or exuberant; but have received those which by different writers have been differently formed, as *viscid*, and *viscidity*, *viscous*, and *viscosity*.

Compounded or double words I have seldom noted, except when they obtain a signification different from that which the components have in their simple state. Thus *highwayman*, *woodman*, and *horsecourser*, require an explication; but of *thieflike* or *coachdriver* no notice was needed, because the primitives contain the meaning of the compounds.

Words arbitrarily formed by a constant and settled analogy, like diminutive adjectives in *ish*, as *greenish*, *bluish*, adverbs in *ly*, as *dully*, *openly*, substantives in *ness*, as *vileness*, *faultiness*, were less diligently sought, and sometimes have been omitted, when I had no authority that invited me to insert them; not that they are not genuine and regular offsprings of *English* roots, but because their relation to the primitive being always the same, their signification cannot be mistaken.

The verbal nouns in *ing*, such as the *keeping* of the *castle*, the *leading* of the *army*, are always neglected, or placed only to illustrate the sense of the verb, except when they signify things as well as actions, and have therefore a plural number, as *dwelling*, *living*; or have an absolute and abstract signification, as *colouring*, *painting*, *learning*.

The participles are likewise omitted, unless, by signifying rather habit or quality than action, they take the nature of adjectives; as a *thinking* man, a man of prudence; a *pacing* horse, a horse that can pace: these I have ventured to call *participial adjectives*. But neither are these always inserted, because they are commonly to be understood, without any danger of mistake, by consulting the verb.

Obsolete words are admitted, when they are found in authours not obsolete, or when they have any force or beauty that may deserve revival.

As composition is one of the chief characteristicks of a language, I have endeavoured to make some reparation for the universal negligence of my predecessors, by inserting great numbers of compounded words, as may be found under *after*, *fore*, *new*, *night*, *fair*, and many more. These, numerous as they are, might be multiplied, but that use and curiosity are here satisfied, and the frame of our language and modes of our combination amply discovered.

Of some forms of composition, such as that by which *re* is prefixed to note *repetition*, and *un* to signify *contrariety* or *privation*, all the examples cannot be accumulated, because the use of these particles, if not wholly arbitrary, is so little limited, that they are hourly affixed to new words as occasion requires, or is imagined to require them.

There is another kind of composition more frequent in our language than perhaps in any other, from which arises to foreigners the greatest difficulty. We modify the signification of many words by a particle subjoined; as to *come off*, to escape by a fetch; to *fall on*, to attack; to *fall off*, to apostatize; to *break off*, to stop abruptly; to *bear out*, to justify; to *fall in*, to comply; to *give over*, to cease; to *set off*, to embellish; to *set in*, to begin a continual tenour; to *set out*, to begin a course or journey; to *take off*, to copy; with innumerable expressions of the same kind, of which some appear wildly irregular, being so far distant from the sense of the simple words, that no sagacity will be able to trace the steps by which they arrived at the present use. These I have noted with great care; and though I cannot flatter myself that the collection is complete, I believe I have so far assisted the students of our language, that this kind of phraseology will be no longer insuperable; and the combinations of verbs and particles, by chance omitted, will be easily explained by comparison with those that may be found.

Many words yet stand supported only by the name of *Bailey*, *Ainsworth*, *Philips*, or the contracted *Dict.* for *Dictionaries* subjoined; of these I am not always certain that they are read in any book but the works of lexicographers. Of such I have omitted many, because I had never read them; and many I have inserted, because they may perhaps exist, though they have escaped my notice: they are, however, to be yet considered as resting only upon the credit of former dictionaries. Others, which I considered as useful, or know to be proper, though I could not at present support them by authorities, I have suffered to stand upon my own attestation, claiming the same privilege with my predecessors of being sometimes credited without proof.

The words, thus selected and disposed, are grammatically considered; they are referred to the different parts of speech; traced, when they are irregularly inflected, through their various terminations; and illustrated by observations, not indeed of great or striking importance, separately considered, but necessary to the elucidation of our language, and hitherto neglected or forgotten by *English* grammarians.

That part of my work on which I expect malignity most frequently to fasten, is the *Explanation*; in which I cannot hope to satisfy those, who are perhaps not inclined to be pleased, since I have not always been able to satisfy myself. To interpret a language by itself is very difficult; many words cannot be explained by synonimes, because the idea signified by them has not more than one appellation; nor by paraphrase, because simple ideas cannot be described. When the nature of things is unknown, or the notion unsettled and indefinite, and various in various minds, the words by which such notions are conveyed, or such things denoted, will be ambiguous and perplexed. And such is the fate of hapless lexicography, that not only darkness, but light, impedes and distresses it; things may be not only too little, but too much known, to be happily illustrated. To explain, requires the use of terms less abstruse than that which is to be explained, and such terms cannot always be found; for as nothing can be proved but by supposing something intuitively known, and evident without proof, so nothing can be defined but by the use of words too plain to admit a definition.

Other words there are, of which the sense is too subtle and evanescent to be fixed in a paraphrase; such are all those which are by the grammarians termed *expletives*, and, in dead languages, are suffered to pass for empty sounds, of no other use than to fill a verse, or to modulate a period, but which are easily perceived in living tongues to have power and emphasis, though it be sometimes such as no other form of expression can convey.

My labour has likewise been much increased by a class of verbs too frequent in the *English* language, of which the signification is so loose and general, the use so vague and indeterminate, and the senses detorted[1] so widely from the first idea, that it is hard to trace them through the maze of variation, to catch them on the brink of utter inanity, to circumscribe them by any limitations, or interpret them by any words of distinct and settled meaning; such are *bear*, *break*, *come*, *cast*, *fall*, *get*, *give*, *do*, *put*, *set*, *go*, *run*, *make*, *take*, *turn*, *throw*. If of these the whole power is not accurately delivered, it must be remembered, that while our language is yet living, and variable by the caprice of every one that speaks it, these words are hourly shifting their relations, and can no more be ascertained in a dictionary, than a grove, in the agitation of a storm, can be accurately delineated from its picture in the water.

The particles are among all nations applied with so great latitude, that they are not easily reducible under any regular scheme of explication: this difficulty is not less, nor perhaps greater, in *English*, than in other languages. I have laboured them with diligence, I hope with success; such at least as can be expected in a task, which no man, however learned or sagacious, has yet been able to perform.

Some words there are which I cannot explain, because I do not understand them; these might have been omitted very often with little inconvenience, but I would not so far indulge my vanity as

---

[1] [*detorted* turned aside.]

to decline this confession: for when *Tully* owns himself ignorant whether *lessus*, in the twelve tables, means a *funeral song*, or *mourning garment*; and *Aristotle* doubts whether οὔρευς, in the Iliad, signifies a *mule*, or *muleteer*, I may surely, without shame, leave some obscurities to happier industry, or future information.

The rigour of interpretative lexicography requires that *the explanation, and the word explained, should be always reciprocal*; this I have always endeavoured, but could not always attain. Words are seldom exactly synonimous; a new term was not introduced, but because the former was thought inadequate: names, therefore, have often many ideas, but few ideas have many names. It was then necessary to use the proximate word, for the deficiency of single terms can very seldom be supplied by circumlocution; nor is the inconvenience great of such mutilated interpretations, because the sense may easily be collected entire from the examples.

In every word of extensive use, it was requisite to mark the progress of its meaning, and show by what gradations of intermediate sense it has passed from its primitive to its remote and accidental signification; so that every foregoing explanation should tend to that which follows, and the series be regularly concatenated from the first notion to the last.

This is specious, but not always practicable; kindred senses may be so interwoven, that the perplexity cannot be disentangled, nor any reason be assigned why one should be ranged before the other. When the radical idea branches out into parallel ramifications, how can a consecutive series be formed of senses in their nature collateral? The shades of meaning sometimes pass imperceptibly into each other; so that though on one side they apparently differ, yet it is impossible to mark the point of contact. Ideas of the same race, though not exactly alike, are sometimes so little different, that no words can express the dissimilitude, though the mind easily perceives it, when they are exhibited together; and sometimes there is such a confusion of acceptations, that discernment is wearied, and distinction puzzled, and perseverance herself hurries to an end, by crouding together what she cannot separate.

These complaints of difficulty will, by those that have never considered words beyond their popular use, be thought only the jargon of a man willing to magnify his labours, and procure veneration to his studies by involution and obscurity. But every art is obscure to those that have not learned it: this uncertainty of terms, and commixture of ideas, is well known to those who have joined philosophy with grammar; and if I have not expressed them very clearly, it must be remembered that I am speaking of that which words are insufficient to explain.

The original sense of words is often driven out of use by their metaphorical acceptations, yet must be inserted for the sake of a regular origination. Thus I know not whether *ardour* is used for *material heat*, or whether *flagrant*, in *English*, ever signifies the same with *burning*; yet such are the primitive ideas of these words, which are therefore set first, though without examples, that the figurative senses may be commodiously deduced.

Such is the exuberance of signification which many words have obtained, that it was scarcely possible to collect all their senses; sometimes the meaning of derivatives must be sought in the mother term, and sometimes deficient explanations of the primitive may be supplied in the train of derivation. In any case of doubt or difficulty, it will be always proper to examine all the words of the same race; for some words are slightly passed over to avoid repetition, some admitted easier and clearer explanation than others, and all will be better understood, as they are considered in greater variety of structures and relations.

All the interpretations of words are not written with the same skill, or the same happiness: things equally easy in themselves, are not all equally easy to any single mind. Every writer of a long work commits errours, where there appears neither ambiguity to mislead, nor obscurity to confound him; and in a search like this, many felicities of expression will be casually overlooked, many convenient parallels will be forgotten, and many particulars will admit improvement from a mind utterly unequal to the whole performance.

But many seeming faults are to be imputed rather to the nature of the undertaking, than the negligence of the performer. Thus some explanations are unavoidably reciprocal or circular, as *hind, the female of the stag*; *stag, the male of the hind*: sometimes easier words are changed into harder, as *burial* into *sepulture* or *interment*, *drier* into *desiccative*, *dryness* into *siccity* or *aridity*, *fit* into *paroxysm*; for the easiest word, whatever it be, can never be translated into one more easy. But easiness and difficulty are merely relative, and if the present prevalence of our language should invite foreigners to this dictionary, many will be assisted by those words which now seem only to increase or produce obscurity. For this reason I have endeavoured frequently to join a *Teutonick* and *Roman* interpretation, as to CHEER, to *gladden*, or *exhilarate*, that every learner of *English* may be assisted by his own tongue.

The solution of all difficulties, and the supply of all defects, must be sought in the examples, subjoined to the various senses of each word, and ranged according to the time of their authours.

When first I collected these authorities, I was desirous that every quotation should be useful to some other end than the illustration of a word; I therefore extracted from philosophers principles of science; from historians remarkable facts; from chymists complete processes; from divines striking exhortations; and from poets beautiful descriptions. Such is design, while it is yet at a distance from execution. When the time called upon me to range this accumulation of elegance and wisdom into an alphabetical series, I soon discovered that the bulk of my volumes would fright away the student, and was forced to depart from my scheme of including all that was pleasing or useful in *English* literature, and reduce my transcripts very often to clusters of words, in which scarcely any meaning is retained; thus to the weariness of copying, I was condemned to add the vexation of expunging. Some passages I have yet spared, which may relieve the labour of verbal searches, and intersperse with verdure and flowers the dusty desarts of barren philology.

The examples, thus mutilated, are no longer to be considered as conveying the sentiments or doctrine of their authours; the word for the sake of which they are inserted, with all its appendant clauses, has been carefully preserved; but it may sometimes happen, by hasty detruncation, that the general tendency of the sentence may be changed: the divine may desert his tenets, or the philosopher his system.

Some of the examples have been taken from writers who were never mentioned as masters of elegance or models of stile; but words must be sought where they are used; and in what pages, eminent for purity, can terms of manufacture or agriculture be found? Many quotations serve no other purpose, than that of proving the bare existence of words, and are therefore selected with less scrupulousness than those which are to teach their structures and relations.

My purpose was to admit no testimony of living authours, that I might not be misled by partiality, and that none of my cotemporaries might have reason to complain; nor have I departed from this resolution, but when some performance of uncommon excellence excited my veneration, when my memory supplied me, from late books, with an example that was wanting, or when my heart, in the tenderness of friendship, solicited admission for a favourite name.

So far have I been from any care to grace my pages with modern decorations, that I have studiously endeavoured to collect examples and authorities from the writers before the restoration, whose works I regard as *the wells of English undefiled*, as the pure sources of genuine diction. Our language, for almost a century, has, by the concurrence of many causes, been gradually departing from its original *Teutonick* character, and deviating towards a *Gallick* structure and phraseology, from which it ought to be our endeavour to recal it, by making our ancient volumes the groundwork of stile, admitting among the additions of later times, only such as may supply real deficiencies, such as are readily adopted by the genius of our tongue, and incorporate easily with our native idioms.

But as every language has a time of rudeness antecedent to perfection, as well as of false refinement and declension, I have been cautious lest my zeal for antiquity might drive me into times too remote, and croud my book with words now no longer understood. I have fixed *Sidney*'s work for the boundary, beyond which I make few excursions. From the authours which rose in the time of *Elizabeth*, a speech might be formed adequate to all the purposes of use and elegance. If the language of theology were extracted from *Hooker* and the translation of the Bible; the terms of natural knowledge from *Bacon*; the phrases of policy, war, and navigation from *Raleigh*; the dialect of poetry and fiction from *Spenser* and *Sidney*; and the diction of common life from *Shakespeare*, few ideas would be lost to mankind, for want of *English* words, in which they might be expressed.

It is not sufficient that a word is found, unless it be so combined as that its meaning is apparently determined by the tract and tenour of the sentence; such passages I have therefore chosen, and when it happened that any authour gave a definition of a term, or such an explanation as is equivalent to a definition, I have placed his authority as a supplement to my own, without regard to the chronological order, that is otherwise observed.

Some words, indeed, stand unsupported by any authority, but they are commonly derivative nouns or adverbs, formed from their primitives by regular and constant analogy, or names of things seldom occurring in books, or words of which I have reason to doubt the existence.

There is more danger of censure from the multiplicity than paucity of examples; authorities will sometimes seem to have been accumulated without necessity or use, and perhaps some will be found, which might, without loss, have been omitted. But a work of this kind is not hastily to be charged with superfluities: those quotations, which to careless or unskilful perusers appear only to repeat the same sense, will often exhibit, to a more accurate examiner, diversities of signification, or, at least, afford different shades of the same meaning: one will shew the word applied to persons, another to things; one will express an ill, another a good, and a third a neutral sense; one will prove the expression genuine from an ancient authour; another will shew it elegant from a modern: a doubtful authority is corroborated by another of more credit; an ambiguous sentence is ascertained by a passage clear and determinate; the word, how often soever repeated, appears with new associates and in different combinations, and every quotation contributes something to the stability or enlargement of the language.

When words are used equivocally, I receive them in either sense; when they are metaphorical, I adopt them in their primitive acceptation.

I have sometimes, though rarely, yielded to the temptation of exhibiting a genealogy of sentiments, by shewing how one authour copied the thoughts and diction of another: such quotations are indeed little more than repetitions, which might justly be censured, did they not gratify the mind, by affording a kind of intellectual history.

The various syntactical structures occurring in the examples have been carefully noted; the licence or negligence with which many words have been hitherto used, has made our stile capricious and indeterminate; when the different combinations of the same word are exhibited together, the preference is readily given to propriety, and I have often endeavoured to direct the choice.

Thus have I laboured by settling the orthography, displaying the analogy, regulating the structures, and ascertaining the signification of *English* words, to perform all the parts of a faithful lexicographer: but I have not always executed my own scheme, or satisfied my own expectations. The work, whatever proofs of diligence and attention it may exhibit, is yet capable of many improvements: the orthography which I recommend is still controvertible, the etymology which I adopt is uncertain, and perhaps frequently erroneous; the explanations are sometimes too much contracted, and sometimes too much diffused, the significations are distinguished rather with subtilty than skill, and the attention is harassed with unnecessary minuteness.

The examples are too often injudiciously truncated, and perhaps sometimes, I hope very rarely, alleged in a mistaken sense; for in making this collection I trusted more to memory, than, in a state of disquiet and embarrassment, memory can contain, and purposed to supply at the review what was left incomplete in the first transcription.

Many terms appropriated to particular occupations, though necessary and significant, are undoubtedly omitted; and of the words most studiously considered and exemplified, many senses have escaped observation.

Yet these failures, however frequent, may admit extenuation and apology. To have attempted much is always laudable, even when the enterprize is above the strength that undertakes it: To rest below his own aim is incident to every one whose fancy is active, and whose views are comprehensive; nor is any man satisfied with himself because he has done much, but because he can conceive little. When first I engaged in this work, I resolved to leave neither words nor things unexamined, and pleased myself with a prospect of the hours which I should revel away in feasts of literature, with the obscure recesses of northern learning, which I should enter and ransack; the treasures with which I expected every search into those neglected mines to reward my labour, and the triumph with which I should display my acquisitions to mankind. When I had thus enquired into the original of words, I resolved to show likewise my attention to things; to pierce deep into every science, to enquire the nature of every substance of which I inserted the name, to limit every idea by a definition strictly logical, and exhibit every production of art or nature in an accurate description, that my book might be in place of all other dictionaries whether appellative or technical. But these were the dreams of a poet doomed at last to wake a lexicographer. I soon found that it is too late to look for instruments, when the work calls for execution, and that whatever abilities I had brought to my task, with those I must finally perform it. To deliberate whenever I doubted, to enquire whenever I was ignorant, would have protracted the undertaking without end, and, perhaps, without much improvement; for I did not find by my first experiments, that what I had not of my own was easily to be obtained: I saw that one enquiry only gave occasion to another, that book referred to book, that to search was not always to find, and to find was not always to be informed; and that thus to persue perfection, was, like the first inhabitants of Arcadia, to chace the sun, which, when they had reached the hill where he seemed to rest, was still beheld at the same distance from them.

I then contracted my design, determining to confide in myself, and no longer to solicit auxiliaries, which produced more incumbrance than assistance: by this I obtained at least one advantage, that I set limits to my work, which would in time be ended, though not completed.

Despondency has never so far prevailed as to depress me to negligence; some faults will at last appear to be the effects of anxious diligence and persevering activity. The nice and subtle ramifications of meaning were not easily avoided by a mind intent upon accuracy, and convinced of the necessity of disentangling combinations, and separating similitudes. Many of the distinctions which to common readers appear useless and idle, will be found real and important by men versed in the school philosophy, without which no dictionary shall ever be accurately compiled, or skilfully examined.

Some senses however there are, which, though not the same, are yet so nearly allied, that they are often confounded. Most men think indistinctly, and therefore cannot speak with exactness; and consequently some examples might be indifferently put to either signification: this uncertainty is not to be imputed to me, who do not form, but register the language; who do not teach men how they should think, but relate how they have hitherto expressed their thoughts.

The imperfect sense of some examples I lamented, but could not remedy, and hope they will be compensated by innumerable passages selected with propriety, and preserved with exactness;

some shining with sparks of imagination, and some replete with treasures of wisdom.

The orthography and etymology, though imperfect, are not imperfect for want of care, but because care will not always be successful, and recollection or information come too late for use.

That many terms of art and manufacture are omitted, must be frankly acknowledged; but for this defect I may boldly allege that it was unavoidable: I could not visit caverns to learn the miner's language, nor take a voyage to perfect my skill in the dialect of navigation, nor visit the warehouses of merchants, and shops of artificers, to gain the names of wares, tools and operations, of which no mention is found in books; what favourable accident, or easy enquiry brought within my reach, has not been neglected; but it had been a hopeless labour to glean up words, by courting living information, and contesting with the sullenness of one, and the roughness of another.

To furnish the academicians *della Crusca* with words of this kind, a series of comedies called *la Fiera*, or *the Fair*, was professedly written by *Buonaroti*; but I had no such assistant, and therefore was content to want what they must have wanted likewise, had they not luckily been so supplied.

Nor are all words which are not found in the vocabulary, to be lamented as omissions. Of the laborious and mercantile part of the people, the diction is in a great measure casual and mutable; many of their terms are formed for some temporary or local convenience, and though current at certain times and places, are in others utterly unknown. This fugitive cant, which is always in a state of increase or decay, cannot be regarded as any part of the durable materials of a language, and therefore must be suffered to perish with other things unworthy of preservation.

Care will sometimes betray to the appearance of negligence. He that is catching opportunities which seldom occur, will suffer those to pass by unregarded, which he expects hourly to return; he that is searching for rare and remote things, will neglect those that are obvious and familiar: thus many of the most common and cursory words have been inserted with little illustration, because in gathering the authorities, I forbore to copy those which I thought likely to occur whenever they were wanted. It is remarkable that, in reviewing my collection, I found the word SEA unexemplified.

Thus it happens, that in things difficult there is danger from ignorance, and in things easy from confidence; the mind, afraid of greatness, and disdainful of littleness, hastily withdraws herself from painful searches, and passes with scornful rapidity over tasks not adequate to her powers, sometimes too secure for caution, and again too anxious for vigorous effort; sometimes idle in a plain path, and sometimes distracted in labyrinths, and dissipated by different intentions.

A large work is difficult because it is large, even though all its parts might singly be performed with facility; where there are many things to be done, each must be allowed its share of time and labour, in the proportion only which it bears to the whole; nor can it be expected, that the stones which form the dome of a temple, should be squared and polished like the diamond of a ring.

Of the event of this work, for which, having laboured it with so much application, I cannot but have some degree of parental fondness, it is natural to form conjectures. Those who have been persuaded to think well of my design, will require that it should fix our language, and put a stop to those alterations which time and chance have hitherto been suffered to make in it without opposition. With this consequence I will confess that I flattered myself for a while; but now begin to fear that I have indulged expectation which neither reason nor experience can justify. When we see men grow old and die at a certain time one after another, from century to century, we laugh at the elixir that promises to prolong life to a thousand years; and with equal justice may the lexicographer be derided, who being able to produce no example of a nation that has preserved their words and phrases from mutability, shall imagine that his dictionary can embalm his language, and secure it from corruption and decay, that it is in his power to change sublunary nature, and clear the world at once from folly, vanity, and affectation.

With this hope, however, academies have been instituted, to guard the avenues of their languages, to retain fugitives, and repulse intruders; but their vigilance and activity have hitherto been vain; sounds are too volatile and subtile for legal restraints; to enchain syllables, and to lash the wind, are equally the undertakings of pride, unwilling to measure its desires by its strength. The *French* language has visibly changed under the inspection of the academy; the stile of *Amelot*'s translation of father *Paul* is observed by *Le Courayer* to be *un peu passè*;[1] and no *Italian* will maintain, that the diction of any modern writer is not perceptibly different from that of *Boccace*, *Machiavel*, or *Caro*.

Total and sudden transformations of a language seldom happen; conquests and migrations are now very rare: but there are other causes of change, which, though slow in their operation, and invisible in their progress, are perhaps as much superiour to human resistance, as the revolutions of the sky, or intumescence of the tide. Commerce, however necessary, however lucrative, as it depraves the manners, corrupts the language; they that have frequent intercourse with strangers, to whom they endeavour to accommodate themselves, must in time learn a mingled dialect, like the jargon which serves the traffickers on the *Mediterranean* and *Indian* coasts. This will not always be confined to the exchange, the warehouse, or the port, but will be communicated by degrees to other ranks of the people, and be at last incorporated with the current speech.

There are likewise internal causes equally forcible. The language most likely to continue long without alteration, would be that of a nation raised a little, and but a little above barbarity, secluded from strangers, and totally employed in procuring the conveniencies of life; either without books, or, like some of the *Mahometan* countries, with very few: men thus busied and unlearned, having only such words as common use requires, would perhaps long

[1] [*un peu passè* somewhat outdated.]

continue to express the same notions by the same signs. But no such constancy can be expected in a people polished by arts, and classed by subordination, where one part of the community is sustained and accommodated by the labour of the other. Those who have much leisure to think, will always be enlarging the stock of ideas, and every increase of knowledge, whether real or fancied, will produce new words, or combinations of words. When the mind is unchained from necessity, it will range after convenience; when it is left at large in the fields of speculation, it will shift opinions; as any custom is disused, the words that expressed it must perish with it; as any opinion grows popular, it will innovate speech in the same proportion as it alters practice.

As by the cultivation of various sciences, a language is amplified, it will be more furnished with words deflected from their original sense; the geometrician will talk of a courtier's zenith, or the excentrick virtue of a wild hero, and the physician of sanguine expectations and phlegmatick delays. Copiousness of speech will give opportunities to capricious choice, by which some words will be preferred, and others degraded; vicissitudes of fashion will enforce the use of new, or extend the signification of known terms. The tropes of poetry will make hourly encroachments, and the metaphorical will become the current sense: pronunciation will be varied by levity or ignorance, and the pen must at length comply with the tongue; illiterate writers will at one time or other, by publick infatuation, rise into renown, who, not knowing the original import of words, will use them with colloquial licentiousness, confound distinction, and forget propriety. As politeness increases, some expressions will be considered as too gross and vulgar for the delicate, others as too formal and ceremonious for the gay and airy; new phrases are therefore adopted, which must, for the same reasons, be in time dismissed. *Swift*, in his petty treatise on the *English* language, allows that new words must sometimes be introduced, but proposes that none should be suffered to become obsolete. But what makes a word obsolete, more than general agreement to forbear it? and how shall it be continued, when it conveys an offensive idea, or recalled again into the mouths of mankind, when it has once become unfamiliar by disuse, and unpleasing by unfamiliarity.

There is another cause of alteration more prevalent than any other, which yet in the present state of the world cannot be obviated. A mixture of two languages will produce a third distinct from both, and they will always be mixed, where the chief part of education, and the most conspicuous accomplishment, is skill in ancient or in foreign tongues. He that has long cultivated another language, will find its words and combinations croud upon his memory; and haste and negligence, refinement and affectation, will obtrude borrowed terms and exotick expressions.

The great pest of speech is frequency of translation. No book was ever turned from one language into another, without imparting something of its native idiom; this is the most mischievous and comprehensive innovation; single words may enter by thousands, and the fabrick of the tongue continue the same, but new phraseology changes much at once; it alters not the single stones of the building, but the order of the columns. If an academy should be established for the cultivation of our stile, which I, who can never wish to see dependance multiplied, hope the spirit of *English* liberty will hinder or destroy, let them, instead of compiling grammars and dictionaries, endeavour, with all their influence, to stop the licence of translatours, whose idleness and ignorance, if it be suffered to proceed, will reduce us to babble a dialect of *France*.

If the changes that we fear be thus irresistible, what remains but to acquiesce with silence, as in the other insurmountable distresses of humanity? It remains that we retard what we cannot repel, that we palliate what we cannot cure. Life may be lengthened by care, though death cannot be ultimately defeated: tongues, like governments, have a natural tendency to degeneration; we have long preserved our constitution, let us make some struggles for our language.

In hope of giving longevity to that which its own nature forbids to be immortal, I have devoted this book, the labour of years, to the honour of my country, that we may no longer yield the palm of philology, without a contest, to the nations of the continent. The chief glory of every people arises from its authours: whether I shall add any thing by my own writings to the reputation of *English* literature, must be left to time: much of my life has been lost under the pressures of disease; much has been trifled away; and much has always been spent in provision for the day that was passing over me; but I shall not think my employment useless or ignoble, if by my assistance foreign nations, and distant ages, gain access to the propagators of knowledge, and understand the teachers of truth; if my labours afford light to the repositories of science, and add celebrity to *Bacon*, to *Hooker*, to *Milton*, and to *Boyle*.

When I am animated by this wish, I look with pleasure on my book, however defective, and deliver it to the world with the spirit of a man that has endeavoured well. That it will immediately become popular I have not promised to myself: a few wild blunders, and risible absurdities, from which no work of such multiplicity was ever free, may for a time furnish folly with laughter, and harden ignorance in contempt; but useful diligence will at last prevail, and there never can be wanting some who distinguish desert; who will consider that no dictionary of a living tongue ever can be perfect, since while it is hastening to publication, some words are budding, and some falling away; that a whole life cannot be spent upon syntax and etymology, and that even a whole life would not be sufficient; that he, whose design includes whatever language can express, must often speak of what he does not understand; that a writer will sometimes be hurried by eagerness to the end, and sometimes faint with weariness under a task, which *Scaliger* compares to the labours of the anvil and the mine; that what is obvious is not always known, and what is known is not always present; that sudden fits of inadvertency will surprize vigilance, slight avocations will seduce attention, and casual eclipses of the mind will darken learning; and that the writer shall often in vain trace his memory at the moment of need, for that which yesterday he knew with intuitive readiness, and which will come uncalled into his thoughts to-morrow.

In this work, when it shall be found that much is omitted, let it not be forgotten that much likewise is performed; and though no book was ever spared out of tenderness to the authour, and the world is little solicitous to know whence proceeded the faults of that which it condemns; yet it may gratify curiosity to inform it, that the *English Dictionary* was written with little assistance of the learned, and without any patronage of the great; not in the soft obscurities of retirement, or under the shelter of academick bowers, but amidst inconvenience and distraction, in sickness and in sorrow. It may repress the triumph of malignant criticism to observe, that if our language is not here fully displayed, I have only failed in an attempt which no human powers have hitherto completed. If the lexicons of ancient tongues, now immutably fixed, and comprised in a few volumes, be yet, after the toil of successive ages, inadequate and delusive; if the aggregated knowledge, and co-operating diligence of the *Italian* academicians, did not secure them from the censure of *Beni*; if the embodied cricticks of *France*, when fifty years had been spent upon their work, were obliged to change its oeconomy, and give their second edition another form, I may surely be contented without the praise of perfection, which, if I could obtain, in this gloom of solitude, what would it avail me? I have protracted my work till most of those whom I wished to please have sunk into the grave, and success and miscarriage are empty sounds: I therefore dismiss it with frigid tranquillity, having little to fear or hope from censure or from praise.

15

NOAH WEBSTER

(1758–1843)

Webster first mentions the causes underlying the discrepancy in English between pronunciation and spelling, and suggests that by the omission of silent letters, the regularization of the use of remaining ones, and the addition of a few diacritical signs, spelling would conform to pronunciation with consequent advantages: the mastery of spelling would be easier and more complete, pronunciation would be rendered uniform throughout the country, books would be shorter, and American spelling would take on a distinctive form. He answers at length a number of objections to his scheme, and appends a letter on the topic by Benjamin Franklin.

'An Essay on the Necessity, Advantages and Practicability of Reforming the Mode of Spelling, and of Rendering the Orthography of Words Consistent to the Pronunciation'

(Appendix to *Dissertations on the English Language*, 1789)

It has been observed by all writers on the English language, that the orthography or spelling of words is very irregular; the same letters often representing different sounds, and the same sounds often expressed by different letters. For this irregularity, two principal causes may be assigned:

1. The changes to which the pronunciation of a language is liable, from the progress of science and civilization.

2. The mixture of different languages, occasioned by revolutions in England, or by a predilection of the learned, for words of foreign growth and ancient origin.

To the first cause, may be ascribed the difference between the spelling and pronunciation of Saxon words. The northern nations of Europe originally spoke much in gutturals. This is evident from the number of aspirates and guttural letters, which still remain in the orthography of words derived from those nations; and from the modern pronunciation of the collateral branches of the Teutonic, the Dutch, Scotch and German. Thus *k* before *n* was once pronounced; as in *knave, know*; the *gh* in *might, though, daughter*, and other similar words; the *g* in *reign, feign*, &c.

But as savages proceed in forming languages, they lose the guttural sounds, in some measure, and adopt the use of labials, and the more open vowels. The ease of speaking facilitates this progress, and the pronunciation of words is softened, in proportion to a national refinement of manners. This will account for the difference between the ancient and modern languages of France, Spain and Italy; and for the difference between the soft pronunciation of the present languages of those countries, and the more harsh and guttural pronunciation of the northern inhabitants of Europe.

In this progress, the English have lost the sounds of most of the guttural letters. The *k* before *n* in *know*, the *g* in *reign*, and in many other words, are become mute in practice; and the *gh* is softened into the sound of *f*, as in *laugh*, or is silent, as in *brought*.

To this practice of softening the sounds of letters, or wholly suppressing those which are harsh and disagreeable, may be added a popular tendency to abbreviate words of common use. Thus *Southwark*, by a habit of quick pronunciation, is become *Suthark*; *Worcester* and *Leicester*, are become *Wooster* and *Lester*; *business*, *bizness*; *colonel, curnel*; *cannot, will not, cant, wont*.[1] In this manner the final *e* is not heard in many modern words, in which it formerly made a syllable. The words *clothes, cares*, and most others of the same kind, were formerly pronounced in two syllables.[2]

---

[1] *Wont* is strictly a contraction of *woll not*, as the word was anciently pronounced.

[2] '*Ta-ke, ma-ke, o-ne, bo-ne, sto-ne, wil-le*, &c. dissyllaba olim fuerunt, quæ nunc habentur pro monosyllabis.'—Wallis.

[*dissyllaba...monosyllabis* were previously disyllables, which are now held to be monosyllables (J. Wallis, *Grammatica Linguæ Anglicanæ* [5th ed. 1688], I. i).]

Of the other cause of irregularity in the spelling of our language, I have treated sufficiently in the first Dissertation. It is here necessary only to remark, that when words have been introduced from a foreign language into the English, they have generally retained the orthography of the original, however ill adapted to express the English pronunciation. Thus *fatigue, marine, chaise*, retain their French dress, while, to represent the true pronunciation in English, they should be spelt *fateeg, mareen, shaze*. Thus thro an ambition to exhibit the etymology of words, the English, in *Philip, physic, character, chorus*, and other Greek derivatives, preserve the representatives of the original Φ and Χ; yet these words are pronounced, and ought ever to have been spelt, *Fillip, fyzzic* or *fizzic, karacter, korus*.[1]

But such is the state of our language. The pronunciation of the words which are strictly *English*, has been gradually changing for ages, and since the revival of science in Europe, the language has received a vast accession of words from other languages, many of which retain an orthography very ill suited to exhibit the true pronunciation.

The question now occurs; ought the Americans to retain these faults which produce innumerable inconveniencies in the acquisition and use of the language, or ought they at once to reform these abuses, and introduce order and regularity into the orthography of the AMERICAN TONGUE?

Let us consider this subject with some attention.

Several attempts were formerly made in England to rectify the orthography of the language.[2] But I apprehend their schemes

---

[1] The words *number, chamber*, and many others in English are from the French *nombre, chambre*, &c. Why was the spelling changed? or rather why is the spelling of *lustre, metre, theatre*, not changed? The cases are precisely similar. The Englishman who first wrote *number* for *nombre*, had no greater authority to make the change, than any modern writer has to spell *lustre, metre* in a similar manner, *luster, meter*. The change in the first instance was a valuable one; it conformed the spelling to the pronunciation, and I have taken the liberty, in all my writings, to pursue the principle in *luster, meter, miter, theater, sepulcher*, &c.

[2] The first by Sir Thomas Smith, secretary of state to Queen Elizabeth: Another by Dr. Gill, a celebrated master of St. Paul's school in London: Another by Mr. Charles Butler, who went so far as to print his book in his proposed orthography: Several in the time of Charles the first; and in the present age, Mr. Elphinstone has published a treatise in a very ridiculous orthography.

failed of success, rather on account of their intrinsic difficulties, than on account of any necessary impracticability of a reform. It was proposed, in most of these schemes, not merely to throw out superfluous and silent letters, but to introduce a number of new characters. Any attempt on such a plan must undoubtedly prove unsuccessful. It is not to be expected that an orthography, perfectly regular and simple, such as would be formed by a 'Synod of Grammarians on principles of science,' will ever be substituted for that confused mode of spelling which is now established. But it is apprehended that great improvements may be made, and an orthography almost regular, or such as shall obviate most of the present difficulties which occur in learning our language, may be introduced and established with little trouble and opposition.

The principal alterations, necessary to render our orthography sufficiently regular and easy, are these:

1. The omission of all superfluous or silent letters; as *a* in *bread*. Thus *bread, head, give, breast, built, meant, realm, friend*, would be spelt, *bred, hed, giv, brest, bilt, ment, relm, frend*. Would this alteration produce any inconvenience, any embarrassment or expense? By no means. On the other hand, it would lessen the trouble of writing, and much more, of learning the language; it would reduce the true pronunciation to a certainty; and while it would assist foreigners and our own children in acquiring the language, it would render the pronunciation uniform, in different parts of the country, and almost prevent the possibility of changes.

2. A substitution of a character that has a certain definite sound, for one that is more vague and indeterminate. Thus by putting *ee* instead of *ea* or *ie*, the words *mean, near, speak, grieve, zeal*, would become *meen, neer, speek, greev, zeel*. This alteration could not occasion a moments trouble; at the same time it would prevent a doubt respecting the pronunciation; whereas the *ea* and *ie* having different sounds, may give a learner much difficulty. Thus *greef* should be substituted for *grief*; *kee* for *key*; *beleev* for *believe*; *laf* for *laugh*; *dawter* for *daughter*; *plow* for *plough*; *tuf* for *tough*; *proov* for

prove; *blud* for *blood*; and *draft* for *draught*. In this manner *ch* in Greek derivatives, should be changed into *k*; for the English *ch* has a soft sound, as in *cherish*; but *k* always a hard sound. Therefore *character*, *chorus*, *cholic*, *architecture*, should be written *karacter*, *korus*, *kolic*, *arkitecture*; and were they thus written, no person could mistake their true pronunciation.

Thus *ch* in French derivatives should be changed into *sh*; *machine*, *chaise*, *chevalier*, should be written *masheen*, *shaze*, *shevaleer*; and *pique*, *tour*, *oblique*, should be written *peek*, *toor*, *obleek*.

3. A trifling alteration in a character, or the addition of a point would distinguish different sounds, without the substitution of a new character. Thus a very small stroke across *th* would distinguish its two sounds. A point over a vowel, in this manner, *à*, or *ò*, or *ī*, might answer all the purposes of different letters. And for the dipthong *ow*, let the two letters be united by a small stroke, or both engraven on the same piece of metal, with the left hand line of the *w* united to the *o*.

These, with a few other inconsiderable alterations, would answer every purpose, and render the orthography sufficiently correct and regular.

The advantages to be derived from these alterations are numerous, great and permanent.

1. The simplicity of the orthography would facilitate the learning of the language. It is now the work of years for children to learn to spell; and after all, the business is rarely accomplished. A few men, who are bred to some business that requires constant exercise in writing, finally learn to spell most words without hesitation; but most people remain, all their lives, imperfect masters of spelling, and liable to make mistakes, whenever they take up a pen to write a short note. Nay, many people, even of education and fashion, never attempt to write a letter, without frequently consulting a dictionary.

But with the proposed orthography, a child would learn to spell, without trouble, in a very short time, and the orthography being very regular, he would ever afterwards find it difficult to make a mistake. It would, in that case, be as difficult to spell *wrong*, as it is now to spell *right*.

Besides this advantage, foreigners would be able to acquire the pronunciation of English, which is now so difficult and embarrassing, that they are either wholly discouraged on the first attempt, or obliged, after many years labor, to rest contented with an imperfect knowledge of the subject.

2. A correct orthography would render the pronunciation of the language, as uniform as the spelling in books. A general uniformity thro the United States, would be the event of such a reformation as I am here recommending. All persons, of every rank, would speak with some degree of precision and uniformity.[1] Such a uniformity in these states is very desireable; it would remove prejudice, and conciliate mutual affection and respect.

3. Such a reform would diminish the number of letters about one sixteenth or eighteenth. This would save a page in eighteen; and a saving of an eighteenth in the expense of books, is an advantage that should not be overlooked.

4. But a capital advantage of this reform in these states would be, that it would make a difference between the English orthography and the American. This will startle those who have not attended to the subject; but I am confident that such an event is an object of vast political consequence. For,

The alteration, however small, would encourage the publication of books in our own country. It would render it, in some measure, necessary that all books should be printed in America. The English would never copy our orthography for their own use; and consequently the same impressions of books would not answer for both countries. The inhabitants of the present generation would read the English impressions; but posterity, being taught a different spelling, would prefer the American orthography.

Besides this, a *national language* is a band of *national union*. Every

[1] I once heard Dr. Franklin remark, 'that those people spell best, who do not know how to spell;' that is, they spell as their ears dictate, without being guided by rules, and thus fall into a regular orthography.

engine should be employed to render the people of this country *national*; to call their attachments home to their own country; and to inspire them with the pride of national character. However they may boast of Independence, and the freedom of their government, yet their *opinions* are not sufficiently independent; an astonishing respect for the arts and literature of their parent country, and a blind imitation of its manners, are still prevalent among the Americans. Thus an habitual respect for another country, deserved indeed and once laudable, turns their attention from their own interests, and prevents their respecting themselves.

OBJECTIONS

1. 'This reform of the Alphabet would oblige people to relearn the language, or it could not be introduced.'

But the alterations proposed are so few and so simple, that an hour's attention would enable any person to read the new orthography with facility; and a week's practice would render it so familiar, that a person would write it without hesitation or mistake. Would this small inconvenience prevent its adoption? Would not the numerous national and literary advantages, resulting from the change, induce Americans to make so inconsiderable a sacrifice of time and attention? I am persuaded they would.

But it would not be necessary that men advanced beyond the middle stage of life, should be at the pains to learn the proposed orthography. They would, without inconvenience, continue to use the present. They would read the *new* orthography, without difficulty; but they would write in the *old*. To men thus advanced, and even to the present generation in general, if they should not wish to trouble themselves with a change, the reformation would be almost a matter of indifference. It would be sufficient that children should be taught the new orthography, and that as fast as they come upon the stage, they should be furnished with books in the American spelling. The progress of printing would be proportioned to the demand for books among the rising generation.

This progressive introduction of the scheme would be extremely easy; children would learn the proposed orthography more easily than they would the old; and the present generation would not be troubled with the change; so that none but the obstinate and capricious could raise objections or make any opposition. The change would be so inconsiderable, and made on such simple principles, that a column in each newspaper, printed in the new spelling, would in six months, familiarize most people to the change, show the advantages of it, and imperceptibly remove their objections. The only steps necessary to ensure success in the attempt to introduce this reform, would be, a resolution of Congress, ordering all their acts to be engrossed in the new orthography, and recommending the plan to the several universities in America; and also a resolution of the universities to encourage and support it. The printers would begin the reformation by publishing short paragraphs and small tracts in the new orthography; school books would first be published in the same; curiosity would excite attention to it, and men would be gradually reconciled to the plan.

2. 'This change would render our present books useless.'

This objection is, in some measure, answered under the foregoing head. The truth is, it would not have this effect. The difference of orthography would not render books printed in one, illegible to persons acquainted only with the other. The difference would not be so great as between the orthography of Chaucer, and of the present age; yet Chaucer's works are still read with ease.

3. 'This reformation would injure the language by obscuring etymology.'

This objection is unfounded. In general, it is not true that the change would obscure etymology; in a few instances, it might; but it would rather restore the etymology of many words; and if it were true that the change would obscure it, this would be no objection to the reformation.

It will perhaps surprize my readers to be told that, in many particular words, the modern spelling is less correct than the ancient. Yet this is a truth that reflects dishonor on our modern refiners of the language. Chaucer, four hundred years ago, wrote *bilder* for *builder*; *dedly* for *deadly*; *ernest* for *earnest*; *erly* for *early*; *brest* for *breast*; *hed* for *head*; and certainly his spelling was the most agreeable to the pronunciation.[1] Sidney wrote *bin, examin, sutable,* with perfect propriety. Dr. Middleton wrote *explane, genuin, revele,* which is the most easy and correct orthography of such words; and also *luster, theater,* for *lustre, theatre.* In these and many other instances, the modern spelling is a corruption; so that allowing many improvements to have been made in orthography, within a century or two, we must acknowlege also that many corruptions have been introduced.

In answer to the objection, that a change of orthography would obscure etymology, I would remark, that the etymology of most words is already lost, even to the learned; and to the unlearned, etymology is never known. Where is the man that can trace back our English words to the elementary radicals? In a few instances, the student has been able to reach the primitive roots of words; but I presume the radicals of one tenth of the words in our language, have never yet been discovered, even by Junius, Skinner, or any other etymologist. Any man may look into Johnson or Ash, and find that *flesh* is derived from the Saxon *floce*; *child* from *cild*; *flood* from *flod*; *lad* from *leode*; and *loaf* from *laf* or *hlaf.* But this discovery will answer no other purpose, than to show, that within a few hundred years, the spelling of some words has been a little changed: We should still be at a vast distance from the primitive roots.

In many instances indeed etymology will assist the learned in understanding the composition and true sense of a word; and it throws much light upon the progress of language. But the true sense of a complex term is not always, nor generally, to be learnt from the sense of the primitives or elementary words. The current meaning of a word depends on its use in a nation. This true sense is to be obtained by attending to good authors, to dictionaries and

[1] In Chaucer's life, prefixed to the edition of his works 1602, I find *move* and *prove* spelt almost correctly, *moove* and *proove.*

to practice, rather than to derivation. The former *must* be *right*; the latter *may* lead us into *error*.

But to prove of how little consequence a knowlege of etymology is to most people, let me mention a few words. The word *sincere* is derived from the Latin, *sine cera*, without wax; and thus it came to denote *purity of mind*. I am confident that not a man in a thousand ever suspected this to be the origin of the word; yet all men, that have any knowlege of our language, use the word in its true sense, and understand its customary meaning, as well as Junius did, or any other etymologist.

Yea or *yes* is derived from the imperative of a verb, *avoir* to have, as the word is now spelt. It signifies therefore *have*, or *possess*, or *take* what you ask. But does this explication assist us in using the word? And does not every countryman who labors in the field, understand and use the word with as much precision as the profoundest philosophers?

The word *temper* is derived from an old root, *tem*, which signified *water*. It was borrowed from the act of *cooling*, or moderating heat. Hence the meaning of *temperate*, *temperance*, and all the ramifications of the original stock. But does this help us to the modern current sense of these words? By no means. It leads us to understand the formation of languages, and in what manner an idea of a visible action gives rise to a correspondent abstract idea; or rather, how a word, from a literal and direct sense, may be applied to express a variety of figurative and collateral ideas. Yet the customary sense of the word is known by practice, and as well understood by an illiterate man of tolerable capacity, as by men of science.

The word *always* is compounded of *all* and *ways*; it had originally no reference to time; and the etymology or composition of the word would only lead us into error. The true meaning of words is that which a nation in general annex to them. Etymology therefore is of no use but to the learned; and for them it will still be preserved, so far as it is now understood, in dictionaries and other books that treat of this particular subject.

4. 'The distinction between words of different meanings and similar sound would be destroyed.'

'That distinction,' to answer in the words of the great Franklin, 'is already destroyed in pronunciation.' Does not every man pronounce *all* and *awl* precisely alike? And does the sameness of sound ever lead a hearer into a mistake? Does not the construction render the distinction easy and intelligible, the moment the words of the sentence are heard? Is the word *knew* ever mistaken for *new*, even in the rapidity of pronouncing an animated oration? Was *peace* ever mistaken for *piece*; *pray* for *prey*; *flour* for *flower*? Never, I presume, is this similarity of sound the occasion of mistakes.

If therefore an identity of *sound*, even in rapid speaking, produces no inconvenience, how much less would an identity of *spelling*, when the eye would have leisure to survey the construction? But experience, the criterion of truth, which has removed the objection in the first case, will also assist us in forming our opinion in the last.

There are many words in our language which, with the *same orthography*, have two or more *distinct meanings*. The word *wind*, whether it signifies *to move round*, or *air in motion*, has the *same spelling*; it exhibits no distinction to the *eye* of a silent reader; and yet its meaning is never mistaken. The construction shows at sight in which sense the word is to be understood. *Hail* is used as an expression of joy, or to signify frozen drops of water, falling from the clouds. *Rear* is to raise up, or it signifies the hinder part of an army. *Lot* signifies fortune or destiny; a plat of ground; or a certain proportion or share; and yet does this diversity, this contrariety of meanings ever occasion the least difficulty in the ordinary language of books? It cannot be maintained. This diversity is found in all languages;[1] and altho it may be considered as a defect, and occasion some trouble for foreign learners, yet to natives it produces no sensible inconvenience.

5. 'It is idle to conform the orthography of words to the pronunciation, because the latter is continually changing.'

---

[1] In the Roman language *liber* had four or five different meanings; it signified *free*, *the inward bark of a tree*, *a book*, sometimes *an epistle*, and also *generous*.

This is one of Dr. Johnson's objections, and it is very unworthy of his judgement. So far is this circumstance from being a real objection, that it is alone a sufficient reason for the change of spelling. On his principle of *fixing the orthography*, while the *pronunciation is changing*, any *spoken language* must, in time, lose all relation to the *written language*; that is, the sounds of words would have no affinity with the letters that compose them. In some instances, this is now the case; and no mortal would suspect from the spelling, that *neighbour, wrought*, are pronounced *nabur, rawt*. On this principle, Dr. Johnson ought to have gone back some centuries, and given us, in his dictionary, the primitive Saxon orthography, *wol* for *will*; *ydilnesse* for *idleness*; *eyen* for *eyes*; *eche* for *each*, &c. Nay, he should have gone as far as possible into antiquity, and, regardless of the changes of pronunciation, given us the primitive radical language in its purity. Happily for the language, that doctrine did not prevail till his time; the spelling of words changed with the pronunciation; to these changes we are indebted for numberless improvements; and it is hoped that the progress of them, in conformity with the national practice of speaking, will not be obstructed by the erroneous opinion, even of Dr. Johnson. How much more rational is the opinion of Dr. Franklin, who says, 'the orthography of our language began to be fixed too soon.' If the pronunciation must vary, from age to age, (and some trifling changes of language will always be taking place) common sense would dictate a correspondent change of spelling. Admit Johnson's principles; take his pedantic orthography for the standard; let it be closely adhered to in future; and the slow changes in the pronunciation of our national tongue, will in time make as great a difference between our *written* and *spoken* language, as there is between the pronunciation of the present English and German. The *spelling* will be no more a guide to the pronunciation, than the orthography of the German or Greek. This event is actually taking place, in consequence of the stupid opinion, advanced by Johnson and other writers, and generally embraced by the nation.

All these objections appear to me of very inconsiderable weight, when opposed to the great, substantial and permanent advantages to be derived from a regular national orthography.

Sensible I am how much easier it is to *propose* improvements, than to *introduce* them. Every thing *new* starts the idea of difficulty; and yet it is often mere novelty that excites the appearance; for on a slight examination of the proposal, the difficulty vanishes. When we firmly *believe* a scheme to be practicable, the work is *half* accomplished. We are more frequently deterred by fear from making an attack, than repulsed in the encounter.

Habit also is opposed to changes; for it renders even our errors dear to us. Having surmounted all difficulties in childhood, we forget the labor, the fatigue, and the perplexity we suffered in the attempt, and imagin the progress of our studies to have been smooth and easy.[1] What seems intrinsically right, is so merely thro habit.

Indolence is another obstacle to improvements. The most arduous task a reformer has to execute, is to make people *think*; to rouse them from that lethargy, which, like the mantle of sleep, covers them in repose and contentment.

But America is in a situation the most favorable for great reformations; and the present time is, in a singular degree, auspicious. The minds of men in this country have been awakened. New scenes have been, for many years, presenting new occasions for exertion; unexpected distresses have called forth the powers of invention; and the application of new expedients has demanded every possible exercise of wisdom and talents. Attention is roused; the mind expanded; and the intellectual faculties invigorated. Here men are prepared to receive improvements, which would be rejected by nations, whose habits have not been shaken by similar events.

[1] Thus most people suppose the present mode of spelling to be really the *easiest* and *best*. This opinion is derived from habit; the new mode of spelling proposed would save three fourths of the labor now bestowed in learning to write our language. A child would learn to spell as well in one year, as he can now in four. This is not a supposition—it is an assertion capable of proof; and yet people, never knowing, or having forgot the labor of learning, suppose the present mode to be the easiest. No person, but one who has taught children, has any idea of the difficulty of learning to spell and pronounce our language in its present form.

Now is the time, and *this* the country, in which we may expect success, in attempting changes favorable to language, science and government. Delay, in the plan here proposed, may be fatal; under a tranquil general government, the minds of men may again sink into indolence; a national acquiescence in error will follow; and posterity be doomed to struggle with difficulties, which time and accident will perpetually multiply.

Let us then seize the present moment, and establish a *national language*, as well as a national government. Let us remember that there is a certain respect due to the opinions of other nations. As an independent people, our reputation abroad demands that, in all things, we should be federal; be *national*; for if we do not respect *ourselves*, we may be assured that *other nations* will not respect us. In short, let it be impressed upon the mind of every American, that to neglect the means of commanding respect abroad, is treason against the character and dignity of a brave independent people.

To excite the more attention to this subject, I will here subjoin what Dr. Franklin has done and written to effect a reform in our mode of spelling. This sage philosopher has suffered nothing useful to escape his notice. He very early discovered the difficulties that attend the learning of our language; and with his usual ingenuity, invented a plan to obviate them. If any objection can be made to his scheme,[1] it is the substitution of *new* characters, for *th*, *sh*, *ng*, &c. whereas a small stroke, connecting the letters, would answer all the purposes of new characters; as these combinations would thus become single letters, with precise definite sounds and suitable names.

A specimen of the Doctor's spelling cannot be here given, as I have not the proper types;[2] but the arguments in favor of a reformed mode of spelling shall be given in his own words.

[1] See his Miscellaneous Works. p. 470. Ed. Lond. 1779.

[2] This indefatigable gentleman, amidst all his other employments, public and private, has compiled a Dictionary on his scheme of a Reform, and procured types to be cast for printing it. He thinks himself too old to pursue the plan; but has honored me with the offer of the manuscript and types, and expressed a strong desire that I should undertake the task. Whether this project, so deeply interesting to this country, will ever be effected; or whether it will be defeated by indolence and prejudice, remains for my countrymen to determine.

Copy of a Letter from Miss S—, *to Dr.* FRANKLIN, *who had sent her his Scheme of a Reformed Alphabet. Dated, Kensington (England) Sept. 26,* 1768.

DEAR SIR,

I have transcribed your alphabet, &c. which I think might be of service to those who wish to acquire an accurate pronunciation, if that could be fixed; but I see many inconveniences, as well as difficulties, that would attend the bringing your letters and orthography into common use. All our etymologies would be lost; consequently we could not ascertain the meaning of many words; the distinction too between words of *different meaning* and *similar* sound would be useless,[1] unless we living writers publish new editions. In short, I believe we must let people spell on in their old way, and (as we find it easiest) do the same ourselves.—With ease and with sincerity I can, in the old way, subscribe myself,

Dear Sir,

Your faithful and affectionate Servant,

Dr. Franklin.   M. S.

Dr. FRANKLIN'S *Answer to Miss* S—.

DEAR MADAM,

The objection you make to rectifying our alphabet, 'that it will be attended with inconveniences and difficulties,' is a very natural one; for it always occurs when any reformation is proposed, whether in religion, government, laws, and even down as low as roads and wheel carriages. The true question then is not, whether there will be no difficulties or inconveniences; but whether the difficulties may not be surmounted; and whether the conveniences will not, on the whole, be greater than the inconveniences. In this case, the difficulties are only in the beginning of the practice; when they are once overcome, the advantages are lasting. To either you or me, who spell well in the present mode, I imagin the difficulty

---

[1] This lady overlooked the other side of the question; viz. that by a reform of the spelling, words now spelt alike and pronounced differently, would be distinguished by their letters; for the nouns *abuse* and *use* would be distinguished from the verbs, which would be spelt *abuze, yuze*; and so in many instances. See the answer below.

of changing that mode for the new, is not so great, but that we might perfectly get over it in a week's writing. As to those who do not spell well, if the two difficulties are compared, viz. that of teaching them true spelling in the present mode, and that of teaching them the new alphabet and the new spelling according to it, I am confident that the latter would be by far the least. They naturally fall into the new method already, as much as the imperfection of their alphabet will admit of; their present *bad* spelling is only bad, because contrary to the present *bad* rules; under the new rules it would be *good*.[1] The difficulty of learning to spell well in the old way is so great, that few attain it; thousands and thousands writing on to old age, without ever being able to acquire it. It is besides, a difficulty continually increasing;[2] as the sound gradually varies more and more from the spelling; and to foreigners it makes the learning to pronounce our language, as written in our books, almost impossible.

Now as to the inconveniences you mention: The first is, 'that all our etymologies would be lost; consequently we could not ascertain the meaning of many words.' Etymologies are at present very uncertain; but such as they are, the old books still preserve them, and etymologists would there find them. Words in the course of time, change their meaning, as well as their spelling and pronunciation; and we do not look to etymologies for their present meanings. If I should call a man a *knave* and a *villain*, he would hardly be satisfied with my telling him, that one of the words originally signified a *lad* or *servant*, and the other an under *plowman*, or the inhabitant of a village. It is from present usage only, the meaning of words is to be determined.

Your second inconvenience is, 'the distinction between words of different meaning and similar sound would be destroyed.' That distinction is already destroyed in pronouncing them; and we rely on the sense alone of the sentence to ascertain which of the several

---

[1] This remark of the Doctor is very just and obvious. A countryman writes *aker* or *akur* for *acre*; yet the countryman is *right*, as the word *ought* to be spelt; and we laugh at him only because *we* are accustomed to be *wrong*.

[2] This is a fact of vast consequence.

words, similar in sound, we intend. If this is sufficient in the rapidity of discourse, it will be much more so in written sentences, which may be read leisurely, and attended to more particularly in case of difficulty, than we can attend to a past sentence, while the speaker is hurrying us along with new ones.

Your third inconvenience is, 'that all the books already written would be useless.' This inconvenience would only come on gradually in a course of ages. I and you and other now living readers would hardly forget the use of them. People would long learn to read the old writing, tho they practised the new. And the inconvenience is not greater than what has actually happened in a similar case in Italy. Formerly its inhabitants all spoke and wrote Latin; as the language changed, the spelling followed it. It is true that at present, a mere unlearned Italian cannot read the Latin books, tho they are still read and understood by many. But if the spelling had never been changed, he would now have found it much more difficult to read and write his own language;[1] for written words would have had no relation to sounds; they would only have stood for things; so that if he would express in writing the idea he has when he sounds the word *Vescovo*, he must use the letters *Episcopus*.[2]

In short, whatever the difficulties and inconveniences now are, they will be more easily surmounted now, than hereafter; and some time or other it must be done, or our writing will become the same with the Chinese, as to the difficulty of learning and using it. And it would already have been such, if we had continued the Saxon spelling and writing used by our forefathers.

I am, my dear friend,
Your's affectionately,
B. FRANKLIN.

London, Craven Street, Sept. 28, 1768.

[1] That is, if the language had retained the old *Roman* spelling, and been pronounced as the modern *Italian*. This is a fair state of facts, and a complete answer to all objections to a reform of spelling.

[2] In the same ridiculous manner, as *we* write, *rough, still, neighbor, wrong, tongue, true, rhetoric,* &c. and yet pronounce the words, *ruf, stil, nabur, rong, tung, tru, retoric.*

16

BENJAMIN FRANKLIN
(1706–1790)

Franklin's letter congratulates Webster on his *Dissertations*, and goes on to cite
a number of 'popular errors' he would like to see corrected: new uses of
existing words, and the employment of nouns as verbs. Reflecting on the
advantages to France in the international use of French by polite and learned
society, he recommends that every difficulty in the study of English as a foreign
language be removed, and mentions in particular a number of typographical
innovations he disapproves of. The text is from the collected *Works* of 1793.

'On Modern Innovations in the English Language and in Printing' (1789)

To NOAH WEBSTER, *jun. Esq. at* HARTFORD.

Philadelphia, Dec. 26, 1789.

DEAR SIR,

I received, some time since, your *Dissertations on the English Language*. It is an excellent work, and will be greatly useful in turning
the thoughts of our countrymen to correct writing. Please to
accept my thanks for it, as well as for the great honour you have
done me in its dedication. I ought to have made this acknowledgment sooner, but much indisposition prevented me.

I cannot but applaud your zeal for preserving the purity of our
language both in its expression and pronunciation, and in correcting the popular errors several of our states are continually falling
into with respect to both. Give me leave to mention some of
them, though possibly they may already have occurred to you.
I wish, however, that in some future publication of yours, you
would set a discountenancing mark upon them. The first I remember, is the word *improved*. When I left New-England in the

year 1723, this word had never been used among us, as far as I
know, but in the sense of *ameliorated*, or *made better*, except once
in a very old book of Dr. Mather's, entitled *Remarkable Providences*.
As that man wrote a very obscure hand, I remember that when
I read that word in his book, used instead of the word *employed*,
I conjectured that it was an error of the printer, who had mistaken
a short *l* in the writing for an *r*, and a *y* with too short a tail for
a *v*, whereby *employed* was converted into *improved*: but when I
returned to Boston in 1733, I found this change had obtained
favour, and was then become common; for I met with it often in
perusing the newspapers, where it frequently made an appearance
rather ridiculous. Such, for instance, as the advertisement of a
country house to be sold, which had been many years *improved*
as a tavern; and in a character of a deceased country gentleman, that he had been, for more than thirty years, *improved*
as a justice of the peace. This use of the word *improve* is
peculiar to New England, and not to be met with among any
other speakers of English, either on this or the other side of the
water.

During my late absence in France, I find that several other new
words have been introduced into our parliamentary language.
For example, I find a verb formed from the substantive *notice*.
I should not have noticed *this, were it not that the gentleman*, &c.
Also another verb, from the substantive *advocate*; *The gentleman
who* advocates, *or who has* advocated *that motion*, &c. Another
from the substantive *progress*, the most awkward and abominable
of the three: *The committee having* progressed, *resolved to adjourn*.
The word *opposed*, though not a new word, I find used in a new
manner, as, *The gentlemen who are* opposed *to this measure, to which
I have also myself always been* opposed. If you should happen to be
of my opinion with respect to these innovations, you will use your
authority in reprobating them.

The Latin language, long the vehicle used in distributing knowledge among the different nations of Europe, is daily more and
more neglected; and one of the modern tongues, viz. French,

seems, in point of universality, to have supplied its place. It is spoken in all the courts of Europe; and most of the literati, those even who do not speak it, have acquired knowledge of it, to enable them easily to read the books that are written in it. This gives a considerable advantage to that nation. It enables its authors to inculcate and spread through other nations, such sentiments and opinions, on important points, as are most conducive to its interests, or which may contribute to its reputation, by promoting the common interests of mankind. It is, perhaps, owing to its being written in French, that Voltaire's Treatise on Toleration has had so sudden and so great an effect on the bigotry of Europe, as almost entirely to disarm it. The general use of the French language has likewise a very advantageous effect on the profits of the book-selling branch of commerce, it being well known, that the more copies can be sold that are struck off from one composition of types, the profits increase in a much greater proportion than they do in making a greater number of pieces in any other kind of manu-facture. And at present there is no capital town in Europe without a French bookseller's shop corresponding with Paris. Our English bids fair to obtain the second place. The great body of excellent printed sermons in our language, and the freedom of our writings on political subjects, have induced a great number of divines of different sects and nations, as well as gentlemen concerned in public affairs, to study it, so far at least as to read it. And if we were to endeavour the facilitating its progress, the study of our tongue might become much more general. Those who have em-ployed some part of their time in learning a new language, must have frequently observed, that while their acquaintance with it was imperfect, difficulties, small in themselves, operated as great ones in obstructing their progress. A book, for example, ill printed, or a pronunciation in speaking not well articulated, would render a sentence unintelligible, which from a clear print, or a distinct speaker, would have been immediately comprehended. If, there-fore, we would have the benefit of seeing our language more generally known among mankind, we should endeavour to remove all the difficulties, however small, that discourage the learning of it. But I am sorry to observe that, of late years, those difficulties, instead of being diminished, have been augmented.

In examining the English books that were printed between the restoration and the accession of George the Second, we may observe, that all substantives were begun with a capital, in which we imitated our mother tongue, the German. This was more particularly useful to those who were not well acquainted with the English, there being such a prodigious number of our words that are both verbs and substantives, and spelt in the same manner, though often accented differently in pronunciation. This method has, by the fancy of printers, of late years been entirely laid aside; from an idea, that suppressing the capitals shews the character to greater advantage; those letters, prominent above the line, disturbing its even, regular appearance. The effect of this change is so considerable, that a learned man of France, who used to read our books, though not perfectly acquainted with our language, in conversation with me on the subject of our authors, attributed the greater obscurity he found in our modern books, compared with those of the period above mentioned, to a change of style for the worse in our writers; of which mistake I convinced him, by marking for him each substantive with a capital, in a paragraph, which he then easily understood, though before he could not comprehend it. This shews the inconvenience of that pretended improvement.

From the same fondness for an uniform and even appearance of characters in the line, the printers have of late banished also the Italic types, in which words of importance to be attended to in the sense of the sentence, and words on which an emphasis should be put in reading, used to be printed. And lately another fancy has induced other printers to use the round *s* instead of the long one, which formerly served well to distinguish a word readily by its varied appearance. Certainly the omitting this prominent letter makes a line appear more even, but renders it less immediately legible; as the paring of all men's noses might smooth and level their faces, but would render their physiognomies less distinguish-able. Add to all these improvements backwards, another modern fancy, that *grey* printing is more beautiful than black. Hence the English new books are printed in so dim a character as to be read with difficulty by old eyes, unless in a very strong light, and with good glasses. Whoever compares a volume of the Gentleman's Magazine, printed between the years 1731 and 1740, with one of those printed in the last ten years, will be convinced of the much greater degree of perspicuity given by black than by the grey. Lord Chesterfield pleasantly remarked this difference to Faulkener, the Printer of the Dublin Journal, who was vainly making en-comiums on his own paper, as the most complete of any in the world. 'But, Mr. Faulkener,' says my lord, 'don't you think it might be still farther improved, by using paper and ink not quite so near of a colour?'—For all these reasons I cannot but wish that our American printers would, in their editions, avoid these fancied improvements, and thereby render their works more agreeable to foreigners in Europe, to the great advantage of our bookselling commerce.

Farther, to be more sensible of the advantage of clear and distinct printing, let us consider the assistance it affords in reading well aloud to an auditory. In so doing the eye generally slides forward three or four words before the voice. If the sight clearly dis-tinguishes what the coming words are, it gives time to order the modulation of the voice to express them properly. But if they are obscurely printed, or disguised by omitting the capitals and long *s*'s, or otherwise, the reader is apt to modulate wrong; and finding he has done so, he is obliged to go back and begin the sentence again; which lessens the pleasure of the hearers. This leads me to mention an old error in our mode of printing. We are sensible that when a question is met with in the reading, there is a proper variation to be used in the management of the voice. We have, therefore, a point, called an interrogation, affixed to the question, in order to distinguish it. But this is absurdly placed at its end, so that the reader does not discover it till he finds that he has wrongly modulated his voice, and is therefore obliged to begin again the sentence. To prevent this, the Spanish printers, more sensibly, place an interrogation at the beginning as well as at the end of the question. We have another error of the same kind in printing plays, where something often occurs that is marked as spoken *aside*. But the word *aside* is placed at the end of the speech, when it ought to precede it, as a direction to the reader, that he may govern his voice accordingly. The practice of our ladies in meeting five or six together, to form little busy parties, where each is employed in some useful work, while one reads to them, is so commendable in itself, that it deserves the attention of authors and printers to make it as pleasing as possible, both to the reader and hearers.

My best wishes attend you, being, with sincere esteem,

Sir,

Your most obedient and
very humble servant,

B. FRANKLIN.

17

WILLIAM COBBETT

(1763–1835)

Cobbett's *Grammar*, in a series of letters to his son, was 'intended for the use of...soldiers, sailors, apprentices, and plough-boys', and this section substantiates his boast: 'How many false pretenders to erudition have I exposed to shame merely by my knowledge of grammar! How many of the insolent and ignorant, great and powerful, have I pulled down and made little and despicable!' His examples, and some of his conclusions, reflect his radical political views. The text is from the London edition of 1819.

'Syntax, as Relating to Nouns'

(Letter XVI from *A Grammar of the English Language*, 1818)

MY DEAR JAMES,

164. Read again Letter V, the subject of which is the Etymology of Nouns. Nouns are *governed*, as it is called, by verbs and prepositions; that is to say, these latter sorts of words *cause nouns to be in such or such a case*; and there must be a *concord*, or an *agreement*, between the nouns and the other words, which, along with the nouns, compose a sentence.

165. But these matters will be best explained when I come to the *Syntax of Verbs*; for, until we take the verb into account, we cannot go far in giving rules for the forming of sentences. Under the present head, therefore, I shall content myself with doing little more than to give some further account of the manner of using the *Possessive Case* of nouns; that being the only case to denote which our nouns *vary their endings*.

166. This possessive case was pretty fully spoken of by me in the Letter just referred to; but, there are certain other observations to make with regard to the using of it in sentences. When the noun, which is in the possessive case, is expressed by a circum-

locution; that is to say, by many words in lieu of one, the sign of
the possessive case is joined to the last word: as, '*John*, the old
farmer's, wife. *Oliver*, the spy's, evidence.' It is, however, much
better to say, 'the wife of *John*, the old farmer. The evidence of
Oliver, the spy.'

167. When two or more nouns in the possessive case follow
each other and are joined by a conjunctive conjunction, the sign
of the possessive case is, when the thing possessed is the same, put
to the last noun only: as, 'Peter, Joseph, and Richard's estate.'
In this example the thing possessed being one and the same thing,
the sign applies equally to each of the three possessive nouns. But,
'Peter's, Joseph's, and Richard's estate,' implies that *each* has an
estate; or, at least, it will admit of that meaning being given to it,
while the former phrase will not.

168. Sometimes the sign of the possessive case is left out, and a
hyphen is used in its stead: as, 'Reynolds, the *government-spy*.' That
is to say, 'the government's spy;' or 'the spy *of the* government.'
These two words, joined in this manner, are called a *compound
noun*; and, to this compounding of nouns our language is very
much prone. We say, '*chamber-floor, horse-shoe, dog-collar*;' that is
to say *chamber's* floor, *horse's* shoe, *dog's* collar.

169. This is an advantage peculiar to our language. It enables
us to say much in few words, which always gives strength to
language; and, after *clearness*, strength is the most valuable quality
that writing or speaking can possess. 'The Yorkshire-men flew to
arms.' If we could not compound our words, we must say, 'the
men of the shire of York flew to arms.' When you come to learn
French, you will soon see how much the English language is better
than the French in this respect.

170. You must take care, when you use the possessive case, not
to use after it words which create a confusion in meaning. HUME
has this sentence: 'They flew to arms and attacked *Northumberland's* house, *whom* they put to death.' We know what is *meant*,
because *whom* can relate to *persons* only; but, if it had been an
attack on Northumberland's *men*, the meaning would have been,

that the *men were put to death*. However, the sentence, as it stands, is sufficiently incorrect. It should have been: 'They flew to arms, attacked the house of Northumberland, and put him to death.'

171. A passage from DOCTOR HUGH BLAIR, the author of *Lectures on Rhetoric*, will give you another instance of error in the use of the possessive case. I take it from the 24th Lecture: 'In comparing Demosthenes and Cicero, most of the French critics are disposed to give the preference to the latter. P. Rapin the jesuit, in the parallels which he has drawn between some of the most eminent Greek and Roman writers, uniformly decides in favour of the Roman. For the preference which he gives to Cicero, he assigns, and lays stress on one reason of a pretty extraordinary nature, viz. that Demosthenes could not possibly have so clear an *insight* as Cicero *into* the manners and passions of men; Why? because *he* had not the advantage of *perusing Aristotle's Treatise of Rhetoric*, wherein, says our critic, *he* has fully laid open *that mystery*: and to support this weighty argument, *he* enters into a controversy with A. Gellius, in order to prove that Aristotle's Rhetoric was not published till after Demosthenes had spoken, *at least*, his most considerable orations.' It is surprising that the Doctor should have put such a passage as this upon paper, and more surprising that he should leave it in this state after having perused it with that care, which is usually employed in examining writings that are to be put into print, and especially writings in which every word is expected to be used in a proper manner. In Bacon, in Tull, in Blackstone, in Hume, in Swift, in Bolingbroke; in all writers, however able, we find errors. Yet, though many of their sentences will not stand the test of strict grammatical criticism, the *sense* generally is clear to our minds: and we read on. But, in this passage of Doctor Blair, *all is confusion*: the mind is puzzled: we, at last, hardly know *whom* or *what* the writer is talking about; and we fairly come to a stand.

172. In speaking of the many faults in this passage, I shall be obliged to make here observations which would come under the head of pronouns, verbs, adverbs, and prepositions. The first two

of the three sentences are, in themselves, rather obscure, and are well enough calculated for ushering in the complete confusion that follows. The *he* which comes immediately after the word *because* may relate to Demosthenes; but to what noun does the second *he* relate? It would, when we first look at it, seem to relate to the same noun as the first *he* relates to; for, the Doctor cannot call *Aristotle's Treatise of Rhetoric* a *he*. No: in speaking of this the Doctor says, '*wherein;*' that is to say, *in which*. He *means*, I dare say, that the *he* should stand for *Aristotle*; but it does not stand for Aristotle. This noun is not a *nominative* in the sentence; and it cannot have the pronoun relating to it as such. This *he* may relate to *Cicero*, who may be supposed to have laid open a mystery in the perusing of the treatise; and the words which follow the *he* would seem to give countenance to this supposition; for, *what* mystery is meant by the words '*that* mystery?' Is it the mystery of *Rhetoric*, or the mystery *of the manners and passions of men*? This is not all, however; for the Doctor, as if bewitched by the love of confusion, must tack on another long member to the sentence, and bring forward another *he* to stand for P. *Rapin*, whom and whose argument we have, amidst the general confusion, wholly forgotten. There is an error also in the use of the active participle, *perusing*. 'Demosthenes could not have so complete an insight as Cicero, because he *had not* the advantage *of perusing*.' That is to say, the advantage of being engaged *in perusing*. But this is not what is meant. The Doctor means, that he *had not had* the advantage *of perusing*; or, rather, that he *had not* the advantage *of having perused*. In other words, that Demosthenes could not have, or possess, a certain kind of knowledge, at the time when he made his orations, because, at that time, he had not, or did not possess, the advantage of *having perused*, or having *finished to peruse*, the treatise of Aristotle. Towards the close of the last sentence the adverb, '*at least,*' is put in a wrong place. The Doctor means, doubtless, that the adverb should apply to *considerable*, and not to *spoken*; but, from its being wrong placed, it applies to the latter, and not to the former. He means to say, that Demosthenes had spoken the most considerable, *at least*, of his orations; but, as the words now stand, they mean, that he had *done the speaking part to them*, if he had done nothing more. There is an error in the use of the word '*insight*,' followed, as it is, by '*into*.' We may have a *look*, or *sight*, *into* a house; but not an *insight*. This would be to take an *inside view of an inside*.

173. We have, here, a pretty good proof, that a knowledge of the Greek and Latin is not sufficient to prevent men from writing bad English. Here is a *profound scholar*, a teacher of rhetoric, discussing the comparative merits of Greek and Latin writers, and disputing with a French critic: here he is, writing English in a manner more incorrect than you will, I hope, be liable to write it at the end of your reading of this little book. Lest it should be supposed, that I have taken great pains to hunt out this erroneous passage of Doctor Blair, I will inform you, that I have hardly looked into his book. Your brothers, in reading it through, marked a great number of erroneous passages, from amongst which I have selected the passage just cited. With what propriety, then, are the Greek and Latin languages called the '*learned* languages?'

18

WILLIAM HAZLITT

(1778–1830)

Hazlitt's essay attacks writers and teachers of his time for failing to adjust their views to advances in philology, but much of what he criticizes is still a common-place of textbooks. He rejects the analogy of Greek and Latin grammar as irrelevant to the description of English, and illustrates the shortcomings of defining parts of speech by meaning. Instead he outlines a system of definition by inflection, and—somewhat less accurately—by etymology. He concludes by regretting that Horne Tooke (like Hobbes and Locke) described language largely in terms of 'names'.

'English Grammar'

(*The Atlas*, 15 March 1829)

This is one of those subjects on which the human understanding has played the fool, almost as egregiously, though with less dire consequences, than on many others; or rather one on which it has not chosen to exert itself at all, being hoodwinked and led blind-fold by mere precedent and authority. Scholars who have made and taught from English grammars were previously and syste-matically initiated in the Greek and Latin tongues, so that they have, without deigning to notice the difference, taken the rules of the latter and applied them indiscriminately and dogmatically to the former. As well might they pretend that there is a *dual number* in the Latin language because there is one in the Greek.

The *Definitions* alone are able to corrupt a whole generation of ingenuous youth. They seem calculated for no other purpose than to *mystify* and *stultify* the understanding, and to inoculate it betimes with a due portion of credulity and verbal sophistry. After repeating them by rote, to maintain that two and two make five is easy, and a thing of course. What appears most extraordinary is, that notwithstanding the complete exposure of their fallacy and nonsense by HORNE TOOKE and others, the same system and method of instruction should be persisted in; and that grammar succeeds grammar and edition edition, re-echoing the same point-blank contradictions and shallow terms. Establishments and endowments of learning (which subsist on a 'foregone conclusion') may have something to do with it; independently of which, and for each person's individual solace, the more senseless the absurdity and the longer kept up, the more reluctant does the mind seem to part with it, whether in the greatest things or mere trifles and technicalities; for in the latter, as the retracting an error could produce no startling sensation, and be accompanied with no redeeming enthusiasm, its detection must be a pure loss and pitiful mortification. One might suppose, that out of so many persons to have their attention directed to this subject, some few would find out their mistake and protest against the common practice; but the greater the number of professional labourers in the vineyard, who seek not truth but a livelihood, and can *pay with words* more currently than with things, the less chance must there be of this, since the majority will always set their faces against it, and insist upon the old *Mumpsimus* in preference to the new *Sumpsimus*. A schoolmaster who should go so far out of his way as to take the DIVERSIONS OF PURLEY for a text-book, would be regarded by his brethren of the rod as 'a man of Ind,' and would soon have the dogs of the village bark at him. It is said without blushing, by both masters and ushers who do not chuse to be 'wise above what is written,' that a noun is the name of a *thing*, *i. e.* substance, as if *love*, *honour*, *colour*, were the names of substances. An adjective is defined to be the name of a quality; and yet in the expressions, a *gold* snuff-box, a *wooden* spoon, an *iron* chest, &c., the words *gold*, *wooden*, *iron*, are allowed by all these profound writers, grammarians, and logicians, to be essentially adjectives. A verb is likewise defined to be a word denoting *being*, *action*, or *suffering*; and yet the words *being*, *action*, *suffering* (or passion), are all substantives; so that these words cannot be supposed to have any reference to the things whose names they bear, if it be the peculiar and sole office of the verb to denote them. If a system were made in burlesque and purposely to call into question and expose its own nakedness, it could not go beyond this, which is gravely taught in all seminaries, and patiently learnt by all school-boys as an exercise and discipline of the intellectual faculties. Again, it is roundly asserted that there are *six cases* (why not seven?) in the English language; and a case is defined to be a peculiar termination or inflection added to a noun to show its position in the sentence. Now in the Latin language there are no doubt a number of cases, inasmuch as there are a number of inflections;[1] and for the same reason (if words have a meaning) in the English language there are none, or only one, the genitive; because if we except this, there is no inflection or variety whatever in the terminations. Thus to instance in the present noun—A case, Of a case, To a case, A case, O case, From a case—they tell you that the word *case* is here its own nominative, genitive, dative, accusative, vocative, and ablative, though the deuce of any case—that is, inflection of the noun—is there in the case. Nevertheless, many a pedagogue would swear till he was black in the face that it is so; and would lie awake many a restless night boiling with rage and vexation that any one should be so lost to shame and reason as to suspect that there is here also a distinction without a difference. In strictness, in the Latin word there are only four, *casus, casui, casum, casu*; and the rest are conceded out of uniformity with other cases where the terminations are six times varied:[2] but why insist on the full complement, where there is no case in the whole language (but for the arbitrary one already excepted) to bear it out? Again, it is agreed on all hands, that English nouns have genders. Except with a few, where the termination is borrowed from another language, such as *Empress*, &c., there is no possibility of generally telling the sex implied from the form of the termination: but men looking

[1] This was necessary in Latin, where no order was observed in the words of a sentence: in English the juxtaposition generally determines the connection.

[2] *Quere*, Is the vocative ever a case?

at the point with their Latin eyes, see genders wherever they have been accustomed to find them in a foreign tongue. The difference of sex is vernacularly conveyed in English by a different word— *man, woman, stag, deer, king, queen*, &c.; and there is no such thing as conventional gender in neutral things—*house, church, field*, and so on. All this might be excusable as a prejudice or oversight; but then why persist in it in the thirty-eighth edition of a standard book published by the great firm[1] in Paternoster-row? We sometimes think mankind have a propensity to lying not more in matters-of-fact than theory. They maintain what they know to be without a shadow of foundation, and in the sheer spirit of contradiction, or because they hate to be convinced. In the same manner as the cases and genders of nouns, the whole ramification of the verb is constructed, and hung up for the admiration of the credulous upon the ideal model of the Latin and Greek verb, with all its tenses, persons, moods, and participles, whether there be anything more than a mere skeleton of a resemblance to suspend all this learned patch-work upon or not. 'I *love*, thou *lovest*, he *loves*; we, ye, they *love*.' There is a difference in the three first, so that from announcing the verb, you know the prefix: but in the three last, what difference is there, what sign of separation from one another, or from the first person singular? 'I *loved*,' is the past tense doubtless: it is a difference of inflection denoting time: but 'I *did* love, I *have loved*, I *will, can, shall, would* love,' are not properly tenses or moods of the verb *love*, but other verbs with the infinitive or participle of the first verb appended to them. Thus is our irregular verb professionally licked into regularity and shape. When the thing is wanting, it is supplied by the name. *Empedocles was a cobbler, even when he did not cobble.* A conjunction is held to be a part of speech without any meaning in itself, but that serves to connect sentences together, such as *that, and*, &c. It is proved by Mr. HORNE TOOKE, that the conjunction *that* is no other than the pronoun *that* (with the words *thing* or *proposition*

---

[1] [*the great firm* Longman's; the book was Lindley Murray's *English Grammar*, first published in 1795.]

understood)—as *and* is the imperative of the old Saxon verb, *anandad* (to add), upon a similar principle—'I say this *and* (or add) that'—and though it is above fifty years since this luminous discovery was published to the world, no hint of it has crept into any Grammar used in schools, and by authority. It seems to be taken for granted that all sound and useful knowledge is by rote, and that if it ceased to be so, the Church and State might crumble to pieces like the conjunctions *and* and *that*. There may be some truth in that.

It is strange that Mr. HORNE TOOKE, with all his logical and etymological acuteness, should have been so bad a metaphysician as to argue that all language was merely a disjointed tissue of names of objects (with certain abbreviations), and that he should have given or attempted no definition of the verb. He barely hints at it in one place, *viz.*—that the verb is *quod loquimur*, the noun *de quo*;[1] that is, the noun expresses the name of any thing or points out the object; the verb signifies the opinion or will of the speaker concerning it. What then becomes of the *infinitive mood*, which neither affirms, denies, nor commands any thing, but is left like a log of wood in the high road of grammar, to be picked up by the first jaunting-car of 'winged words' that comes that way with its moods, persons, and tenses, flying, and turned to any use that may be wanted? Mr. TOOKE was in the habit of putting off his guests at Wimbledon with promising to explain some *puzzle* the following Sunday; and he left the world in the dark as to the definition of the verb, much in the same spirit of *badinage* and mystery. We do not know when the deficiency is likely to be supplied, unless it has been done by Mr. FEARN in his little work called ANTI-TOOKE. We have not seen the publication, but we know the author to be a most able and ingenious man, and capable of lighting upon nice distinctions which few but himself would ever dream of. An excess of modesty, which doubts every thing, is much more favourable to the discovery of truth than that spirit of dogmatism which presumptuously takes every thing for granted;

[1] [*quod...quo* what we speak...of what.]

but at the same time it is not equally qualified to place its conclusions in the most advantageous and imposing light; and we accordingly too often find our quacks and impostors collecting a crowd with their drums, trumpets, and *placards* of themselves at the end of a street, while the 'still, small' pipe of truth and simplicity is drowned in the loud din and bray, or forced to retire to a distance to solace itself with its own low tones and fine-drawn distinctions. Having touched upon this subject, we may be allowed to add that some of our most eminent modern writers, as, for instance, Mr. MACULLOCH with his *Principles of Political Economy*, and Mr. MILL with his *Elements of Political Economy*, remind us of two barrel-organ grinders in the same street, playing the same tune and contending for precedence and mastery. What is MOZART to any of the four?

19

RALPH WALDO EMERSON
(1803–1882)

Emerson was a transcendentalist, believing that 'the world is emblematic'. He begins by agreeing with Hobbes and Locke that words are signs of things, but goes on to suggest that things themselves are signs. Consequently all language, dependent on a symbolic nature, is naturally symbolic, and most symbolic when most natural. Corrupt men speak corrupt language, devoid of images, full of words standing for nonentities. Good speech is picturesque, the best is allegorical; all parts of speech are metaphors, for the world they refer to is a metaphor. Proverbs represent a high employment of language: in them a natural fact illustrates a general truth.

'Language'

(Chapter IV from *Nature*, 1836)

A third use which Nature subserves to man is that of Language. Nature is the vehicle of thought, and in a simple, double, and threefold degree.

1. Words are signs of natural facts.
2. Particular natural facts are symbols of particular spiritual facts.
3. Nature is the symbol of spirit.

1. Words are signs of natural facts. The use of natural history is to give us aid in supernatural history. The use of the outer creation is to give us language for the beings and changes of the inward creation. Every word which is used to express a moral or intellectual fact, if traced to its root, is found to be borrowed from some material appearance. *Right* originally means *straight*; *wrong* means *twisted*. *Spirit* primarily means *wind*; *transgression*, the crossing of a *line*; *supercilious*, the *raising of the eye-brow*. We say the *heart* to express emotion, the *head* to denote thought; and *thought* and *emotion* are, in their turn, words borrowed from

sensible things, and now appropriated to spiritual nature. Most of the process by which this transformation is made, is hidden from us in the remote time when language was framed; but the same tendency may be daily observed in children. Children and savages use only nouns or names of things, which they continually convert into verbs, and apply to analogous mental acts.

2. But this origin of all words that convey a spiritual import,— so conspicuous a fact in the history of language,—is our least debt to nature. It is not words only that are emblematic; it is things which are emblematic. Every natural fact is a symbol of some spiritual fact. Every appearance in nature corresponds to some state of the mind, and that state of the mind can only be described by presenting that natural appearance as its picture. An enraged man is a lion, a cunning man is a fox, a firm man is a rock, a learned man is a torch. A lamb is innocence; a snake is subtle spite; flowers express to us the delicate affections. Light and darkness are our familiar expression for knowledge and ignorance; and heat for love. Visible distance behind and before us, is respectively our image of memory and hope.

Who looks upon a river in a meditative hour, and is not reminded of the flux of all things? Throw a stone into the stream, and the circles that propagate themselves are the beautiful type of all influence. Man is conscious of a universal soul within or behind his individual life, wherein, as in a firmament, the natures of Justice, Truth, Love, Freedom, arise and shine. This universal soul, he calls Reason: it is not mine or thine or his, but we are its; we are its property and men. And the blue sky in which the private earth is buried, the sky with its eternal calm, and full of everlasting orbs, is the type of Reason. That which, intellectually considered, we call Reason, considered in relation to nature, we call Spirit. Spirit is the Creator. Spirit hath life in itself. And man in all ages and countries, embodies it in his language, as the FATHER.

It is easily seen that there is nothing lucky or capricious in these analogies, but that they are constant, and pervade nature. These are not the dreams of a few poets, here and there, but man is an analogist, and studies relations in all objects. He is placed in the centre of beings, and a ray of relation passes from every other being to him. And neither can man be understood without these objects, nor these objects without man. All the facts in natural history taken by themselves, have no value, but are barren like a single sex. But marry it to human history, and it is full of life. Whole Floras, all Linnæus' and Buffon's volumes, are but dry catalogues of facts; but the most trivial of these facts, the habit of a plant, the organs, or work, or noise of an insect, applied to the illustration of a fact in intellectual philosophy, or, in any way associated to human nature, affects us in the most lively and agreeable manner. The seed of a plant,—to what affecting analogies in the nature of man, is that little fruit made use of, in all discourse, up to the voice of Paul, who calls the human corpse a seed,—'It is sown a natural body; it is raised a spiritual body.' The motion of the earth round its axis, and round the sun, makes the day, and the year. These are certain amounts of brute light and heat. But is there no intent of an analogy between man's life and the seasons? And do the seasons gain no grandeur or pathos from that analogy? The instincts of the ant are very unimportant considered as the ant's; but the moment a ray of relation is seen to extend from it to man, and the little drudge is seen to be a monitor, a little body with a mighty heart, then all its habits, even that said to be recently observed, that it never sleeps, become sublime.

Because of this radical correspondence between visible things and human thoughts, savages, who have only what is necessary, converse in figures. As we go back in history, language becomes more picturesque, until its infancy, when it is all poetry; or, all spiritual facts are represented by natural symbols. The same symbols are found to make the original elements of all languages. It has moreover been observed, that the idioms of all languages approach each other in passages of the greatest eloquence and power. And as this is the first language, so is it the last. This immediate dependence of language upon nature, this conversion of an outward phenomenon into a type of somewhat in human life, never loses its power to affect us. It is this which gives that piquancy to the conversation of a strong-natured farmer or backwoodsman, which all men relish.

Thus is nature an interpreter, by whose means man converses with his fellow men. A man's power to connect his thought with its proper symbol, and so utter it, depends on the simplicity of his character, that is, upon his love of truth and his desire to communicate it without loss. The corruption of man is followed by the corruption of language. When simplicity of character and the sovereignty of ideas is broken up by the prevalence of secondary desires, the desire of riches, the desire of pleasure, the desire of power, the desire of praise,—and duplicity and falsehood take place of simplicity and truth, the power over nature as an interpreter of the will, is in a degree lost; new imagery ceases to be created, and old words are perverted to stand for things which are not; a paper currency is employed when there is no bullion in the vaults. In due time, the fraud is manifest, and words lose all power to stimulate the understanding or the affections. Hundreds of writers may be found in every long-civilized nation, who for a short time believe, and make others believe, that they see and utter truths, who do not of themselves clothe one thought in its natural garment, but who feed unconsciously upon the language created by the primary writers of the country, those, namely, who hold primarily on nature.

But wise men pierce this rotten diction and fasten words again to visible things; so that picturesque language is at once a commanding certificate that he who employs it, is a man in alliance with truth and God. The moment our discourse rises above the ground line of familiar facts, and is inflamed with passion or exalted by thought, it clothes itself in images. A man conversing in earnest, if he watch his intellectual processes, will find that always a material image, more or less luminous, arises in his mind, cotemporaneous with every thought, which furnishes the vestment of the thought. Hence, good writing and brilliant discourse are perpetual allegories. This imagery is spontaneous. It is the blending of experience with the present action of the mind. It is proper creation. It is the working of the Original Cause through the instruments he has already made.

These facts may suggest the advantage which the country-life possesses for a powerful mind, over the artificial and curtailed life of cities. We know more from nature than we can at will communicate. Its light flows into the mind evermore, and we forget its presence. The poet, the orator, bred in the woods, whose senses have been nourished by their fair and appeasing changes, year after year, without design and without heed,—shall not lose their lesson altogether, in the roar of cities or the broil of politics. Long hereafter, amidst agitation and terror in national councils,—in the hour of revolution,—these solemn images shall reappear in their morning lustre, as fit symbols and words of the thoughts which the passing events shall awaken. At the call of a noble sentiment, again the woods wave, the pines murmur, the river rolls and shines, and the cattle low upon the mountains, as he saw and heard them in his infancy. And with these forms, the spells of persuasion, the keys of power are put into his hands.

3. We are thus assisted by natural objects in the expression of particular meanings. But how great a language to convey such pepper-corn informations! Did it need such noble races of creatures, this profusion of forms, this host of orbs in heaven, to furnish man with the dictionary and grammar of his municipal speech? Whilst we use this grand cipher to expedite the affairs of our pot and kettle, we feel that we have not yet put it to its use, neither are able. We are like travellers using the cinders of a volcano to roast their eggs. Whilst we see that it always stands ready to clothe what we would say, we cannot avoid the question, whether the characters are not significant of themselves. Have mountains, and waves, and skies, no significance but what we consciously give them, when we employ them as emblems of our thoughts? The world is emblematic. Parts of speech are metaphors because the whole of nature is a metaphor of the human mind. The laws of moral nature answer to those of matter as face to face in a glass. 'The visible

world and the relation of its parts, is the dial plate of the invisible.' The axioms of physics translate the laws of ethics. Thus, 'the whole is greater than its part;' 'reaction is equal to action;' 'the smallest weight may be made to lift the greatest, the difference of weight being compensated by time;' and many the like propositions, which have an ethical as well as physical sense. These propositions have a much more extensive and universal sense when applied to human life, than when confined to technical use.

In like manner, the memorable words of history, and the proverbs of nations, consist usually of a natural fact, selected as a picture or parable of a moral truth. Thus; A rolling stone gathers no moss; A bird in the hand is worth two in the bush; A cripple in the right way, will beat a racer in the wrong; Make hay whilst the sun shines; 'T is hard to carry a full cup even; Vinegar is the son of wine; The last ounce broke the camel's back; Long-lived trees make roots first;—and the like. In their primary sense these are trivial facts, but we repeat them for the value of their analogical import. What is true of proverbs, is true of all fables, parables, and allegories.

This relation between the mind and matter is not fancied by some poet, but stands in the will of God, and so is free to be known by all men. It appears to men, or it does not appear. When in fortunate hours we ponder this miracle, the wise man doubts, if, at all other times, he is not blind and deaf;

> —— 'Can these things be,
> And overcome us like a summer's cloud,
> Without our special wonder?'

for the universe becomes transparent, and the light of higher laws than its own, shines through it. It is the standing problem which has exercised the wonder and the study of every fine genius since the world began; from the era of the Egyptians and the Brahmins, to that of Pythagoras, of Plato, of Bacon, of Leibnitz, of Swedenborg. There sits the Sphinx at the road-side, and from age to age, as each prophet comes by, he tries his fortune at reading her riddle.

There seems to be a necessity in spirit to manifest itself in material forms; and day and night, river and storm, beast and bird, acid and alkali, preexist in necessary Ideas in the mind of God, and are what they are by virtue of preceding affections, in the world of spirit. A Fact is the end or last issue of spirit. The visible creation is the terminus or the circumference of the invisible world. 'Material objects,' said a French philosopher, 'are necessarily kinds of *scoriæ* of the substantial thoughts of the Creator, which must always preserve an exact relation to their first origin; in other words, visible nature must have a spiritual and moral side.'

This doctrine is abstruse, and though the images of 'garment,' 'scoriæ,' 'mirror,' &c., may stimulate the fancy, we must summon the aid of subtler and more vital expositors to make it plain. 'Every scripture is to be interpreted by the same spirit which gave it forth,' —is the fundamental law of criticism. A life in harmony with nature, the love of truth and of virtue, will purge the eyes to understand her text. By degrees we may come to know the primitive sense of the permanent objects of nature, so that the world shall be to us an open book, and every form significant of its hidden life and final cause.

A new interest surprises us, whilst, under the view now suggested, we contemplate the fearful extent and multitude of objects; since 'every object rightly seen, unlocks a new faculty of the soul.' That which was unconscious truth, becomes, when interpreted and defined in an object, a part of the domain of knowledge,— a new amount to the magazine of power.

20

THOMAS DE QUINCEY

(1785–1859)

De Quincey considers whether any field of human inquiry has not been studied, whether well, as Greek drama, or poorly, as history, and finds that only the English and French languages have been overlooked by scholars who speak them. There is no history of the English language, but the Anglo-Saxon alone is worthy of much further study, both in itself and in its survival in later English. He illustrates the shortcomings of the studies up to his own day. He finds the lack offensive to his patriotism, because it hides the special merits of English. By comparison with other languages, its adequacy for literary purposes is a matter for confidence.

'The English Language'

(*Blackwood's*, April 1839)

French and English literature, which have now been in a high state of activity for two entire centuries, and perhaps as nearly as possible have been subject to the same allowance for lulls arising out of civil agitations, cannot reasonably be supposed to have left any nook or shy recess in the broad field of national interest at this day unvisited. Long after the main highway of waters has felt the full power of the tide, channels running far inland, with thousands of little collateral creeks, may be still under the very process of filling; for two powers are required to those final effects of the tide; the general hydrostatic power for maintaining the equilibrium, and also hydraulic power for searching narrow conduits. On the same analogy many human interests, less obvious or less general, may long linger unnoticed, and survive for a time the widest expansion of intellectual activity. Possibly the aspects of society must shift materially before even the human consciousness, far less a human interest of curiosity, settles upon them with steadiness enough to light up and vivify their relations. For example, odd as it may seem to us, it is certain—that in the Elizabethan age, Political Economy was not yet viewed by any mind, no, not by Lord Bacon's, as even a *possible* mode of speculation. The whole accidents of value and its functions were not as yet separated into a distinct conscious object; nor, if they had been, would it have been supposed possible to trace laws and fixed relations amongst forms apparently so impalpable, and combinations so fleeting. With the growth of society, gradually the same phenomena revolved more and more frequently; something like order and connexion was dimly descried; philosophic suspicion began to stir; observation was steadily applied; reasoning and disputation ran their circle; and at last a science was matured— definite as mechanics, though (like *that*) narrow in its elementary laws.

Thus it is with *all* topics of general interest. Through several generations they may escape notice; for there must be an interest of social necessity visibly connected with them, before a mere vagrant curiosity will attract culture to their laws. And this interest may fail to arise until society has been made to move through various changes, and human needs have assumed attitudes too commanding and too permanent to be neglected. The laws of the drama, that is, of the dramatic fable, how subtle are they! How imperceptible—how absolutely non-existences—in any rude state of society! But let a national theatre arise, let the mighty artist come forward to shake men's hearts with scenic agitations, how inevitably are these laws brightened to the apprehension, searched, probed, analysed. *Sint Mæcenates*, it has been said, *non deerunt (Flacce) Marones.*[1] That may be doubted; and nearer to the probabilities it would be to invert the order of succession. But, however this may be, it is certain from manifold experience, that invariably there will follow on the very traces and fresh footing of the mighty agent (mighty, but possibly

---

[1] [*Sint...Marones* Let there be patrons of literature, Flaccus, and there will be no lack of Virgils (Martial, *Epig.* VIII. 56. 5).]

blind)—the sagacious theorist of his functions—in the very wake and visible path of the awful Æschylus, or the tear-compelling Euripides, producing their colossal effects in alliance with dark forces slumbering in human nature, will step forth the torch-bearing Aristotle, that pure starry intelligence,[1] bent upon searching into those effects, and measuring (when possible) those forces. The same age accordingly beheld the first pompous exhibitions of dramatic power, which beheld also the great speculator arise to trace its limits, proportions, and the parts of its shadowy empire. 'I came, I saw, I conquered'—such might have been Aristotle's vaunt in reviewing his own analysis of the Athenian drama; one generation or nearly so, having witnessed the creation of the Grecian theatre as a fact, and the finest contemplative survey which has yet been taken of the same fact viewed as a problem; of the dramatic laws, functions, powers, and limits.

No great number of generations, therefore, is requisite for the exhaustion of all capital interests in their capital aspects. And it may be presumed, with tolerable certainty, that by this time the plough has turned up every angle of soil, properly national, alike in England or in France. Not that many parts will not need to be tilled over again, and often absolutely *de novo*.[2] Much of what has been done, has been done so ill, that it is as if it had not been done at all. For instance, the history of neither kingdom has yet been written in a way to last, or in a way worthy of the subject. Either it has been slightly written as to research, witness Hume and Mézérai, Smollet and Père Daniel (not but some of these writers lay claim to antiquarian merits); or written inartificially and feebly as regards effect; or written without knowledge as regards the political forces which moved underground at the great æras of our national developement.

Still, after one fashion or another, almost every great theme has received its treatment in both English literature and French; though

---

[1] *That pure starry intelligence.* Aristotle was sometimes called ὁ νοῦς, *the intellect*; and elsewhere, as Suidas records, he was said to dip his pen into the very intellect and its fountains.

[2] [*de novo* from the beginning.]

many are those on which, in the words of the German adage upon psychology, we may truly affirm that 'the first sensible word is yet to be spoken.' The soil is not absolutely a virgin soil; the mine is not absolutely unworked; although the main body of the precious ore is yet to be extracted.

Mean-time, one capital subject there is, and a domestic subject besides, on which, strange to say, neither nation has thought fit to raise any monument of learning and patriotism. Rich, at several eras, in all kinds of learning, neither England nor France has any great work to show upon her own vernacular language. *Res est in integro*:[1] no Hickes in England, no Malesherbes or Menage in France, has chosen to connect his own glory with the investigation and history of his native tongue. And yet each language has brilliant merits of a very different order; and we speak thoughtfully when we say, that, confining ourselves to our own, the most learned work which the circumstances of any known or obvious case allow, the work which presupposes the amplest accomplishments of judgment and enormous erudition, would be a History of the English Language from its earliest rudiments, through all the periods of its growth, to its stationary condition. Great rivers, as they advance and receive vast tributary influxes, change their direction, their character, their very name; and the pompous inland sea bearing navies on its bosom, has had leisure through a thousand leagues of meandering utterly to forget and disown the rocky mountain bed and the violent rapids which made its infant state unfitted to bear even the light canoe. The analogy is striking between this case and that of the English language. In its elementary period, it takes a different name—the name of Anglo-Saxon; and so rude was it and barren at one stage of this rudimental form, that in the *Saxon Chronicle* we find not more than a few hundred words, perhaps from six to eight hundred words, perpetually revolving, and most of which express some idea in close relation to the state of war. The narrow purposes of the *Chronicler* may, in part, it is true, have determined the narrow choice of words; but

---

[1] [*Res est in integro* The matter has not been looked into.]

it is certain, on the other hand, that the scanty vocabulary which then existed, mainly determined the limited range of his purposes. It is remarkable, also, that the idiomatic forms and phrases are as scanty in this ancient *Chronicle*, as the ideas, the images, and the logical forms of connexion or transition. Such is the shallow brook or rivulet of our language in its infant stage. Thence it devolves a stream continually enlarging, down to the Norman æra; through five centuries (commencing with the century of Bede), used as the vernacular idiom for the intercourse of life by a nation expanding gradually under the ripening influence of a pure religion and a wise jurisprudence; benefiting, besides, by the culture it received from a large succession of learned ecclesiastics, who too often adopted the Latin for the vehicle of their literary commerce with the Continent, but also in cases past all numbering[1] wrote (like the great patriot Alfred) for popular purposes in Saxon,—even this rude dialect grew and widened its foundations, until it became adequate to general intellectual purposes. Still, even in this improved state, it would have been found incommensurate to its great destiny. It could not have been an organ corresponding to the grandeur of those intellects, which, in the fulness of time, were to communicate with mankind in oracles of truth or of power. It could not have offered moulds ample enough for receiving that vast literature, which, in less than another five hundred years, was beginning to well forth from the national genius.

Hence, at the very first entrance upon this interesting theme, we stumble upon what we may now understand to have been the blindest of human follies—the peculiar, and, without exaggeration, we may say the providential felicity of the English language has been made its capital reproach—that, whilst yet ductile and capable of new impressions, it received a fresh and large infusion of alien wealth. It is, say the imbecile, a 'bastard' language—a

---

[1] *In cases past all numbering.* To go no further than the one branch of religious literature, vast masses of sacred poetry in the Saxon language are yet slumbering unused, unstudied, almost unknown to the student, amongst our manuscript treasures.

'hybrid' language, and so forth. And thus, for a metaphor, for a name, for a sound, they overlook, as far as depends on *their* will, they sign away the main prerogative and dowry of their mother tongue. It is time to have done with these follies. Let us open our eyes to our own advantages. Let us recognise with thankfulness that fortunate inheritance of collateral wealth, which, by inoculating our Anglo-Saxon stem with the mixed dialect of Neustria, laid open an avenue mediately through which the whole opulence of Roman, and, ultimately, of Grecian thought, play freely through the pulses of our native English. Most fortunately the Saxon language was yet plastic and unfrozen at the era of the Norman invasion. The language was thrown again into the crucible, and new elements were intermingled with its own when brought into a state of fusion.[1] And this final process it was, making the language at once rich in matter and malleable in form, which created that composite and multiform speech—fitted, like a mirror, to reflect the thoughts of the myriad-minded Shakspeare [ὁ ἀνὴρ μυριόνους],[2] and yet at the same time with enough remaining of its old forest stamina for imparting a masculine depth to the sublimities of Milton, or the Hebrew prophets, and a patriarchal simplicity to the Historic Scriptures.

Such being the value, such the slow developement of our noble language, through a period of more than twice six hundred years, how strange it must be thought, that not only we possess at this day no history, no circumstantial annals, of its growth and condition at different eras, a defect which even the German literature of our language has partially supplied; but that, with one solitary exception, no eminent scholar has applied himself even to a single function of this elaborate service. The solitary exception, we need scarcely say, points to Dr Johnson—whose merits and whose de-

[1] *When brought into a state of fusion.* Let not the reader look upon this image, when applied to an unsettled language, as pure fanciful metaphor: were there nothing more due to a superinduction of one language upon another, merely the confusion of inflexional forms between the two orders of declensions, conjugations, &c., would tend to recast a language, and virtually to throw it anew into a furnace of secondary formation, by unsettling the old familiar forms.

[2] [ὁ...μυριόνους the manifold man.]

merits, whose qualifications and disqualifications, for a task of this nature, are now too notorious to require any illustration from us. The slenderness of Dr Johnson's philological attainments, and his blank ignorance of that particular philology which the case particularly required—the philology of the northern languages, are as much matters of record, and as undeniable as, in the opposite scale, are his logical skill, his curious felicity of distinction, and his masculine vigour of definition. Working under, or over, a commission of men more learned than himself, he would have been the ablest of agents for digesting and organising their materials. To *inform*, or invest with *form*, in the sense of logicians—in other words, to impress the sense and trace the presence of principles—that was Dr Johnson's peculiar province; but to assign the *matter*, whether that consisted in originating the elements of thought, or in gathering the affinities of languages, was suited neither to his nature nor to his habits of study. And, of necessity, therefore, his famous dictionary is a monument of powers unequally yoked together in one task—skill in one function of his duty 'full ten times as much as there needs;' skill in others—sometimes feeble, sometimes none at all.

Of inferior attempts to illustrate the language, we have Ben Jonson's Grammar, early in the seventeenth century; Wallis, the mathematician's, Grammar (written in Latin, and patriotically designed as a polemic grammar against the errors of foreigners), towards the end of the same century; Bishop Lowth's little School-Grammar in the eighteenth century; Archdeacon Nares's Orthoepy; Dr Crombie's Etymology and Syntax; Noah Webster's various essays on the same subject, followed by his elaborate Dictionary, all written and first published in America. We have also, and we mention it on account of its great but most unmerited popularity, the grammar of Lindley Murray—an American, by the way, as well as the eccentric Noah. This book, full of atrocious blunders (some of which, but with little systematic learning, were exposed in a work of the late Mr Hazlitt's), reigns despotically through the young ladies' schools, from the Orkneys to the

Cornish Scillys. And of the other critical grammars, such as the huge 4to of Green, the smaller one of Dr Priestley, many little abstracts prefixed to portable dictionaries, &c., there may be gathered, since the year 1680, from 250 to 300; not one of which is absolutely[1] without value—some raising new and curious questions, others showing their talent in solving old ones. Add to these the occasional notices of grammatical niceties in the critical editions of our old poets, and there we have the total amount of what has hitherto been contributed towards the investigation of our English language in its grammatical theory. As to the investigation of its history, of its gradual rise and progress, and its relations to neighbouring languages, *that* is a total blank; a title pointing to a duty absolutely in arrear, rather than to any performance ever undertaken as yet, even by way of tentative essay. At least, any fractional attempt in that direction is such as would barely form a single section, or sub-section, in a general history. For instance, we have critical essays of some value on the successive translations, into English, of the Bible. But these rather express, *in modulo parvo*,[2] the burden of laborious research which awaits such a task pursued comprehensively, than materially diminish it. Even the history of *Slang*, whether of domestic or foreign growth, and the record of the capricious influxes, at particular epochs, from the Spanish, the French,[3] &c., would

---

[1] So little is the absolute value and learning of such books to be measured by the critical pretensions of the class in which they rank themselves, or by the promises of their title-pages, that we remember to have seen some very acute remarks on pronunciation, on the value of letters, &c., in a little Edinburgh book of rudiments, meant only for children of four or five years old. It was called, we think, *The Child's Ladder*.

[2] [*in...parvo* in small measure.]

[3] By the way, it has long been customary (and partly in compliance with foreign criticism, unlearned in our elder literature, and quite incompetent to understand it), to style the period of Queen Anne, and the succeeding decade of years, our Augustan age. The graver errors of thought in such a doctrine are no present concern of ours. But, as respects the purity of our language, and its dignity, never did either suffer so long and gloomy an eclipse as in that period of our annals. The German language, as written at that time in books, is positively so disfigured by French and Latin embroideries—that it becomes difficult at times to say which language is meant for the ground, and which for the decoration. Our English is never so bad as that; but the ludicrous introduction of foreign forms, such, for example, as '*his Intimados*,' '*his Privados*,' goes far to denationalize the tone of the diction. Even the familiar allusions and abbreviations of that age, some of

furnish materials for a separate work. But we forbear to enter upon the long list of parts, chapters, and sections, which must compose the architectural system of so elaborate a work, seeing that the whole edifice itself is hitherto a great idea, *in nubibus*,[1] as regards our own language. The French, as we have observed, have little more to boast of. And, in fact, the Germans and the Italians, of all nations the two who most cordially hate and despise each other, in this point agree—that they only have constructed many preparatory works, have reared something more than mere scaffolding towards such a systematic and national monument.

1. It is painful and humiliating to an Englishman, that, whilst all other nations show their patriotism severally in connexion with their own separate mother tongues, claiming for them often merits which they have not, and overlooking none of those which they have, his own countrymen show themselves ever ready, with a dishonourable levity, to undervalue the English language, and always upon no fixed principles. Nothing to ourselves seems so remarkable—as that men should dogmatise upon the pretensions of this and that language in particular, without having any general notions previously of what it is that constitutes the value of a language universally. Without some preliminary notice, abstractedly, of the precise qualities to be sought for in a language, how are we to know whether the main object of our question is found, or not found, in any given language offered for examination? The Castilian is pronounced fine, the Italian effeminate, the English harsh, by many a man who has no shadow of a reason for his opinions beyond some vague association of chivalaresque qualities with the personal bearing of Spaniards; or, again, of special adaptation to operatic music in the Italian; or (as regards the English),

which became indispensable to the evasion of what was deemed pedantry, such as '*tis* and '*twas*, are rank with meanness. In Shakspeare's age the diction of books was far more pure, more compatible with simplicity, and more dignified. Amongst our many national blessings, never let us forget to be thankful that in that age was made our final translation of the Bible, under the State authority. How ignoble, how unscriptural, would have been a translation made in the age of Pope!

[1] [*in nubibus* in the clouds.]

because he has heard, perhaps, that the letter *s*, and crowded clusters of consonants and monosyllabic words prevail in it.

Such random and fantastic notions would be entitled to little attention; but, unfortunately, we find that men of distinguished genius—men who have contributed to sustain and extend the glory of this very English language, are sometimes amongst its notorious depreciators. Addison, in a well-known passage of his critical essays, calls the English, in competition with the Greek language, brick against marble. Now, that there is a vocal[1] beauty in the Greek, which raises it in that particular point above all modern languages, and not exclusively above the English, cannot be denied; but this is the lowest merit of a language—being merely its *sensuous* merit (to borrow a word of Milton's); and, beyond all doubt, as respects the higher or intellectual qualities of a language, the English greatly excels the Greek, and especially in that very case which provoked the remark of Addison; for it happens, that some leading ideas in the *Paradise Lost*—ideas essential to the very integrity of the fable, cannot be expressed in Greek; or not so expressed as to convey the same thought impregnated with the same weight of passion. But let not our reverence for the exquisite humour of Addison, and his admirable delicacy of pencil in delineating the traits of character, hide from us the fact that he was a very thoughtless and irreflective critic; that his criticisms, when just, rested not upon principles, but upon mere fineness of tact; that he was an absolute ignoramus as regarded the literature of his own country; and that he was a mere bigot as regarded the antique literature of Pagan Greece or Rome. In

[1] *A vocal beauty in the Greek language.* This arises partly from the musical effect of the mere inflexions of the verbs and participles, in which so many dactylic successions of accent are interchanged with spondaic arrangements, and partly also from the remarkable variety of the vowel sounds which run through the whole gamut of possible varieties in that point, and give more luxury of sound to the ear than in any other known language; for the fact is, that these varieties of vowel or diphthong sounds, succeed to each other more immediately and more constantly than in any other Southern dialect of Europe, which universally have a distinction in mere vocal or audible beauty, not approached by any Northern language, unless (as some people allege) by the Russian; and this, with the other dialects of the Sclavonian family, is to be classed as belonging to Eastern, rather than to Northern Europe.

fact, the eternal and inevitable schism between the *Romanticists* and the *Classicists*, though not in name, had already commenced in substance; and where Milton was not free from grievous error and consequent injustice, both to the writers of his country and to the language, how could it be expected that the far feebler mind of Addison, should work itself clear of a bigotry and a narrowness of sympathy as regards the antique, which the discipline and training of his whole life had established? Even the merit of Addison is not sufficient to waive his liability to one plain retort from an offended Englishman—viz. that, before he signed away with such flagrant levity the pretensions of his native language, at all events, it was incumbent upon him to show that he had fathomed the powers of that language, had exhausted its capacity, and had wielded it with commanding effect. Whereas, we all know that Addison was a master of the humble and unpretending English, demanded, or indeed suffered by his themes; but for that very reason little familiar with its higher or impassioned movements.

2. But Addison, like most other critics on languages, overlooked one great truth, which should have made such sweeping undervaluations impossible as applied to any language; this truth is—that every language, every language at least in a state of culture and developement, has its own separate and incommunicable qualities of superiority. The French itself, which, in some weighty respects, is amongst the poorest of languages, had yet its own peculiar merits—not attainable or approachable by any other. For the whole purposes of what the French understand by the word *causer*, for all the delicacies of social intercourse, and the *nuances* of manners, no language *but* the French possesses the requisite vocabulary. The word *causer* itself is an illustration. Marivaux and other novelists, tedious enough otherwise, are mere repertories of phrases untranslatable—irrepresentable by equivalents in any European language. And some of our own fashionable English novels, which have been fiercely arraigned for their French embroidery as well as for other supposed faults, are thus far justifiable—that,

in a majority of instances, the English could not have furnished a corresponding phrase with equal point or piquancy—sometimes not at all.

3. If even the French has its function of superiority, so, and in a higher sense, have the English and other languages more decidedly northern. But the English, in particular, has a special dowry of power in its double-headed origin. The Saxon part of the language fulfils one set of functions, the Latin another. Meantime, it is a great error on the part of Lord Brougham (and we remember the same error in others) to direct the student in his choice of words towards the Saxon part of the language by preference. Nothing can be more unphilosophic, or built on more thorough misconception of the case. Neither part of the language is good or bad absolutely, but in its relation to the subject, and according to the treatment which the subject is meant to receive. It is an error even to say that the Saxon part is more advantageously used for cases of passion. Even that requires further limitation. Simple narration, and a pathos resting upon artless circumstances, elementary feelings, homely and household affections,—these are most suitably managed by the old indigenous Saxon vocabulary. But a passion which rises into grandeur, which is complex, elaborate, and interveined with high meditative feelings, would languish or absolutely halt, without aid from the Latin moiety of our language. Mr Coleridge remarks—that the writings of all reflective or highly subjective poets, overflow with Latin and Greek polysyllables, or what the uneducated term 'dictionary words.'

4. Again, if there is no such thing in *rerum natura*[1] as a language radically and universally without specific powers; if every language, in short, is and must be, according to the circumstances under which it is moulded, an organ *sui generis*,[2] and fitted to sustain with effect some function or other of the human intellect,—so, on the other hand, the very advantages of a language, those which are most vaunted, become defects under opposite relations.

[1] [*rerum natura* the nature of things.]   [2] [*sui generis* of its own sort.]

The power of running easily into composition, for instance, on which the Germans show so much *fierté*, when stating the pretensions of their own mother tongue, is in itself injurious to the simplicity and natural power of their poetry, besides being a snare, in many cases, to the ordinary narrator or describer, and tempting him aside into efforts of display which mar the effect of his composition. In the early stages of every literature, not simplicity (as it is thought) but elaboration and complexity, and tumid artifice in the structure of the diction, are the besetting vices of the poet: witness the Roman fragments of poetry anterior to Ennius. Now the fusile capacity of a language for running into ready coalitions of polysyllables aids this tendency, and almost of itself creates such a tendency.

5. The process by which languages grow is worthy of deep attention. So profound is the error of some men on this subject, that they talk familiarly of language as of a thing deliberately and consciously 'invented' by the people who use it. A language never was invented[1] by any people; that part which is not borrowed from adjacent nations arises under instincts of necessity and convenience. We will illustrate the matter by mentioning three such modes of instinct in which has lain the parentage of at least three words out of four in every language. First, the instinct of abbreviation, prompted continually by hurry or by impatience. Secondly, the instinct of *onomatopœia*, or more generally, the instinct of imitation applied directly to sounds, indirectly to motion, and by the aid of analogies more or less obvious applied to

[1] Mean-time, a few insulated words have been continually nourished by authors; that is, transferred to other uses, or formed by thoughtful composition and decomposition, or by skilful alterations of form and inflexion. Thus Mr Coleridge introduced the fine word *ancestral*, in lieu of the lumbering word *ancestorial*, about the year 1798. Milton introduced the indispensable word *sensuous*. Daniel, the truly philosophic poet and historian, introduced the splendid *class* of words with the affix of *inter*, to denote reciprocation, *e. g. interpenetrate*, to express mutual or interchangeable penetration; a form of composition which is deeply beneficial to the language, and has been extensively adopted by Coleridge. We ourselves may boast to have introduced the word *orchestric*, which we regard with parental pride, as a word expressive of that artificial and pompous music which attends, for instance, the elaborate hexameter verse of Rome and Greece, in comparison with the simpler rhyme of the more exclusively accentual metres in modern languages; or expressive of any organised music, in opposition to the natural warbling of the woods.

many other classes of objects. Thirdly, the instinct of distinction—sometimes for purposes of necessity, sometimes of convenience. This process claims by far the largest application of words in every language. Thus, from *propriety* (or the abstract idea of annexation between two things by means of fitness or adaptation), was struck off by a more rapid pronunciation and a throwing back of the accent, the modern word, *property*, in which the same general idea is limited to appropriations of pecuniary value; which, however, was long expressed by the original word *propriety*, under a modified enunciation. So again, *major* as a military designation, and *mayor* as a civil one, have split off from the very same original word by varied pronunciations. And these divergencies into multiplied derivatives from some single radix, are, in fact, the great source of opulence to one language by preference to another. And it is clear that the difference in this respect between nation and nation will be in a compound ratio of the complexity and variety of situations into which men are thrown (whence the necessity of a complex condition of society to the growth of a truly fine language)—in the ratio, we say, of this complexity on the one hand; and, on the other, of the intellectual activity put forth to seize and apprehend these fleeting relations of things and persons. Whence, according to the vast inequalities of national minds, the vast disparity of languages.

6. Hence we see the monstrosity of claiming a fine or copious language, for any rude or uncultivated, much more for any savage people, or even for a people of mountaineers, or for a nation subsisting chiefly by hunting, or by agriculture and rural life exclusively, or in any way sequestered and monotonous in their habits. It is philosophically impossible that the Gaelic, or the Hebrew, or the Welsh, or the Manx, or the Armoric, could, at any stage, have been languages of compass or general poetic power. In relation to a few objects peculiar to their own climates, or habits, or superstitions, any of these languages may have been occasionally gifted with a peculiar power of expression; what language is *not* with regard to some class of objects? But a language

of power and compass cannot arise except amongst cities and the habits of luxurious people. 'They talked,' says John Paul, speaking of two rustic characters, in one of his sketches,—'they talked, as country people are apt to talk, concerning—nothing.' And the fact is, universally, that rural occupations and habits, unless counteracted determinately by intellectual pursuits, tend violently to torpor. Social gatherings, social activity, social pleasure—these are the parents of language. And there is but the one following exception to the rule—That such as is the activity of the national intellect in arresting fugitive relations, such will be the language resulting; and this exception lies in the *mechanical* advantages offered by some inflexions compared with others for generating and educing the possible modifications of each primitive idea. Some modes of inflexions easily lend themselves, by their very mechanism, to the adjuncts expressing degrees, expressing the relations of time, past, present, and future; expressing the modes of will, desire, intention, &c. For instance, the Italians have terminal forms, *ino*, *ello*, *acchio*, &c., expressing all gradations of size above or below the ordinary standard. The Romans, again, had frequentative forms, inceptive forms, forms expressing futurition and desire, &c. These short-hand expressions performed the office of natural symbols, or hieroglyphics, which custom had made universally intelligible. Now, in some cases this machinery is large, and therefore extensively auxiliary to the popular intellect in building up the towering pile of a language; in others it is meagre, and so far it is possible that, from want of concurrency in the mechanic aids, the language may, in some respects, not be strictly commensurate to the fineness of the national genius.

7. Another question, which arises upon all languages, respects their degrees of fitness for poetic and imaginative purposes. The mere question of fact is interesting; and the question as to the causal agency which has led to such a result is still more so. In this place we shall content ourselves with drawing the reader's attention to a general phenomenon which comes forward in all non-

poetic languages—viz. that the separation of the two great fields, prose and poetry, or of the mind, impassioned or unimpassioned, is never perfectly accomplished. This phenomenon is most striking in the Oriental languages, where the common edicts of government or provincial regulations of police assume a ridiculous masquerade dress of rhetorical or even of poetic animation. But amongst European languages this capital defect is most noticeable in the French, which has no resources for elevating its diction when applied to cases and situations the most lofty or the most affecting. The single misfortune of having no neuter gender, by compelling the mind to distribute the colouring of life universally; and by sexualising in all cases, neutralises the effect, as a special effect, for any case. To this one capital deformity, which presents itself in every line, many others have concurred. And it might be shown convincingly, that the very power of the French language, as a language for social intercourse, is built on its impotence for purposes of passion, grandeur, and native simplicity. The English, on the other hand, besides its double fountains of words, which furnishes at once two separate keys of feeling, and the ready means of obtaining distinct movements for the same general passion, enjoys the great advantage above southern languages of having a neuter gender, which, from the very first establishing a mode of shade, establishes, by a natural consequence, the means of creating light, and a more potent vitality.

STUDY QUESTIONS

1. WILLIAM CAXTON

1 Explain Caxton's punctuation, taking account of the full stop, colon, diagonal stroke, capital letters, and paragraph sign.

2 What do you find strange about Caxton's vocabulary (e.g. 'achieued' in the first line), and how do you explain it?

3 How would you express Caxton's first sentence in 'our englysshe now vsid'? Explain the points of difference between your version and his, and how you decided where his first sentence ended. Is your task like the one imposed on him by the abbot of Westminster?

4 How far have Caxton's interests as a translator and publisher influenced his linguistic viewpoint? Do his inflections and spellings succeed in being 'stedfaste'?

5 Do you know of linguistic problems today which parallel that of the man who asked for eggs? Are they matters of geography alone, or do they include class and professional differences?

6 Caxton admires French and Latin models. Can you find evidences of this admiration in his style?

7 Compare Skelton's language (if possible, in his *Phyllyp Sparowe*, lines 769–812) with Caxton's. Why would Caxton wish him to correct his book?

2. RICHARD MULCASTER

1 Compare Mulcaster's punctuation and spelling with Caxton's and Harrison's.

2 Mulcaster admitted his style was 'difficult'. How would you characterize it?

3 Read Richard Carew's 'The Excellencie of the English Tongue' (ed. G. G. Smith, *Elizabethan Critical Essays*, 1904, II, 285 ff.) and Sir John Cheke's letter to Thomas Hoby (ed. W. E. Henley, *Tudor Translations*, XXIII) and compare their ideas with Mulcaster's.

4 Find present-day examples of the conditions Mulcaster describes in the first sentence of his third paragraph. Would Webster's plan have satisfied him?

5 What does Mulcaster mean by 'art', 'custom', 'reason', 'matter' and 'artificial'?

6 How would you explain Mulcaster's four arguments? Has their relevance changed since he wrote?

7 'Wherefor I maie well conclude....' Examine Mulcaster's exposition as the development of an argument.

STUDY QUESTIONS

3. WILLIAM HARRISON

1 How helpful is Bodinus' third rule (paragraph 1) in discovering 'the originall of euerie kingdome and nation' today? Have political and demographic changes since the sixteenth century influenced the application of this rule?
2 What other 'relikes' of Anglo-Saxon can you add to Harrison's example –*here*? Study a few pages of a good etymological dictionary, and specify in what aspects of our language the Saxon inheritance seems richest.
3 Do Harrison's remarks about the 'hard and rough kind of speech...now changed with vs into a farre more fine' conflict with his later criticism of 'affectation of forren and strange words'?
4 Do his remarks on the linguistic nationalism of the Normans conflict with his later praise of the way 'in our time the Scottish language endeuoreth to come neere...our toong in finenesse of phrase'?
5 Do Harrison's observations on the linguistic virtuosity of those who speak English, and the difficulty foreigners have in learning our tongue, correspond with your own?
6 How do you explain Harrison's interest throughout this chapter in matters of nationality?

4. WILLIAM CAMDEN

1 Camden and Harrison cover some of the same ground. Draw up a comparative table of contents to show how their interests differ.
2 Contrast Camden's use of earlier texts with Sir Thomas Browne's.
3 Has Camden noted all the Latin-based words in the Wycliffite translation of the Lord's Prayer? How many more are there in the King James and later versions? Is this a good test-passage to choose for this purpose?
4 Check Camden's etymologies of Old and Modern English words. Does he overlook the difference between 'descended' and 'borrowed' words?
5 Compare Camden's four reasons for change in language with the reasons given by Swift and Dr Johnson.
6 Do Sir Thomas Smith's proposed rules for reformed spelling, as Camden reports them, give us any insight into the sounds of English in the late sixteenth century, and the problems of representing them in type?
7 Do Camden's four 'kinds' of English in the last paragraph correspond with the levels mentioned by Caxton, or with any of your own experience in literature, official documents, newspapers, etc.?

5. BEN JONSON

1 Compare Jonson's use of the monetary simile for language with Defoe's. How helpful is analogy for this kind of argument? List some of Jonson's other similes for language.

2 Discuss Jonson's idea of authority and use of authorities.

3 How does Jonson distinguish between the role of speech and the role of writing?

4 Is Jonson's prose true to his stylistic theory?

5 How do Jonson's literary preoccupations influence his linguistic opinions?

6 'The Instrument of *Society*.' How does Jonson apply this idea of language? Is it like Hobbes's, or Locke's?

7 Read Francis Bacon's *Novum Organum* (1620), I, 59–60, and *Advancement of Learning* (1605), I, iv, 1–4. How does Jonson use Bacon's ideas?

6. THOMAS HOBBES

1 How much does Hobbes depend on observation, and how much on tradition, in his account of speech?

2 Compare Hobbes's linguistic philosophy with Locke's and Emerson's. How does each treat pre-verbal cogitation, that is, thought without words?

3 Describe Hobbes's notion of the place of language in a theory of knowledge.

4 Hobbes is famous as a prose stylist. How would you characterize his style?

5 Do you find Hobbes's list of four uses and four abuses adequate?

6 How do Hobbes's 'foure generall heads' relate to parts of speech? Are they categories of form or of meaning?

7. JOHN DRYDEN

1 Dryden groups linguistic and dramatic faults together. Why, and with what result?

2 Do you agree with all Dryden's criticisms of Jonson? How might Jonson have defended himself?

3 How does Dryden view the conflicting claims of custom and rule in linguistic propriety?

4 Read the letter of John Evelyn, Dryden's fellow member of the Royal Society committee on the English language, to Sir Peter Wyche (1665) (ed. J. E. Spingarn, *Critical Essays of the Seventeenth Century*, 1908, II, 310 ff.). What light does it throw on Dryden's ideas?

5 Dryden said in the Dedication to *Troilus and Cressida* (1679) that he had to translate an idea into Latin in order to find the correct way to express it in English. What evidence of this attitude do you find in the present essay? Take the first and last paragraphs as examples, paying particular attention to the vocabulary. In which parts of speech did Dryden most often employ Latin derivatives?

6 Explain the syntax and sense of the paragraph beginning 'For *Ben. Johnson*, the most judicious of Poets...'.

8. SIR THOMAS BROWNE

1 Who were Vossius, Casaubon, Verstegan, Buxtorfius, Scaliger, and what did each contribute to philology?

2 What is Browne's attitude toward the causes and effects of linguistic change? Are his views influenced by his religious and political opinions?

3 How does the scientist Browne treat linguistic 'data' in Old English, East Anglian dialects, the Strasbourg Oaths ('the League between *Charles* and *Lewis*'), etc.?

4 Had the idea of 'families' of languages developed since Harrison and Camden wrote? How far is it compatible with Browne's ideas of 'preservation' and 'commixture'?

5 Why has English spelling become so settled in the century since Mulcaster that Browne's looks almost entirely familiar to us, although three hundred years old?

6 Why do writers like Camden and Browne concern themselves so particularly with the etymology of royal titles?

9. JOHN LOCKE

1 Locke looks on language as God-given. What are the implications of this theory for the study of language (e.g. learning in children, dialects, etymological change, etc.)?

2 Paraphrase paragraph 2 of chapter II.

3 How do Locke's ideas about definitions compare with Hobbes's? What would Locke hold to be the function of a dictionary?

4 What does Locke have in mind in the sentence beginning "'Tis true, common use...'? Is he right?

5 Is Locke right in believing that the 'primary signification' of words like 'imagine', 'apprehend', etc., implies that these 'had their first rise from sensible *Ideas*'?

6 How does paragraph 7 of chapter II relate to what we now call 'jargon'? Does it also relate to the language of advertising, political propaganda, and the like?

10. DANIEL DEFOE

1 Read the excerpt from Sprat's *History of the Royal Society* (ed. J. E. Spingarn, *Critical Essays of the Seventeenth Century*, 1908, II, 112 ff.). What reflections of this project do you find in Defoe's plan?

2 What parallels does the excursus on swearing have in the essays of Addison and Swift?

3 Explain the two sentences beginning '*Custom*, which is now our best Authority', and discuss Defoe's ideas of usage and authority.

4 What are the literary implications of Defoe's plan?

5 How much of the plan of his academy do you think Defoe has borrowed from the French? What bodies supply the lack of such an academy today?

6 How do you account for Defoe's several references to Latin?

7 What does Defoe mean by '*Cadence in Expression*, which we call speaking *Sense*'?

II. JOSEPH ADDISON

1 How do you think Addison pronounced 'Liberty', 'Conspiracy', 'Theatre', 'Orator'? What does his choice of examples reveal about him?

2 What are the originals of *Mob.*, *rep.*, *pos.*, *incog.*? Which of these shortened forms still survive? How many shortened forms do you use (look up, for example, the etymology of *lord*)? Is Addison consistent about shortened forms?

3 Explain the meaning of 'by the best Authorities and Rules drawn from the Analogy of Languages [an academy] shall settle all Controversies between Grammar and Idiom'.

4 Compare Addison's account of the 'personality' of English with Otto Jespersen's in chapter I of his *Growth and Structure of the English Language*.

5 Read also *Spectator* 78 and 80 (1711).

6 Evaluate the facts and logic of the paragraph beginning 'I might here observe'. Why does Addison's impression of the foreign grasp of English differ from Harrison's?

12. JONATHAN SWIFT

1 Read Swift's *Treatise on Polite Conversation*, his *Discourse to Prove the Antiquity of the English Tongue*, and his contribution to *Tatler* 230 (1710). How do they relate to the *Proposal*?

2 Compare Swift's programme with Defoe's.

3 Compare Swift's views on spelling with Johnson's.

4 Describe the role of history—linguistic, political, and religious—in this essay.

5 What is the 'tone' of the essay? Does it vary from one part to another?

6 What does Swift's list of 'Causes'—the Court, Dunces, Poets, etc.—reveal about his linguistic concerns?

7 Have Swift's predictions, that his praises of Lord Oxford would become unintelligible after two centuries or so, come true? Explain your answer.

13. LORD CHESTERFIELD

1 What is Chesterfield's idea of a 'lawful standard of our language'?

2 Discuss Chesterfield's linguistic nationalism.

3 Read Johnson's letter to Chesterfield (7 February 1755).

4 Does Chesterfield share the popular image of 'sifting, winnowing... purifying, and finally fixing our language'? What relationship do these terms bear to Swift's title?

5 What works had Johnson published by 1754? Why should they lead Chesterfield to believe Johnson to be highly qualified? What is Chesterfield's notion of a dictionary-maker? Is it yours?

6 Paraphrase the last paragraph before the postscript. In what points of vocabulary, spelling, punctuation, and grammar does your paraphrase differ from the original? Do these points suggest a failure in Chesterfield's hopes of 'fixing' English?

14. SAMUEL JOHNSON

1 What similar concerns are expressed in the first and last paragraphs, and how does Johnson link the two?

2 Compare this Preface with those in the *Oxford English Dictionary* and any important twentieth-century dictionary.

3 How do the 'rules' of 'experience and analogy' operate in Johnson's method?

4 What assumptions underlie paragraphs 7 and 8? How do they affect paragraph 9?

5 Does Johnson's distinction between primitives and derivatives adequately reflect etymological processes?

6 List examples of Johnson's 'formal' grammatical description.

7 To what does Johnson attribute linguistic change?

8 The phrase 'well of English undefiled' was first used by Spenser (*Faerie Queene*, IV, ii, 32) about Chaucer. Why does Johnson use it about the writers from Sidney to the Restoration?

9 Read Johnson's *Plan of a Dictionary of the English Language* (1747). How does it help you to understand the growth of his linguistic philosophy?

15. NOAH WEBSTER

1 Do you find Webster's reasons for the 'irregularity' of English spelling convincing? What view of language as an aspect of human society does he take? Is it like Emerson's?

2 What relationship between spelling and pronunciation does Webster assume in his three 'alterations' and four 'advantages'?

3 '*Now* is the time, and *this* the country.' Explain.

4 How is the argument under objection 3 constructed? What is distinctive about Webster's idea of 'meaning'? Does he deal fairly with Dr Johnson under objection 5? Can you think of any other objections?

5 Transcribe the first paragraph of Webster's 'Essay' in his reformed spelling, and ask a friend to do the same. Compare your results. How near have you come to Mulcaster's spelling?

6 What does Franklin mean by his reference to Chinese in the last paragraph Webster quotes? Are Franklin's arguments here like Webster's?

16. BENJAMIN FRANKLIN

1 How does Franklin's 'zeal for preserving the purity of our language' agree with his desire for reform in spelling?

2 How many of the 'innovations' Franklin condemns are still current? Do you find any of his usages unfamiliar?

3 How much did Franklin's patriotism and his knowledge of printing assist his linguistic insight, and how much did they impair it?

4 Outline, on the basis of this letter and the one reproduced at the end of no.15, Franklin's ideas about the relation of writing to speech. Did any particular purposes influence these ideas?

5 With the help of the *Oxford English Dictionary*, trace the history of 'improve', 'notice', 'advocate', 'progress' and 'oppose'. With this advantage of perspective over Franklin, how would you criticize his remarks?

6 How would you rewrite the sentence beginning 'The general use of the French language'?

17. WILLIAM COBBETT

1 Do you agree with Cobbett's criticism of Blair? To what extent does Cobbett commit 'faults' of his own?

2 What are the signs that, despite his belief that 'a knowledge of the Greek and Latin is not sufficient to prevent men from writing bad English', Cobbett based his grammar on that of the '*learned* languages'?

3 On the evidence of this chapter, how would you explain the great popularity and influence that Cobbett's *Grammar* enjoyed?

4 To what extent does Cobbett base his grammar on formal description? How far do the conventions of writing enter into it?

5 'In all writers, however able, we find errors.' Does Cobbett, although a critic of Swift in this very sentence, agree with him about the standard for authority?

6 What other phrases might have been condemned on the basis of the logic in Cobbett's criticism of 'insight into' (paragraph 172)? Consider 'compare with', 'deduce from', and more examples.

18. WILLIAM HAZLITT

1 Are there any virtues in a Latin-based grammar to make up for the faults Hazlitt finds in it?

2 What hints do Hazlitt's criticisms of Latinate grammar contain for a more realistic account of English structure?

3 Describe Horne Tooke's contributions to philology. Has Hazlitt quoted any of his errors in the belief that they were right?

4 How does Hazlitt use traditional phrases like 'foregone conclusion', 'labourers in the vineyard', 'old *Mumpsimus*', 'licked into...shape'?

5 How do you account for the slowness, which Hazlitt condemns, of teachers and publishers to accept the findings of linguistic science?

6 Look at the definitions of parts of speech in several grammars (including Hazlitt's own, 1809). Which ones might have met with Hazlitt's approval?

19. RALPH WALDO EMERSON

1 Comment on Emerson's equation of primitive and infant language. What about the infants in primitive societies?

2 Is Emerson justified in regarding the system of language as analogous to the system of nature?

3 What are the artistic implications of Emerson's idea of poetic symbolism?

4 What do the two paragraphs beginning 'Thus is nature an interpreter' have to do with linguistic purity and propriety?

5 'The idioms of all languages approach each other in passages of the greatest eloquence and power.' What is Emerson suggesting here? Is he right, in your experience?

6 How does the paragraph beginning 'We are thus assisted' bear on the idea of language as a medium of human communication?

20. THOMAS DE QUINCEY

1 Is there any parallel between the history of the study of Political Economy, or of dramatic criticism, and that of the study of language?

2 How accurate are De Quincey's notions of Anglo-Saxon language and literature?

3 Was De Quincey justified in regarding his own language as 'stationary'?

4 Do you agree with De Quincey's criticism of Dr Johnson?

5 Why does De Quincey hold a higher opinion of the 'purity' of Elizabethan English than Dryden did?

6 What is the topic of each of the sections numbered 1 to 7? How are they arranged?

7 Do De Quincey's 'three...modes of instinct' account adequately for 75 per cent of the words in English? Try them on a few sentences.

8 Read also (in Masson's 1897 edition) De Quincey's 'Orthographic Mutineers' (xi, 437 f.), 'Language' (x, 246 f.), and 'English Dictionaries' (x, 430 f.).

SELECT INDEX OF
LITERARY AND LINGUISTIC TOPICS